CREATING SINGLE-PARTY DEMOCRACY

CREATING
SINGLE-PARTY
DEMOCRACY

Japan's Postwar Political System

Edited and with
an introduction by
Kataoka Tetsuya

HOOVER INSTITUTION PRESS
Stanford University
Stanford, California

Hoover Institution Press Publication 403
Copyright © 1992 by the Board of Trustees of the
    Leland Stanford Junior University

First printing, 1992
98 97 96 95 94 93 92   9 8 7 6 5 4 3 2 1
Simultaneous first paperback printing, 1992
98 97 96 95 94 93 92   9 8 7 6 5 4 3 2 1

Manufactured in the United States of America
Printed on acid-free paper

Library of Congress Cataloging-in-Publication Data
Creating single-party democracy : Japan's postwar political
system / edited by Tetsuya Kataoka.
        p.   cm. — (Hoover Press publication : 403)
    Includes bibliographical references and index.
    ISBN 0-8179-9111-5. — ISBN 0-8179-9112-3
    1. Political parties—Japan. 2. Japan—Politics and
government—1945–   I. Kataoka, Tetsuya.
JQ1698.A1C74 1992   91-26081
324.252—dc20   CIP

Contents

Contributors   vii

1 | Introduction   1
    Kataoka Tetsuya

2 | The 1955 System: 34
    Origin and Transformation
    Masumi Junnosuke

3 | Rearmament Controversies and   55
    Cultural Conflicts in Japan:
    The Case of the Conservatives
    and the Socialists
    Otake Hideo

4 | The Japan Socialist Party   79
    before the Mid-1960s:
    An Analysis of Its Stagnation
    Tani Satomi

5 | Shigemitsu Mamoru   100
    and the 1955 System
    Ito Takashi

6 | Toward the Liberal Democratic Party Merger: Conservative Policies and Politics   119
    Tsutsui Kiyotada

7 | Did *Kokutai* Change? Problems of Legitimacy in Postwar Japan   133
    Nagao Ryuichi

8 | The 1955 System: The Origin of Japan's Postwar Politics   151
    Kataoka Tetsuya

Index   169

Contributors

ITO TAKASHI is a graduate of Tokyo University and a professor of Japanese history at Tokyo University. He is widely known for his biographical studies of Japan's prewar and postwar leaders.

KATAOKA TETSUYA is a graduate of Waseda University and the University of Chicago, a senior research fellow at the Hoover Institution, and was formerly a professor of Tsukuba University and Vassar College. He has written on the Chinese revolution and Japan's postwar politics.

MASUMI JUNNOSUKE is a graduate of Tokyo University and a professor of political science at Tokyo City University. He has written several major works of political history dealing with prewar and postwar Japan.

NAGAO RYUICHI is a graduate of Tokyo University and a professor of constitutional law at Tokyo University, Komaba campus. He has written on Hans Kelsen; on Japan's constitutions, both imperial and postwar; and on U.S.-Japan relations.

OTAKE HIDEO is a graduate of Kyoto Univeresity and a professor of Tohoku University in Sendai. He has written extensively on Japan's domestic politics.

TANI SATOMI is an associate professor of general education at Okayama University and a specialist on the history of the socialist movement in Japan.

TSUTSUI KIYOTADA is a graduate of Kyoto University and an associate professor of sociology at Nara Womens' College. He has written on the politics of both prewar and postwar Japan.

1 | Introduction

Kataoka Tetsuya

IN 1988, WHEN I ORGANIZED THE SMALL WORKSHOP THAT LED TO THE publication of this book, two things were uppermost in my mind. The first was that I was challenging a system of belief very dear to the hearts of my professional colleagues. That belief—the founding myth that legitimizes the postwar Japanese regime—consists of an interpretation of Japan's postwar history, particularly its political history, that has become universally accepted. That interpretation—a eulogy and apology for Prime Minister Yoshida Shigeru and his policies that dominate Japan today—is bound up with the interests of the existing power structure and maintained by Yoshida's students among the so-called conservative mainstream in the Liberal Democratic party and the members of the Realist school of academics.

The Realists' powerful allies in America are represented by Professor Edwin O. Reischauer of Harvard, the acclaimed dean of Japanese studies in the United States, who until recently represented the consensus U.S. policy toward Japan. This consensus is sustained by the State and Defense departments, Harvard University, the *New York Times*, and the New York financial world, a formidable list.

The second thing on my mind in the spring of 1988 was that, unknown to its defenders, the 1955 System was teetering on the edge of disaster. To those of us who knew that Japan's domestic political system was a creature of the cold war and of America's cold war policies in particular, there were ample signs of a sea change. President Reagan's arms buildup, paid for in part by loans from Japan, was accompanied by strident charges against Japan's alleged military free ride. Having become a debtor nation in 1985, the United States dealt several "Japan-bashing" blows in the next few years. The stock market on Wall Street crashed in October of 1987. Mr. Reagan was in search of a peaceful monument to adorn his eight years in office, and things were taking a surprising turn at Reykjavik.

Further, in the spring of 1988, Clyde V. Prestowitz, Jr., and Karel van Wolferen were writing books on Japan. Although I was not sure what Prestowitz was going to say, I could guess van Wolferen's approach from his article, "The Japan Problem," in *Foreign Affairs* in 1985. None of us could have known that the cold war regimes in Eastern Europe would come tumbling down. The ending of the cold war spelled trouble for Japan because, as I mentioned earlier, today's Japan is a creature of the cold war, and thus the 1955 System would be on a chopping block.

Unlike Reischauer's generation, which had seen and taken part in the founding of Japan, Americans such as Prestowitz and James Fallows (of the *Atlantic*), who know only today's Japan, are convinced that it is exploiting the American connection and that it should stop. Not only do they not know how Japan has come to be what it is, but they seem to have no idea of the part U.S. policies toward Japan played in shaping it or the reasons for those policies. In railing at Japan's ruling party, the FSX project (fighter support experimental aircraft that Japan wanted to develop but that Washington vetoed), the trade surplus, or the new consumer tax, these critics are chipping away at the tip of a huge iceberg whose submerged portion they scarcely comprehend. Now that the iceberg seems to have begun slowly drifting away with the defeat of the Liberal Democratic party in the July 1988 upper house election, they should know precisely what they have been attacking and why.

To argue for change, critics must show that change is superior to the existing conditions. This is not an argument against change—far from it; instead it is a plea that the terms of the debate be made clear and comprehensive.

To show the origin of the postwar Japanese regime without favor or prejudice and to contribute to the rationality of the debate were the purposes of the conference. That conference and this volume are mere beginnings, but, by showing the direction of future research, I hope to blaze a trail.

The 1955 System

Let us begin by briefly defining the term *the 1955 System*, bearing in mind that its full significance will not become evident until the end of the volume. Conventionally, the 1955 System refers to the standoff between the Liberal Democratic party (LDP) majority and the Japan Socialist party (JSP) minority that came into existence in 1955, when the conservatives merged into the LDP and the Socialists merged into the JSP, with little chance for an alternating of power. The JSP was radical, orthodox Marxist, anti-American, neutralist, and adamantly opposed to the U.S. military bases in Japan and the U.S.-Japan security treaty. Because the conservatives and the business community clung to the American connection as the only hope for Japan's future, they brooked no interference from the Socialists over bilateral ties. By definition, then, the 1955 System was dominated by the LDP; at least this is the popular view.

In actuality, however, the standoff was far from stable because the factors that produced it—the war-renouncing constitution of 1947 and the security treaty concluded in 1951 in San Francisco—were themselves in the process of change. Uchida Kenzo, Masumi Junnosuke, and I are among the few who view the two institutions as the cornerstones of the 1955 System.[1] As we see it, the 1955 System refers to a political process bounded by the two basic laws and interacting with them in the constitutional development of postwar Japan. In those turbulent years following the occupation, all three elements were in flux; not until the upheaval of the security treaty revision in 1960 did the three become solidly institutionalized and enter the maturation stage.

The basic alignment of Japan's postwar politics was a three-way division created by Douglas MacArthur's purge program. As Hans H. Baerwald makes clear, the purge, by labeling the Japanese government "ultranationalist," decimated the political and military part of it. Those who were purged in the military never returned to public life; the professional politicians returned when the occupation ended. The ensuing vacuum in the government was filled by two major groups, one of which was the Socialists. MacArthur, obsessed by the desire to perpetuate his constitution, favored the Socialists because he felt that only they—the beneficiaries of the purge—would defend the constitution. Certainly he could not count on the purged "ultranationalists" to

---

[1]Uchida Kenzo, *Sengo Nihon no hoshu seiji* (Postwar Japan's conservative politics) (Tokyo: Iwanami Shoten, 1969).

come to its defense. The second group favored by the purge—the civilian career officers in the central-ministry bureaucracies—were largely spared because their administrative expertise was indispensable to the occupation's success and because it was important for MacArthur to maintain the fiction of "indirect rule." This important fiction, also called self-government, legitimized the constitution and other occupation reforms by disguising their origins.[2]

The purge administration's lack of fairness began a three-way tug of war between the bureaucrats, the Socialists, and the professional politicians. The mutual enmities that resulted were reinforced when MacArthur showered favors first on the Socialists and later on Yoshida and his bureaucratic followers. By the time the occupation was over, the three groups had come to represent radically different policies.

The constitution was defended by the JSP, the mainstay of *kakushin* (radical-liberal forces), that included a small group of Japan Communist party (JCP) members. The JSP's existence as a neutralist party was justified by the constitution. By late 1948, when the U.S. government had begun to reverse its earlier occupation policies, however, it became axiomatic at both the State and the Defense departments that the constitution was out of place. In 1951, when the shape of the security treaty became known, many Japanese assumed that it was incompatible with the disarmament clause, if not the whole spirit, of the constitution and that the military treaty would negate the constitution or vice versa. The professional politicians (whom I have labeled Gaullists-revisionists or simply revisionists) took the position that the treaty would negate the constitution, whereas the Socialists felt that the constitution would negate the treaty.

A third way of dealing with the tension between the constitution and the security treaty—Yoshida's and MacArthur's way—was to straddle them. The tension between the constitution and the security treaty arose out of the contradiction between the early U.S. occupation policy and the containment policy (what the Japanese called the reverse course). Thus any analysis of America's early occupation policy must begin with the genealogy of the constitution—the capstone of that policy of disarming and "democratizing" Japan—which means going back to Japan's surrender to the Allied powers. The best overview of that early occupation policy is National Security Council (NSC) 150/4, Initial Postsurrender Policy toward Japan; the best critical review of that policy

---

[2]Hans H. Baerwald, *The Purge of Japanese Leaders under the Occupation* (Berkeley: University of California Press, 1959).

is in the *Memoirs* of George F. Kennan, who, as director of policy planning for the State Department, authored NSC 13/2 of 1948, which set the containment policy in motion for Japan.[3] The tension between the two policies began here and steadily increased as the cold war accelerated.

That tension could have been eradicated if the State and Defense departments had been able to complete the reverse course by revising the constitution a second time. MacArthur, however, with the political power of a potential Republican presidential candidate, vetoed that. The tension split Japan politically as the Korean War plunged it into a national debate on the shape and character of the peace and security treaties with the United States. Japan confronted a series of related political issues whose magnitude, gravity, and number were overwhelming. No polity could have remained tranquil saddled with such issues, which were as follows:

1. Should Japan conclude a peace treaty with one side in the cold war or with all the former belligerents? The former alternative would involve Japan in the cold war; the latter would leave Japan a neutral.

2. If even a partial peace is desirable or practical, should Japan agree to military self-help and regional collective security under U.S. hegemony? Why should Japan rearm against the Soviet Union and China?

3. If such a partial peace were to come to pass, should Japan have the right to open diplomatic ties with Moscow and Peking? Why should Japan not enjoy the same right as Britain, France, and other allies of the United States?

4. Should the constitution—banning rearmament—be revised or rewritten? Or should the security treaty be declared unconstitutional, null, and void?

5. Is accommodating 1,300 U.S. military installations under the security treaty the same thing as continuing the occupation? What should be done about the U.S. armed forces' rights to extraterritoriality, to wage war from the Japanese bases without Japan's consent, to militarily intervene in Japan's domestic disorder and other unequal features of the security treaty?

6. To what extend should the occupation reforms be kept or amended now that Japan is becoming independent?

7. By means of the purge, the occupation created the three political groups. Who should rule Japan, the professional politicians or

---

[3]George F. Kennan, *Memoirs, 1925–1950* (Boston: Little, Brown, 1967).

the bureaucratic politicians? Should there be Diet supremacy or bureaucratic supremacy?

8. If the constitution is to be retained as Yoshida insisted, the Socialists had to be retained also. What is their place in the polity? Can they be entrusted with power when they are adamantly opposed to the Japan-U.S. relations? Is it possible to have an alternating two-party system in which the JSP takes part? Should the JSP-conservative coalition of 1947–1948 be revived to create a moderate loyal opposition? Or should the JSP be eliminated through gerrymandering or some such device (as attempted in 1956)? If the Socialists defend their minority position by means of the constitution and yet a full democracy in Japan calls for a moderate loyal opposition, should not party reform point to constitutional revision as well?

9. Should the conservatives remain in power permanently? How can they if they are torn between Yoshida and the Gaullists? What if the Socialists, who are not fully integrated into the system, choose to vote with one wing or the other of the conservatives? How can Japan have a coherent, stable, and accountable decision-making system on the basis of this three-way division?

Issues 1 through 6 concern Japan's relationship with the United States; issues 7, 8, and 9 are domestic, but their resolution would affect the resolution of the other issues.

These political issues reinforced the three-way division in Japan's politics that remains to this day.

I. The JSP
   Supported the constitution
   Supported early occupation reforms
   Opposed NSC 13/2 and the reverse course altogether
   Opposed rearmament
   Favored by the Supreme Commander for the Allied Powers (SCAP) until 1948
   Neutralist, anti-American, and semirevolutionary after 1949
II. The Yoshida faction of the conservatives
   Supported the constitution
   Supported NSC 13/2 and the reverse course only with respect to domestic institutions (excluding the constitution)
   Pro-American but adamantly opposed to the U.S. policy of full rearmament
   Covertly nationalistic

Bureaucratic in origin

Favored by SCAP after 1949

III. The Gaullist-revisionists

Core of professional politicians, who were supplanted by the
Socialists and bureaucrats because of the purge

Supported constitutional revision

Supported NSC 13/2 and all the reverse course, domestic or
foreign

Supported regional security and rearmament

Basically pro-American but openly nationalistic

Favored a two-party system and Diet supremacy, rather than
bureaucratic supremacy

The 1955 System, then, was a two-party system in appearance only.
In the actual three-way division of power, a majority was necessarily
based on a coalition of two groups: the peace and security treaties were
supported by Yoshida and the revisionists; the constitution was defended by Yoshida and the JSP; revision of the security treaty was
endorsed by the revisionists and the Socialists; and rapprochement with
Moscow and Peking was supported by the revisionists and the JSP.

No combination of two groups could eliminate a minority, however,
because the issue cleavages did not overlap. A minority was a minority
only on one issue but not on another. Thus Japan was saddled with an
enormously difficult political system with built-in tension and instability. To say that there was "viscosity" in the system was an
understatement.[4]

The foregoing describes the 1955 System in its early stages. I now
offer a very brief recapitulation of history between 1945 and 1960 to
show how these issues were resolved, to produce the mature system.
(See a more detailed analysis in chapter 7.)

History, 1945–1960

This period begins with the no-war constitution. In the confusion
surrounding the terms of Japan's surrender, the safety of Japan's emperor
had to be negotiated with Douglas MacArthur, SCAP, a skeleton in the
closet of what I call standard history—the prevailing orthodoxy in the

---

[4]Mike Mochizuki, *Managing and Influencing the Japanese Legislative Process:
The Role of Parties and the National Diet* (Ph.D. dissertation, Harvard University, 1982).

postwar history of Japan upheld by both Japanese and U.S. scholars. John W. Dower, in an excellent biography of Yoshida (and an outstanding example of standard history), argues correctly that Yoshida was a nationalist, a royalist, and an imperialist but that, because of a run-in with Kempeitai (Japanese military police) during the war, he became a pacifist and a defender of the no-war constitution.[5] Dower, however, overlooks the fact that Yoshida opposed the MacArthur draft of the constitution to the bitter end because he felt it was a way for the United States to eliminate the monarchy and put the emperor on trial for war crimes. Yoshida consented to it only when ordered to do so by the emperor[6] and when promised by Douglas MacArthur that the war-renouncing clause would be exchanged for the emperor's safety.

Both for the Japanese government and Yoshida, then, the new constitution's first use was to serve the specific, instrumental purpose of saving the person of the emperor. Later, when the issue of rearmament was raised by Washington, MacArthur and Yoshida used the constitution to dodge that issue.

Japan's postwar politics began with five political parties. The JCP and the JSP were called the "democratic forces" (minshu seiryoku) until the general strike of February 1, 1947, was put down by SCAP, at which time they acquired the label of "radical-liberal forces" (kakushin seiryoku).[7] Then there were three conservative parties, two of which were carryovers from the prewar major parties, Seiyukai and Minseito. As figure 1.1 indicates, these two parties were the major actors on the conservative side until they merged into the LDP. But before that happened, the conservatives, like the Socialists, were to go through numerous splits, mergers, and realignments. These shifting alignments, however, did not seem to alter their self-identification as descendants of Seiyukai and Minseito. Hence, I have decided to call them Seiyukai and Minseito until they become the Liberal party and the Democratic party, respectively. This convention—and it is no more than that—will help focus attention on the macropicture.

In the wake of the Korean War, U.S.-Japan negotiations on the peace and security treaties began. Here MacArthur intervened a fourth and final time to preserve his constitution. Using his political influence over the Republicans in the U.S. Senate, who held the power of ratifi-

---

[5]John W. Dower, *Empire and Aftermath: Yoshida Shigeru and the Japanese Experience, 1878–1954* (Cambridge, Mass.: Harvard University Press, 1979).

[6]Shidehara heiwa zaidan, *Shidehara Kijuro* (Tokyo: Diet Library, 1955), p. 656.

[7]Shinobu Seizaburo, *Sengo Nihon seiji* (Japan's postwar politics) (Tokyo: Sokei Shobo, 1966), 2:542.

Figure 1.1

Genealogy of the Conservative Political Parties

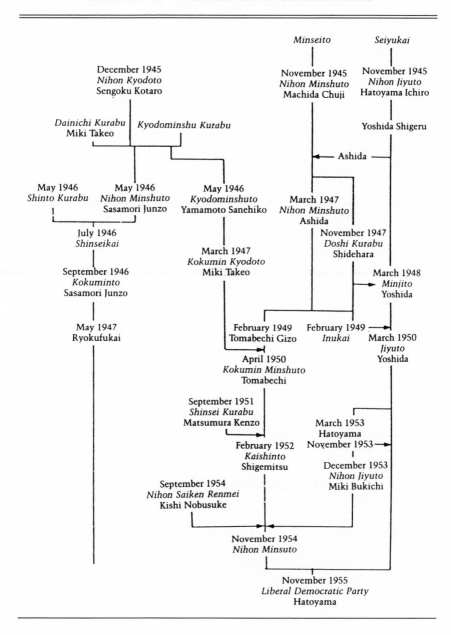

cation over the two treaties, he successfully prevailed on John Foster Dulles, the U.S. negotiator, to accept the constitution as an implicit premise of the security treaty.[8]

Dulles promised Yoshida a protectorate arrangement without the Far Eastern clause (which enabled the United States to wage war from Japan without Japan's consent) or the domestic intervention clause. But when MacArthur was dismissed by Truman in April 1951, Dulles reneged on his promise; the final treaty draft included both clauses. This was Dulles's penalty for Yoshida's rejection of military self-help, a penalty made possible by the disappearance of MacArthur, Yoshida's patron.

The partial peace, which antagonized Moscow and Peking and cut Japan from the China market, and the unequal military treaty split Japan. The 1955 System, with a domestic 38th parallel drawn down the middle, had emerged. Professional politicians, many of whom were returning to public life after the purge, joined the Socialists to call for a revision of the just-concluded security treaty. Dulles supported the revisionists in their call for rearmament and constitutional revision.[9] Underneath the treaty and rearmament controversy, however, swirled the domestic conflict between the professional politicians and the bureaucratic politicians. This conflict, too, was bequeathed by the occupation.

Chalmers A. Johnson correctly points out that the power of the postwar government bureaucracies was a legacy of the imperial counterpart. He goes on to say that it was the occupation's reliance on indirect rule that preserved the prewar institutions. But he goes no further.[10] Reading NSC 150/4, the Initial Postsurrender Policy toward Japan, today, it is difficult to see how the imperial bureaucracies could have survived the reforms or the purge; except for the Ministry of Interior, which was liquidated, however, most of them did. How did they survive and how did their survival affect Japan's politics?

During the occupation, Douglas MacArthur boasted that he was the sovereign, and above both the Meiji Constitution and his own. He was the source of all power and authority in Japan. Yet it became apparent that administering Japan was impossible without the assistance of the

---

[8]Kataoka Tetsuya, *The Price of a Constitution: The Origin of Japan's Postwar Politics* (unpublished manuscript), chapter 4.

[9]Tsutsui Kiyotada, *Ishibashi Tanzan: ichi jiyushugi seijika no kiseki* (Ishibashi Tanzan: A liberal politician's record) (Tokyo: Chuo Koronsha, 1986), chapter 1.

[10]Chalmers A. Johnson, *MITI and the Japanese Miracle: The Growth of Industrial Policy, 1925–1975* (Stanford: Stanford Univeristy Press, 1982), p. 43.

imperial bureaucracy. Foreign Ministry bureaucrats were particularly indispensable because they were among the few people who understood English, a prerequisite for liaison with an alien conqueror. During the nearly seven years of occupation, Japan produced five prime ministers: Higashikuni, Shidehara Kijuro, Yoshida, Katayama Tetsu, and Ashida Hitoshi. Of them, Shidehara, Yoshida, and Ashida were career diplomats; the other two together lasted less than a year.

At the apex of the power structure in occupied Japan was the SCAP; beneath him were SCAP sections that corresponded roughly to their Japanese counterparts; and beneath them were Japanese bureaucracies of the central ministries. At the very bottom came the new Diet, a latecomer created by the constitution of 1947 that, although supposed to be supreme, was a mere rubber stamp.

More than 90 percent of the bills were originated by the SCAP, whose officials consulted the Japanese bureaucrats in the drafting process and later administrative oversight. SCAP officials often went to the Diet floor to lobby for their favorite bills. MacArthur could also issue executive orders called SCAPINs, short for SCAP instructions. The new police reserve (the forerunner of the Self-Defense Forces) was created by such an executive order, which circumvented the constitution.

Setbacks for the bureaucracies included the liquidation of the Ministry of Interior. Some prewar bureau chiefs and above were also purged, but SCAP could not decimate the bureaucrats as he had the politicians: The occupation reforms—including the purge itself—were administered by the bureaucracies, which meant that the bureaucracies were purging the politicians.

This, then, is how the legacy of the imperial bureaucracies survived and why there was such enmity between the bureaucratic officials such as Yoshida and the professional politicians like Hatoyama Ichiro, Kono Ichiro, and others in the Seiyukai who believed that Yoshida's maneuverings had something to do with their purge.[11] The Seiyukai politicians had fought the imperial bureaucracies and *zaibatsu* financiers in an effort to expand democracy in the Taisho era, only to have their hopes dashed by the militarists. The politicians reemerged after the war to claim the power that was rightfully theirs but found themselves under the thumb of a new emperor and his mandarins.

Thus, the politician-bureaucrat rivalry for power began during the occupation.[12] From the standpoint of the professional politicians, many

---

[11]Hatoyama Ichiro, *Hatoyama Ichiro kaikoroku* (Hatoyama Ichiro's memoir) (Tokyo: Bungei Shunjusha, 1957), pp. 93–97.

[12]In *Ishibashi Tanzan*, chapter 2, Tsutsui Kiyotada mentions the Liberal Dem-

of whom would later become revisionists, the Americans were friends of their enemies, the bureaucrats. Yoshida, the quintessential bureaucrat who owed his long tenure in power to his friendship with MacArthur after 1949, made countless appointments both in politics and in the bureaucracies. This was particularly true of the Foreign Ministry, where he exercised the so-called Item Y purge to ensure its fealty. (SCAP's purge directive classified several categories of purge liability in alphabetical order, with Item A standing for class A war crimes such as crime against peace and so on. In jest, Yoshida's appointment policy in the Foreign Ministry was called an internal purge under Item Y.) The same result obtained at the Ministry of Finance, to which Yoshida appointed his trusted protégé Ikeda Hayato. These two ministries would become the most pro-American of all the bureaucracies.

In 1952 and 1953 Japan held two general elections in six months but failed to produce a stable majority. To overcome the situation, the conservative merger was proposed. There were three major interrelated motives: A merger of Hatoyama and Yoshida would not solve the problem; therefore, a large majority of conservatives, including many in Yoshida's own party, agreed that he had to go, making the proposed merger on Hatoyama's terms.[13] Then there was the fear of the expanding Socialists. Most promoters of the conservative merger wanted a two-party system, but they had abandoned the hope of a moderate Socialist party and felt that the only solution was to contain the Socialists with an LDP monopoly. In late 1954, Yoshida was overthrown; the LDP was born the following year.

But the new prime minister, Hatoyama Ichiro, ran afoul of Dulles, now President Eisenhower's secretary of state. Hatoyama proposed a peace treaty with Moscow to outshine Yoshida's treaty with Washington, but Dulles vetoed it in a 1956 demarche.[14] Yoshida, who knew how to deal with Washington, sided with Dulles and thus rebounded into the ring.

In late 1956, the revisionists failed in their coup to gerrymander the Socialists into impotence. The LDP's bill to replace the multi-member districts with a single-member, winner-take-all system was tabled by

---

ocratic party wrangle over the appointment of Fukunaga Kenji as secretary-general, an example of such rivalry.

[13]The best explanation for the merger's anti-Yoshida nature is in Mitearai Tatsuo, *Miki Bukichi den* (Miki Bukichi: A biography) (Tokyo: Shikisha, 1958).

[14]The United States threatened to take Okinawa if Japan ceded Kunashiri and Etorofu to the Soviet Union, as Hatoyama proposed. See *New York Times*, August 28, 1956, p. 1; *Asahi Shimbun*, August 29, 1956, p. 1.

House Speaker Masutani, a Yoshida protégé who colluded with the JSP.[15]

After Hatoyama's retirement, the revisionists regrouped around Kishi Nobusuke, who was committed to revising the unequal security treaty. In Kishi Dulles found the ally he had been looking for—neither a "pacifist" Yoshida nor a "neutralist" Hatoyama but someone who promised rearmament and constitutional revision. In 1958, however, Dulles again undermined the revisionists—this time inadvertently—by plunging Japan into the nuclear confrontation over the islands of Quemoy and Matsu in the Taiwan Strait. Although Dulles was using the international crisis to get the kind of security treaty he wanted, the crisis frightened the Socialists, who broke away from the treaty revision coalition with Kishi. At this point, Yoshida came to Kishi's rescue to complete the treaty revision. But Kishi had to pay a price for Yoshida's cooperation: naming Ikeda, Yoshida's protégé, as his successor. Thus ended the reign of the revisionists, which had lasted a mere six years.[16]

The Socialists acquiesced de facto in the security treaty and the U.S. military bases; the revisionists fell silent over the constitution, thus winning the day for Yoshida's interpretation of the constitution and the security treaty. According to that interpretation, Japan's Self-Defense Forces were constitutional as long as they refused to take part in a regional collective security role. The three-way split remained, however, because neither the Socialists nor the revisionists were completely reconciled to the resolution. But the end of the conflict meant that Japan could now concentrate its efforts on economic development. This was not a transformation of the 1955 System but a temporary resolution of the internal tension; it was the final fruition of Yoshida's dream, not its negation.

The Mature 1955 System

As the 1955 System matured, traits that were only immanent in the original system—the LDP's factionalism, the ascendancy of a new breed of professional politicians, and the so-called money politics—were articulated and institutionalized.

The conservative factionalism had its origins in an accident of history: Yoshida and Hatoyama both being in the Seiyukai party, thus splitting the party. The two halves wooed like-minded members of Minseito, the conservative opposition, splitting it and creating a four-

---

[15]See Kataoka, *The Price of a Constitution*, chapter 6.
[16]Ibid.

way division. Had Yoshida been in Minseito and Hatoyama been in Seiyukai, that would have reinforced the existing party identification. The three-way division on substantive issues, then, was the primary cause of factionalism and was merely reinforced by the system of multi-member, medium-size election districts.[17]

The ultimate fate of factionalism depended on the outcome of the Hatoyama-Yoshida conflict. Yoshida's policy, which presupposed the JSP's anti-U.S. stance, necessarily called for the LDP's one-party dominance that exists to this day. Hatoyama, in contrast, being a veteran professional politician of Seiyukai, wanted an alternating two-party system minus the JSP. So not until the final demise of the Hatoyama government in 1956 did formal factionalism make its appearance, in the form of "the seven divisions and two regiments." The occasion for all this was the 1956 LDP presidential election that named Ishibashi Tanzan to succeed Hatoyama. Apologists for Yoshida maintain that the LDP's factionalism is necessary if the LDP is to monopolize power, in which case, a change of government can take place only among the factions in the LDP. On the other hand, factions would be weakened by the so-called responsible two-party system that periodically throws out the "rascals."

The LDP's factions are frequently likened to independent parties with all their trappings: headquarters, independent sources of funds, candidates for prime minister, shadow cabinets, shadow party administrations, and so forth. As Watanabe Tsuneo maintains, at times the factions behave as if they are independent political parties. But it is misleading to suggest that they will become political parties: In all the years of the LDP's existence, no faction has ever declared its independence from the party. Instead, all the factions cooperate on key votes to maintain the security treaty against the JSP and other opposition parties. Thus, the LDP's factionalism is balanced by the continued and vital presence of the party, the mark of the 1955 System after its maturation.

The second development, which came after 1960, was the return of Diet supremacy. The Diet was a rubber stamp only during the occupation and its immediate aftermath. As things returned to normal, the

---

[17]Watanabe Tsuneo gives the standard history interpretation: that the LDP's factionalism is attributable to the multi-member, medium-size election districts. This is questionable, for Watanabe ignores the issues that tore Japan asunder and blames the electoral system. That system, however, had been in force since 1947, but factions did not appear until 1956. See Watanabe Tsuneo, *Habatsu* (Factions) (Tokyo: Kobundo, 1964).

professional politicians began testing the limits of their power under the constitution. Masumi Junnosuke in chapter 2 provides a nice exposition of this point. As electoral democracy reached its full flood, the vote-getters began to ascend in power. Finally this development produced Tanaka Kakuei, a politicians' politician hailing, ironically, from a bureaucratic faction.

The political-bureaucratic contest is still going on in muted form. The memory of the occupation has been erased, and the contest is institutionalized. But there are exceptions even today. In 1986, Prime Minister Nakasone Yasuhiro, a disciple of Kono Ichiro, took a leaf from Reagan's book and began deregulating: cutting up, abolishing, and privatizing a host of government bureaucracies. The demolition of the Japan National Railway decimated the railway workers' union, which had been the backbone of Sohyo, a labor federation that had in turn propped up the JSP. This was Nakasone's way of "settling accounts with the postwar" period.

The principle of Diet supremacy will remain shackled until political parties begin to alternate in power. As long as the LDP, still made up of a substantial number of bureaucratic politicians, retains power, the bureaucracies will be kept on a long leash. If, however, their political masters were to change periodically, the bureaucracies would be forced to retreat to strict neutrality. That last mile toward Diet supremacy has yet to be traveled.

The third development, which came after 1960, was money politics, and is tied into almost every aspect of the 1955 System: one-party dominance, factionalism, the pacifist diplomacy of the Japanese government, the Yoshida faction's policy of income doubling, and so on. Money politics is especially associated with factionalism because of the correspondence between a faction's numerical strength and the ability of its captain to raise funds. Naturally, there have been frequent cases of corruption in the LDP, the most notable examples being the Lockheed bribery scandal and the Recruit case.

In the wake of the Recruit scandal, public opinion is demanding a scuttling of the 1955 System and a return to a responsible two-party system. But that calls for Tweedledees and Tweedledums, capable of swapping places. In other words the JSP has to be integrated into that system. That in turns calls for a final resolution of the tension between the constitution and defense policy, as the Gaullists had demanded.

History in Postwar Japan

The two major schools of history in postwar Japan correspond to the two political forces in the three-way division of power. One is Marxist, and the other is what I call standard history, history from Yoshida's perspective, and propounded by the Realists in Japan and adherents of the modernization paradigm in the United States. Standard history, which came into existence to combat Marxist history and influence in Japan, succeeded in that task but also managed to distort a substantial part of the postwar history of Japan. That distortion minimizes or denies altogether the roles played by the revisionists and the United States in shaping the 1955 System. The true history of postwar Japanese politics, I suggest, cannot be written until we get out from under the spell of standard history.

The Marxist Rampage

Marxism, which burst on defeated Japan and nearly overwhelmed the intellectuals, had as its high point massive "participatory" and violent demonstrations against the revision of the U.S.-Japan security treaty in 1960. Many Americans assume that the postwar Japanese were what they are stereotyped as today—a nation of smiling, equivocating, apologetic, and apolitical people interested primarily in commerce and consensus. Until 1960, however, the Japanese were angry. They marched into the imperial palace demanding to see what the emperor was eating when the rest of the nation was starving, they sabotaged and wrecked trains (prompting Chalmers Johnson to write a book on one such incident),[18] and they thrust their fists into the air shouting, "Yankee, go home." A good deal of the animus for these actions was Marxism, a category including progressives, existentialists, radical liberals, and socialists of various descriptions who spoke of class, monopoly capital, and imperialism.

Marxism was popular in defeated Japan for three reasons. First, Japan was defeated in a very special kind of war, one in which the victor was cast in the role of crusader and the vanquished accused of war crimes. Whereas the entire Japanese nation was held guilty and in disgrace, the Communists enjoyed clear consciences: They had endured incarceration to prove their fidelity to the idea of overthrowing the emperor

---

[18]*Conspiracy at Matsukawa* (Berkeley: University of California Press, 1972). How tense and intense Japan's intellectuals were can be also seen in filmmaker Shohei Imamura's 1961 black farce, *Pigs and Battleships*.

system. Second and equally important, the Japanese left was cultivated as an instrument of U.S. occupation policy. The Initial Postsurrender Policy toward Japan (SWNCC 150/4) envisioned a major upheaval—directed at the imperial prerogative enshrined in the Meiji Constitution—as the crux of the "democratization" of Meiji Japan. Theodore Cohen called it "the American occupation as new deal."[19] But at the time only the hard-bitten Stalinists in Fuchu Prison would collaborate with such a policy.

Third, for its part, the SCAP bureaucracy, despite all the post hoc pretenses to the contrary, saw Japan's surrender as unconditional. Thus the occupation reforms rested on the doctrine articulated by President Roosevelt after Casablanca wherein wars of aggression were crimes committed by nations saddled with feudalism. (The Junkers in Germany were an example of such a feudal social structure.) In Japan feudalism meant the emperor system; therefore, the struggle against feudalism brought together Marxism and the messianic doctrine of unconditional surrender. As illustrated by Andrew Roth and Owen Lattimore, the zeal to punish became indistinguishable from the zeal to reform.[20]

Reading Cohen's account of the origin of SWNCC 150/4, one can see how E. H. Norman's book became the bible of the reformers. Himself a Communist,[21] Norman theorized about feudalism in Japan, taking his cue from the works of Kozaha, the school that provided revolutionary theories to the Japan Communist party (JCP).[22] At a congress of the Comintern in 1932, Stalin called for a two-stage revolution. Arguing that, because of the presence of the monarchy, the aristocracy, and other "feudal" remnants, Japan's bourgeois-democratic revolution was in an arrested state, Stalin called for the overthrow of the emperor system before the revolution could proceed to the higher stage. This lèse-majesté thesis split the Japanese Marxists in the Comintern into two factions: Kozaha remained loyal to Stalin and came to constitute the JCP. Ronoha, the workers' and peasants' faction, bolted the Comintern

[19]Theodore Cohen, *Remaking Japan: The American Occupation as New Deal* (New York: The Free Press, 1987).

[20]Andrew Roth, *Dilemma in Japan* (Boston: Little, Brown, 1945). E. Herbert Norman's influence is clear in Owen Lattimore's *Solutions in Asia* (Boston: Little, Brown, 1945), wherein Lattimore called for decapitation of the emperor.

[21]James Barros, *No Sense of Evil: The Espionage Case of E. Herbert Norman* (Toronto: Ivy, 1988).

[22]John W. Dower, ed., *Origins of the Modern Japanese State: Selected Writings of E. H. Norman* (New York: Random House, 1975).

and produced a thesis calling for a one-stage revolution in an effort to fudge the question of the monarchy. So the common Marxist paradigm brought together the victor and the Japanese pariah against the Japanese establishment.

Then Douglas MacArthur wiped the slate clean with the purge that began in 1946. The end was to create a "moderate force" between the Communists and the decimated conservatives. Almost in spite of itself, the JSP emerged as the party of plurality in the general election of 1947, whereupon SCAP thrust it into government. Yoshida was persona non grata at SCAP general headquarters (GHQ) at the time[23] because he had opposed the constitutional revision and obstructed the Socialists. In the meantime, the Ronoha faction moved into the left wing of the JSP and before long took over the whole party, making Marxism the guiding doctrine of Japan's major opposition party.

This was the background for the ascendancy of the left in postwar Japanese historiography. Public opinion at that time is indicated by a remark made by Inoki Masamichi, at the time a young professor of Seikei University and affiliated with the right-wing Socialists, later the doyen of conservative intellectuals and a biographer of Yoshida Shigeru. In the April 1949 issue of *Chuo Koron*, Inoki averred that there were two specters abroad in Japan, one communism and the other Yoshida.[24] How is it that Inoki, later the champion of Yoshida, began as Inoki, the enemy of Yoshida? Did Inoki change? Or did Japan lean much more to the left in those early postwar years?

In January 1946 a group of proletarian writers published *Kindai Bungaku* (Modern Literature), which heralded the postwar trend in literary and intellectual works.[25] That group, the keynoters of *après-guerre* intellectuals, delved into a series of controversies that began with the autonomy debate (that is, the autonomy of self in dialectical materialism) and went on to the war guilt debate (recriminations against fellow writers). In the meantime, Minshushugi Kagakusha Kyokai or Minka (the Democratic Scientists Association) was founded by Marxist scholars, chief among whom were Ishimoda Shou and Ogura Hirokatsu. With notables such as Yokota Kisaburo and Suekawa Hiroshi (president of

---

[23]This was the contemporary observation of Ashida Hitoshi in Shindo Eiichi, ed., *Ashida Hitoshi nikki* (Diaries of Ashida Hitoshi) (Tokyo: Iwanami Shoten, 1986), 2:130.

[24]"Shakai minshushugi no shimei to unmei" (The mission and fate of social democracy), *Chuo Koron*, April 1949, p. 13.

[25]Kuno Osamu, *Sengo Nihon no shiso* (Postwar Japan's ideology) (Tokyo: Sokei Shobo, 1966), chapter 1.

Ritsumeikan College) as officers, Minka exerted considerable influence on academic research and political proselytizing.

Once the occupation was over, the sounding board for the Marxist pardigm was Iwanami Books, the powerhouse of early postwar journalism.[26] In 1946 Iwanami's chief editor, Yoshino Genzaburo, began publishing the journal *Sekai* with the original design to address the "old liberalists" at the center or center-left. (Professor Inoki was a member of this audience.) But when the cold war began polarizing Japan, Iwanami's audience split also. One group, including Inoki, moved farther right, and the other, including Yoshino, went left.

Before the war, Iwanami gave currency to Kozaha, the Stalinist faction of Japanese Communists. (Kozaha, which means lecture faction, was taken from Iwanami's multivolume *Lecture* series of books.) Between 1953 and 1955, Iwanami mobilized two hundred theoreticians to update the prewar *Lecture* series. The postwar version intoned, "The primary condition controlling postwar Japanese capitalism was the fact that Japan is placed under conditions of colonial slavery."[27]

All Marxists and many Socialists shared a revulsion against what they called *emperor-system fascism*, a term denoting the prewar Japanese political system with the emperor at the apex. In a substantial number of cases, the rejection was an act of personal expiation for having collaborated with the wartime government, an act the Stalinists never forgave. But in addition to rejecting prewar Japan, those Marxists and Socialists were highly negative toward postwar Japan on the grounds that a full blossoming of occupation democracy had been stymied by the cold war reversal (labeled the *reverse course*), engineered jointly by the U.S. and Japanese governments. According to Hayashi Kentaro, a noted conservative social critic, Japanese intellectuals felt almost without exception that "Japan was in a 'backward,' 'dark,' or 'wrong' condition."[28] That such views were fashionable can be seen in the fact that most of the prominent faculty members of the Tokyo University opposed the establishment, criticizing the government and the reverse

---

[26]Yasue Ryosuk, *Sengo heiwa-ron no genryu* (The fountainhead of postwar pacifism), *Sekai*, special 40th anniversary issue, July 1985.

[27]Suzuki Hiroshi, "Sengo kozaha no shiso" (Postwar Kozaha's ideology) in Hidaka Hiroshi, ed., *Sengo Nihon no shiso* (Postwar Japanese ideology) (Tokyo: Gendai shisosha, 1962), 2:88.

[28]Hayashi Kentaro, "Gendai shakai to Marukusu-shugi" (Today's society and Marxism), in Hayashi Kentaro, et al., *Higeki wa hajimatte iru* (Tragedy in the making) (Tokyo: Takagi Shobo, 1972), p. 29.

course. Their leader was Maruyama Masao, a professor of political science at the university, whose crusade culminated in the 1960 upheaval.

It is hardly necessary to describe the role Maruyama played between 1948, when he and Iwanami Books jointly took the initiative to organize the Peace Problem Symposium, and 1960. Whether he was a Marxist may be disputed, although a scholar as eminent as Hayashi Kentaro did not hesitate to call him one. In the area where theory intersects with politics, the arena in which he was operating, however, Maruyama's stand was clear: He was the chief spokesman of the peace movement, of which the JSP left wing was the political backbone, and he stood for opposition to rearmament and to the peace and security treaties with the United States.

Three tenets of Marxist history served important political purposes in the contemporary society. First, it was the font of anti-U.S. nationalism. The Japanese had some serious complaints about the occupation (although standard history has erased them from memory) but lacked the self-confidence to air them. The JCP was an exception. For one thing, it was aligned with Moscow, another victor. More important, to a nation overwhelmed by U.S. power, wealth, and culture and suffering from an inferiority complex, Marxism, matter-of-factly and with scientific pretensions, taught that one form of capitalist monopoly was no better or worse than another and that "American imperialism" over Japan, Korea, and Vietnam was just as evil as the Japanese variety over China.[29] Those tenets found fertile soil among all Japanese.

Second, Marxism taught that history and politics are a struggle for power, which, although not exceptional, had special cogency and relevance at this time. During the occupation, the United States dealt with Japan in terms of absolute power without apology, whereas the rest of Asia appeared to be consummating a war against Western colonialism, which the imperial Japanese government had vowed as its official purpose. Japan at the time was also a class society, with great injustice and unspeakable poverty beating down the poor and helpless. Power, class struggle, proletarian internationalism, and other such concepts fascinated large numbers of Japanese. The theme of power has been expunged from standard history as a consequence of the conservatives' victory over Marxism. But it seems legitimate to ask—as John Dower does—if power should not have been thrown out along with Marxism.[30] Standard

---

[29]Kamiyama Shunpei, *Dai-toa senso no imi* (The significance of the Greater East-Asia War) (Tokyo: Chuo Koronsha, 1964).
[30]See introduction to Dower, ed., *Origins of the Modern Japanese State*.

history—with its stress on consensus, the new middle mass, peace-loving Japan, and commerce—is dull. American revisionists like van Wolferen underscore Dower's point by saying that today's Japan is not a state but a system, implying that Japan was different before Yoshida's victory.

Third, Marxist history as practiced by the Socialists is anti-American only because the United States betrayed its original commitment to New Deal utopia in Japan. In other words, the JSP was anti-American because it favored everything that preceded the reverse course. This rationale emerged only after the JSP turned against the United States; at the time, it dithered before coming out in favor of the constitution.

This curious and nostalgic attachment to a supposedly pristine past has become the definitive trait of the Socialists. With but slight exaggeration, one can say that their only goal is a return to that early postwar domestic order. If the external world is compatible with it, well and good; but if it is not, they are prepared to ignore it. An example is Nakano Yoshio, a respected literary critic, who, in 1952, in choosing between an early peace through alignment with the United States in the cold war and continued occupation, said: "I would rather take the continuation of the occupation than to rearm and reenter the world."[31] Otake Hideo skillfully captures this aspect of the Socialists in chapter 3, wherein he shows that the Socialists debated not rearmament itself so much as the domestic consequences of rearmament. Repulsed by the "traditional style" of those who advocated rearmament, the Socialists irrationally decided the rearmament issue on this basis.

Rational or not, in 1951 the Socialists became immensely popular after they adopted the Four Principles of Peace (opposition to rearmament and to U.S. bases, support for neutrality and all-around peace), voted against the security treaty, and rallied to the defense of the constitution. The sudden increase of U.S.-Japan tension as the two nations began to collide over rearmament caused the Socialists—even though split into two factions—to expand at an alarming pace at the polls. Yoshida, having to resist Washington without MacArthur's patronage, began enlisting the Socialists in a coalition to defend the constitution at a time when only the left-wing JSP was unequivocally committed to constitutional defense. In 1951 Yoshida sent an emissary to Suzuki Mosaburo and Katsumada Seiichi, both of the left wing, to request a staging of antirearmament demonstrations. Suddenly, the Socialists

---

[31] "Mushiro senryo no keizoku o erabu" (I would rather take the continuation of the occupation), *Chuo Koron*, April 1952, pp. 40–45.

found themselves serving Japan's national interests against "American imperialism."[32]

For Yoshida's purpose, the JSP had to be strong enough to poll one-third of the Diet seats needed to block constitutional revision but not much stronger. The Socialists met that condition successfully, thereby shielding Yoshida's Japan from external pressure.

The Conservative Counteroffensive

It is hard to imagine that John Foster Dulles, the quintessential cold warrior, was not alarmed by the neutralist trend in Japan, as he negotiated with the Japanese over the peace and security treaties. It did not escape his notice that the prime minister (Yoshida) was orchestrating it with his "puffball performance," as Dulles called it in disgust. Japan became Dulles's charge once again as he was appointed secretary of state by President Eisenhower. He would try to rearm Japan once and for all.

Something had to be done about the Communists, the neutralists, and the University of Tokyo if the free world was not to lose Japan to the Moscow-Peking axis. So Dulles led the second wave of Americans—after the initial wave of New Dealers—that would try to remodel Japanese ideology. As the United States's new friend, Japan had to be made more presentable than the wartime propaganda picture as a nation of saber-rattling militarists. It was also necessary to disabuse the Japanese of their self-flagellation and give them an injection of self-confidence; some sort of restoration was needed to get away from E. H. Norman and his total rejection of Japan. Dulles's most logical move would have been to revive nationalism. Indeed, while negotiating the peace treaty, he got in touch with the Gaullist-revisionists such as Hatoyama Ichiro and Ishibashi Tanzan, both soon to be prime ministers, apparently to put Yoshida on notice that he could be replaced if he persisted with his foot-dragging on rearmament.[33]

In 1952, then, Dulles enlisted the State Department to set in motion a "psychological program" to combat Marxism. Edwin O. Reischauer and his fellow Japanologists were entrusted with the program. In the hands of the academics, however, the efforts went beyond a psychological program to a search for a new paradigm of Japan's modern history.[34]

---

[32]Igarashi Takeshi, "Peace Making and Party Politics: The Formulation of the Domestic Foreign-Policy System in Postwar Japan," *Journal of Japanese Studies*, Summer 1985, p. 350.

[33]See Tsutsui Kiyotada, *Ishibashi Tanzan*, chapter 1.

[34]Dower, ed., *Origin of the Modern Japanese State*, p. 41.

The answer was the concept of modernization. In the new history based on that paradigm, Japan was no longer the semi-feudal oppressor and aggressor as the Marxists had said. Instead, it was the leading modernizer and the first to introduce constitutional democracy in Asia. Far from deriving from some innate native traits, Japanese militarism was now viewed as an aberration in an otherwise uninterrupted flow of "continuity"; the concept of feudalism was replaced by "tradition" or "early modernity"; and the "secret of Japan's success" was sought in its tradition.

Reischauer's Japan was a happy, presentable, modernizing democracy that could claim the Meiji Restoration and the Tokugawa Japan as its antecedent. But it still carried the cross. As he put it in 1950,

> No matter how feasible it would be to make Japan our military ally, it probably could not be done without seriously endangering Japanese democracy. In view of Japan's strong militaristic tradition and the record of recent history . . . , it would be too much to hope that Japan could be both a military and an ideological ally.[35]

Japan, said Reischauer, was "modern," not "feudal"; but being a race of samurai warriors, Japan nevertheless nursed "militarism" in its "tradition."

Reischauer's politically loaded point conjured up the bogey of "militarism" behind the attempt to rearm postwar Japan. That bogey was created jointly by MacArthur and Yoshida in 1951 when they tried to curb the U.S. government pressure on Japan to rearm while concluding the peace and security treaties. By "militarists" they referred to those who, purged by the occupation, rallied to Dulles's side in an attempt to revise the constitution. Whether the bogey was intended to be part of the modernization paradigm Reischauer constructed is not known. In any case John Foster Dulles's call for an ideology of rearming Japan was not answered: Reischauer chose to side with MacArthur and Yoshida.

Renovating Japanese ideology became urgent after the treaty revision crisis of 1960 rocked the U.S.-Japan tie and ended the reign of Kishi Nobusuke and his fellow revisionists. Having wrested control of the government, Yoshida's followers regrouped and began an ideological renovation under the label of *realism*, embracing Reischauer at the Hakone conferences and undoubtedly preempting him for their partisan ends. Defined as rapid economic growth, "modernization" was unsur-

---

[35]Edwin O. Reischauer, *The United States and Japan* (Cambridge, Mass.: Harvard University Press, 1957), p. xx.

passed as an ideological sanction for a lightly armed merchant state, a modern-day Venice.[36] The crisis induced Washington to abandon any further hopes for Japan's participation in a regional security role. Reischauer was posted to Tokyo as the new ambassador with the self-appointed mission of opening a "dialogue" with Japan's neutralist intellectuals. Thus began the process of converting Marxists into modernists.

The overriding purpose of standard history was to safeguard the new constructions of the security treaty and the Japanese constitution from all critics, Japanese and American.[37] In the first test case of what Kent E. Calder would later call "the crisis and compensation" scheme, Yoshida and his followers decided to deal with their critics on several fronts.[38] To appease the JSP and the left wing, Prime Minister Ikeda Hayato, who succeeded Kishi in 1960, set forth the slogan of "patience and generosity." In Diet politics, this translated into acceptance of "consensus decision making"—decisions by unanimity rather than by majority rule.

This peculiar voting procedure began when the JSP started indulging in obstructionist tactics, such as boycotting sessions and physically preventing voting in the committees and on the floor in the early postoccupation period. Majority rule, by which the LDP would outvote the JSP, was denounced by the media as "violence of numbers." If the government defied the media and forced a vote (kyoko saiketsu) or proceeded alone (tandoku shingi), it could win the vote but lose the mandate. This is what happened to Kishi on the treaty revision vote. Hence the government had to lean over backward to seek unanimity—or consensus. But unanimity involving the Socialists meant that Japan's security policy was at the mercy of the pacifists.

The LDP government thus decided to distance itself from international commitments, the security treaty, politically sensitive matters, and symbols such as equality and sovereignty. Pacifism became semiofficial when endorsed by the LDP; the three principles of nuclear disarmament, the ban on export of arms and weapons, the ban against

---

[36]See Edwin O. Reischauer and Nakayama Ichiro, "Nihon kindai-ka no rekishi-teki hyoka" (Historical assessment of Japan's modernization), Chuo Koron, September 1961, pp. 45–67. Kosaka Masataka, Kaiyo kokka Nihon no koso (Japan as a seafarring nation: A proposal) (Tokyo: Chuo Koronsha, 1974).

[37]Martin Weinstein's Japan's Postwar Defense Policy, 1947–1968 (New York: Columbia University Press, 1969) is a good example.

[38]Kent E. Calder, Crisis and Compensation: Public Policy and Political Stability in Japan, 1949–1986 (Princeton, N.J.: Princeton University Press, 1988).

spending more than 1 percent of gross national product on defense, and the like were all adopted after 1960. Japan's energy came to be absorbed almost wholly in domestic matters, economic development, and social welfare. Ikeda's plan of national income doubling was designed to lull the politicized JSP to sleep. The Realists began promoting the so-called *anpo* utility thesis (*anpo koyoron*), according to which Japan was said to enjoy great fiscal savings by virtue of U.S. military protection.[39]

Social values in Japan began to shift, with material gains being stressed rather than symbolic values. In an amazingly short time, the Japanese became enchanted by "my home," "my car," "the three treasures" (electric washer, refrigerator, television set), and the like. Class tension and the "domestic 38th parallel" were replaced by the consensus of the "new middle mass." Yoshida's mandarins insisted that consensus was part of Japan's native culture and could be traced back in time.[40] Although materialism was a strong antidote to ideological politics, it would soon have its own consequences.

The revisionists, who had also lost power over the treaty revision process, learned another hard lesson. Both Hatoyama and Kishi had sought autonomy, Hatoyama in defiance of Washington and Kishi in close collaboration with it. But they both failed dismally partly because, in the three-way division of power, the revisionists were outvoted two to one. As Miyazawa Kiichi explained:

> In managing politics, we were much troubled by this question: how to dissuade autocratic, reactionary, or militarist demands by old politicians of the prewar persuasions. It is true that as a means to this end, we have often used emotional reactions of the people and the resistance potential of the radical-liberals: it was decisive leverage in restraining the hardliners.[41]

The Realists began revising Japan's postwar history. Typically the Realists were recruited from universities other than Tokyo University, home of Maruyama Masao and the citadel of Marxism. Inoki Masamichi (later president of the Defense College) and Kosaka Masataka, both of Kyoto University, and Nagai Yonosuke, professor at the Tokyo Institute of Technology, were some of the chief protagonists of the Realist school.[42]

---

[39]See Nagai Yonosuke, "Yoshida dokutorin wa eien nari" (The Yoshida doctrine is forever), *Bungei Shunju*, May 1984, pp. 384–405.

[40]Murakimi Yasusuke, Kumon Shunpei, and Sato Seizaburo, *Bunmei toshiteno ie shakai* (The *ie* society as a civilization) (Tokyo: Chuo Koronsha, 1979).

[41]Cited in Uchida Kenzo, *Sengo nihon no hoshu seiji* (Postwar Japan's conservative politics) (Tokyo: Iwanami Shoten, 1960), p. 10.

[42]See Inoki, *Hyoden Yoshida Shigeru* (Yoshida Shigeru: A biography) (Tokyo:

The history of postwar Japan became bland and polite to a fault, as the baby—power—was thrown out with the bathwater of Marxism. In standard history, postwar Japan was a seamless web of good feeling, "consensus," and the "new middle mass" harnessed to the end of industrialization, best described in terms of inanimate macroeconomics. The Yoshida faction's contentions with the revisionists and the Socialists were sanitized and toned down. The JSP was now a marginal, though vital, member of the "consensus" family, defending the constitution. In the new history, embraced by younger Japanese scholars trained in the Anglo-Saxon tradition of empiricism, one can hardly detect the fact that the JSP and Sohyo once harbored revolutionary designs or that it was politically impossible to take a pro-American stance within Japanese universities and colleges until the mid-1970s.[43]

While soft-pedaling conflicts, standard history does not hesitate to show how Yoshida compares favorably to the revisionists. Thus today it is widely assumed that Yoshida founded the LDP. Hatoyama should have been enshrined as the LDP's founding father, but he is dismissed as a nonentity, best ignored;[44] Kishi's politics are seen simply as a reaction to Yoshida's "democracy."[45] In this view democracy in Japan depends on the American people to support Yoshida's developmental policy by absorbing Japan's exports.[46]

The U.S.-Japan tie was said to be a "partnership" or "fruitful partnership" that stresses formal equality and mutuality. Any suggestions to the contrary are downplayed. This illusion, which originated with Douglas MacArthur, viewed Japan in isolation—away from American

---

Yomiuri Shimbunsha, 1978); Kosaka, *Saiso Yoshida Shigeru*. The most recent example is Kozo Yamamura and Yasukichi Yasuba, *The Political Economy of Japan*, vol. 1, *The Domestic Transformation* (Stanford: Stanford University Press, 1987).

[43]In our workshop, I was asked by curious young scholars why I, reputed to be a hardnosed conservative, had invited so many experts on the Socialist party; they did not know how important the JSP was in the early postwar years.

[44]U.S. ambassador John M. Allison's posting to Tokyo, 1953–1957, overlapped the Hatoyama administration's tenure, 1953–1956. But Allison's memoir mentions Hatoyama in only four places. *Ambassador from the Prairie: Or Allison Wonderland* (New York: Houghton Mifflin, 1973).

[45]Mike Mochizuki assumes that the struggle between Yoshida and the revisionists was simply a struggle of democracy vs. reaction. *Managing and Influencing the Japanese Legislative Process: The Role of Parties and the National Diet* (Ph.D. dissertation, Harvard University, 1982), p. 465.

[46]Mike Mochizuki and Richard Samuels, "Japanese Security Requires No Choice between Evils," *New York Times*, December 19, 1982, op-ed page.

influence or power.[47] To conceal the origin of the no-war clause of the constitution, MacArthur created the fiction that Prime Minister Shidehara asked for it. This fiction, a revision of E. H. Norman's thesis of power, became the paradigm of standard history for U.S.-Japan relations.

Two examples of interpretations based on that paradigm are, first, Donald Hellmann's *Japanese Foreign Policy and Domestic Politics: The Peace Agreement with the Soviet Union* (Berkeley: University of California Press, 1969), an excellent pioneering work that remains a useful benchmark and an important source of data. Accurately describing Japan's internal dissension, conflict, and immobilism over the peace treaty with Moscow, to all intents and purposes, the book is about the bilateral negotiation between Tokyo and Moscow. There is not a suggestion, however, that Secretary of State John Foster Dulles objected to the peace treaty and even went to the extent of vetoing it or that the Japanese politicians were divided because the U.S.-Japan tie was at stake in the debate over the rapprochement with Moscow.

The second example is George R. Packard III's *Protest in Tokyo: The Security Treaty Crisis in 1960* (Princeton, N.J.: Princeton University Press, 1966). Here again is a pioneering work that has not been rivaled since. Based on the author's own personal observation, it is extremely rich in detail and offers many valuable insights. But it accepts the JSP's and Yoshida's interpretation of Kishi's downfall, according to which Kishi destroyed his bipartisan coalition with the JSP—a carryover of Hatoyama's bipartisanship over the Soviet rapprochement—by introducing a bill empowering the police in October 1958. This, however, camouflages the JSP's true motive for deserting Kishi: The JSP had determined to abandon Kishi when Secretary Dulles decided to involve Japan in the international crisis over Quemoy that started in August, two months previously. Hence the JSP would have opposed Kishi's police bill in any case. Packard ignores Dulles's decision altogether and blames Kishi's "handling" of domestic opposition or having "tied his fortune" to the treaty revision. Thus Kishi is the villain. That is exactly what Moscow, Peking, Yoshida, and the JSP said at the time. On that basis the political power passed from Kishi to Yoshida's protégé.

In truth Kishi was the deus ex machina that brought the upheaval to a reasonable conclusion, revised the treaty that generated so much animosity to the United States, and enabled Japan to move in the direction of economic development. Without Kishi, the antihero, to

---

[47]Douglas MacArthur, *Reminiscences* (New York: McGraw-Hill, 1964).

dissipate its energy on, the street mobs might have vented their anger at the United States.[48]

Overview of This Volume

Having outlined the 1955 System, its history, and its historiographic issues, let me introduce the individual chapters in this volume. Professor Tsutsui Kiyotada takes a fresh look at Japan's recent past by investigating the political process that led to the conservative merger.[49] A seldom-explored topic is what the occupation reforms, which were designed to alter the character of the Japanese political system, actually accomplished. By looking at the ideology, character, composition, and backgrounds of the political leadership that emerged, we know that the elite included the bureaucracies. Of the two conservative political parties, Seiyukai is better known than Minseito. Tsutsui correctly defines Minseito as a combination of nationalism and socialism, or "revisionist capitalism." (Nakasone Yasuhiro is the only survivor of this strand.) Ashida Hitoshi led the party for awhile, relinquishing leadership to Shigemitsu. But Minseito had more than its share of prewar politicians who did not sit well with Ashida or Miki Takeo, and it did not do well in the elections. In the end, the second conservative party was submerged in the LDP, which was dominated by the Seiyukai tradition.

Tsutsui also reminds us that Seiyukai was more libertarian, anti-bureaucratic, and democratic before Yoshida gained control over it and that Hatoyama and the professional politicians in Seiyukai were not as well connected with the business community as was Yoshida. Of the celebrated triumvirate of government-business-bureaucracy that came to dominate Japan, the bureaucracy might well have been the most critical link.

This chapter admirably demonstrates that (1) the issues of rearmament and constitutional revision were the axis around which postwar politics turned, (2) the presence of Yoshida and Hatoyama in Seiyukai split the party, and (3) they in turn split the Minseito party. But the persistence of the prewar party identification at the grass roots is surprising. During the stage Tsutsui discusses, *jiban* counted at the grass roots, as Tani also shows. Before long, however, *koenkai* displaced *jiban*. How was this done? There is no research at all to answer that.

---

[48]In Martin Weinstein's book, the security treaty of 1960 is simply credited to Yoshida. *Japan's Postwar Defense Policy, 1947–1968* (New York: Columbia University Press, 1969), p. 87.

[49]Ibid.

Tsutsui suggests that in 1955 the conservative parties were agreed on the need for merger and on a common platform, but I believe he underestimates the depth of Yoshida-Hatoyama conflict. The merger's motives were clearly anti-Yoshida, but it failed to contain him because Dulles supported Yoshida on the peace treaty with the Soviets. Thus the platform committee of the LDP was unable to agree on a foreign policy plank by October.[50] Instead of resolving the Yoshida issue,the merger became bogged down by it. Hence the Hatoyama faction went for the ultimate gamble to gerrymander the JSP into impotence and amend the constitution. That was the design behind the 1956 bill to create the single-member district, winner-take-all election system.

Professor Ito Takashi, the leading figure in the movement to take new stock of postwar history in Japan, has done several valuable archival researches (including one on Kishi Nobusuke). Ito's impeccable scholarship is a model to others. His chapter in this volume discusses Shigemitsu Mamoru, a key figure in the early postoccupation days who has long since been forgotten. The following points in Ito's chapter are important.

By 1953–1954 Yoshida represented a small minority among the conservatives, and opinion was nearly unanimous that he had to go. Arrayed against him were Hatoyama Ichiro, Kono Ichiro, Miki Bukichi, Matsumura Kenzo, Ishibashi Tanzan, Shigemitsu Mamoru, Oasa Tadao, Ashida Hitoshi, Ogata Taketora, Miki Takeo, Kitamura Tokutaro, Ono Banboku, and Kishi Nobusuke; but owing to standard history, we hear little of these opponents of Yoshida. Until we know who they were and what they did, postwar history cannot be written, and the same is true for the Socialists.

Ito shows that Shigemitsu saw an alternating two-party system as a vital prerequisite of democracy, as did most of the politicians named above (Miki Bukichi might have been an exception). But because they did not know what to do with the JSP they were stymied; the three-way split was unstable, but the Socialists were too radical to be a coalition partner.

Ito's description of Shigemitsu as a sound nationalist but not anti-American seems credible to me. Yet contemporary U.S. documents (in *Foreign Relations of the United States*, for instance) show that the

---

[50]"Why Conservative Merger Is Difficult: Coordinating Flexible Diplomacy Is the Focus: Neither Side Gives Up Initiative," *Asahi Shimbun*, October 15, 1955, p. 1. On the following day, Hatoyama announced that it was impossible to ask for the return of Kunashiri and Etorofu. But on November 1, 1955, the LDP platform committee demanded the return of Kunashiri and Etorofu.

Americans feared Shigemitsu and others in his company. The blanket suspicion of the depurgees, prewar politicians, militarists, the right wing, and the like became a self-fulfilling prophecy that limited the scope of U.S. foreign policy and forced Washington to accommodate Yoshida on the theory that he was a "safe" conservative.

Known for his meticulous scholarship, Otake Hideo argues that the JSP should undergo a Bad Godesberg–like transformation, which produced a pro-NATO Socialist chancellor (Helmut Schmidt) for the German SPD.[51] If Otake is willing to endorse the West German–type rearmament, he ought to be a bit more charitable toward Ashida, the only conservative politician available as a partner for the Socialists. Just as the U.S. government debated sending Self-Defense Forces to the gulf, the JSP faces the same predicament: either accommodating or facing extinction. But as Otake shows, the Socialists never faced the issue squarely and instead dealt with rearmament as a question of personality.

Professor Masumi accepts the constitution and the security treaty as the cornerstones of the 1955 System, as I do. But he argues that the system was transformed after 1960, without labeling the successor regime and ignoring the fact that the cornerstones remain in place. I differ with him on this point. I believe the 1955 System will continue (1) as long as the two cornerstones exist and (2) as long as that existence preserves the tension in the system or aborts bipartisan foreign policy. The "end of ideology" in 1960 merely signified the maturation of the system, as noted above.

An interesting part of Masumi's chapter is his argument that "money politics," as perfected by Tanaka Kakuei, was not an aberration but a "structural" fulfillment of the system and that corruption and money politics are inherent in the system of one-party dominance. Masumi may be said to have anticipated van Wolferen. He also anticipated Calder's "crisis and compensation" thesis with respect to the LDP's handling of the opposition.

Professor Tani's chapter contains sociological as well as political analyses, with the overall conclusion that the Socialists were incompetent. Their unreadiness to step into power in 1947, however, underscores the difficulty of externally administered social engineering and points up the unfortunate fact that in Japan it is easier to get things done if you team up with the establishment made up of Tokyo University graduates. The Socialists' incompetence suggests that they proba-

---

[51]Otake Hideo, *Adenaua to Yoshida Shigeru* (Adenauer and Yoshida Shigeru) (Tokyo: Chuo Koron, 1986).

bly could not have survived the early cold war if the two wings of the LDP were united; that is to say, they survived because of Yoshida's help.

Tani's analysis of the ascendancy of the JSP left wing is a valuable contribution to our understanding of what happened after 1951. In 1946, SCAP blessed the founding of Sanbestu, a labor federation affiliated with the JCP; but in 1950, alarmed by Communist influence, SCAP organized Sohyo hoping it would be anti-Communist. To prevent the JSP from sliding leftward, Sohyo was ordered to join the JSP en masse. Sohyo became radical, however, thus strengthening the Socialist left wing. Zengakuren and the Japan Teachers' Union, both created by SCAP, became radicalized after the end of the occupation. Together with the JSP and Sohyo, they were to spearhead the pacifist movement, which fully matured after a 1954 incident in which a Japanese fishing vessel was exposed to radioactive fallout near Bikini atoll. At that time pacifism in Japan became institutionalized as part of the collateral development of the 1955 System. After 1960, the LDP itself reinforced the movement with the three principles of nuclear disarmament, the bans on export of weapons, and the capping of defense spending at 1 percent of gross national product.

I do not hesitate to call this an instance of LDP-JSP collusion, although the price—one-party dominance, political corruption, and the "crisis and compensation" mechanism—was dear. Compensation, which began as an appeasement of the Socialists, has extended to appeasing China and Korea. The neutrality plank of the Socialists, a lofty ideal, has been bastardized through collusion. There are good reasons for van Wolferen's appearance.

Tani's grass-roots analysis complements Otake's view of the rearmament controversy. Both Tani and Otake maintain that the right-wing Socialists were vulnerable to the charge of collaboration with the militarists: To prove their Socialist conscience they had to move leftward. Aside from union-steward types like Nishio, the right-wing leaders were intellectuals, full of "affect" but short on instrumental reasons.

Unlike the conservative politicians, who have left an abundance of memoirs and diaries, the Socialists have been taciturn and secretive, probably partly because they were in liaison with Moscow and Peking.[52] Whatever the case, for several important JSP decisions we have only an ideological and formal accounting. The JSP's total silence on the switch from supporting the treaty revision to opposing it, a decision made

---

[52]Hara's recent work is an excellent analysis of the JSP's approach to Peking in 1958. Hara Yoshihisa, *Sengo Nihon to kokusai seiji* (Postwar Japan and international politics) (Tokyo: Chuo Koronsha, 1988).

presumably over the summer of 1958, is most baffling. To oppose the revision meant supporting the 1951 treaty de facto, though the point went unstated. What was the internal debate and why are the Socialists so secretive about this decision?

Professor Nagao's work is the first of its kind to appear in English, although the materials he discusses have been in the constitutional law textbook used in the general education curriculum at Tokyo University for years, making it standard fare for Japan's "elite." No matter how uncomfortable, the origin of that constitution cannot be avoided, either in a "con law" course at Todai or in a discussion of the 1955 System.

The phrasing of the Potsdam declaration and the subsequent notes to the Japanese government legally empowered the U.S. government to either turn Japan into a republic or preserve the emperor system. The declaration spoke of "our terms," but Japan's surrender was unconditional; that was the U.S. intent, and it was so understood by the Japanese government before it accepted the declaration. (See Leon V. Sigal's recent book.[53]) In other words, the United States held the emperor and the monarchy hostage to Japan's good conduct under the occupation, a little known major reason for the occupation's success.

The final chapter (mine) is a summary of the contention between the Gaullists and Yoshida and needs no further comment. Instead let me reflect on the nature of the U.S.-Japan relationship represented by cooperation between MacArthur and Reischauer on the one hand and Yoshida on the other. Without the constitution that relationship would have been different because the reverse course would have been more complete. MacArthur's intervention in the peace treaty negotiation played the most critical part in perpetuating the constitution.

What is the 1955 System's future? That system exists because of the tension between the constitution and the security treaty. The tension was reduced by the settlement of 1960, by which the JSP accepted the treaty de facto. If the JSP can accept the treaty de jure, the tension will disappear—unless the JSP's concession encourages the revisionists to demand constitutional revision.

Lately, however, more formidable foes of the system have emerged: American revisionists such as Chalmers Johnson, Clyde Prestowitz, and James Fallows, who in turn inspired the Japanese revisionists Ishihara Shintaro and "The Japan That Can Say No."

My prediction is that the changes sweeping the world today are so

---

[53]Leon V. Sigal, *Fighting to a Finish: The Politics of War Termination in the United States and Japan, 1945* (Ithaca, N.Y.: Cornell University Press, 1988), p. 154.

great that they will not leave Japan unaffected. Japan, however, is not simply an East Germany, created and supported entirely by an outside power. As this book demonstrates, although the Japanese took an active part in constructing the 1955 System, Japan and its enormous financial and industrial powers are precisely the engine of change. I believe that dusk is settling on the 1955 System and that the Owl of Minerva can now fly.

2 | The 1955 System: Origin and Transformation

Masumi Junnosuke

The 1955 System

In October 1955 the right and left wings of the Japan Socialist party (JSP) merged, and in the following month the two conservative parties, the Democratic party and the Liberal party, merged to form the Liberal Democratic party (LDP). No one doubts that this marked the founding of the 1955 System. The rationale for the mergers was the desire for political power and control of the government. The Socialist party, splintered over the San Francisco peace treaty, increased its Diet strength in the successive elections of 1952, 1953, and 1955 (the advance of the left wing was particularly noteworthy). In the spring of 1955 election, both wings campaigned on platforms promising a merger in the near future. The Diet strength of the conservatives, however, kept shrinking in succeeding elections, and the Democratic party, which had organized the Hatoyama cabinet, fell far short of a majority in 1955. The conservatives resolved to merge to build a stable conservative government and to respond to the Socialists' merger.

The mergers in the two camps, however, were brought about by strong external pressures. Sohyo, the labor federation created by the occupation authority, turned sharply left and became increasingly radical with the coming of the Korean War, directing a large-scale labor campaign against production "rationalization" in many factories. Without Sohyo's total endorsement, the JSP left wing could not have expanded as it did. Without Sohyo's pressure, the JSP would not have come together again.

Having launched itself on a campaign of technology innovation and production rationalization, however, the business community (represented by Keidanren, among others) needed a stable, conservative government to maintain good relationships with Washington, to thwart the JSP's growth, and to cope with the intensifying labor movement. Under this strong business (*zaikai*) pressure the conservatives resolved to combine into a single conservative party. In short, the 1955 System was a confrontational system that emerged against the backdrop of intense labor-management conflict.

Opposition to the mergers in both camps arose out of factional squabbles over hegemony or ulterior motives. In the JSP's case the prime movers behind the merger were Suzuki Mosaburo (of the Ronoha faction) in the left wing and Kawakami Jotaro (of the Nichiro faction) on the right; Wada Hiroo in the left wing and Nishio Suehiro in the right wing opposed the merger. Nishio in particular was critical of the left wing and Sohyo for opposing constitutional revisions. With the backing of the unions affiliated with Domei, Sohyo's conservative rival, Nishio proclaimed the "national party thesis" to oppose the "class party thesis." In the spring of 1960 he would organize the Democratic Socialist party (DSP), thus undoing the merger in less than five years.

On the conservative side, the prime movers were the Democratic party's Executive Committee chairman, Miki Bukichi, and the Liberal Party's secretary-general, Ono Banboku, whereas the Miki Takeo–Matsumura Kenzo faction in the Democratic party and the Yoshida faction in the Liberal party were opposed. Thus the conservatives could not agree on a new president and settled instead on a system of acting commissioners (Hatoyama, Ogata Taketora, Miki Bukichi, and Ono). But the opposition was overcome on both sides by anticommunism (or antisocialism) in the LDP and by the battle cry of class struggle in the JSP's left wing.

This confrontation was based on the inheritance bequeathed by the U.S. occupation—the new constitution (1946) and the security treaty (1951). The constitution was the early occupation period's biggest monument to the democratization of Japan, and the security treaty grew out of U.S.-Soviet tension in the late occupation period. The two did not sit well with each other. The JSP's merger sponsors defended the constitution and wanted to abolish the treaty; the conservatives demanded constitutional revision and the preservation of the treaty. The two monuments, with their twisted interrelationship, were passed on to the third monument—the 1955 System—and became the banners for the LDP and the JSP in their politics of confrontation.

The standoff between the two camps intensified under the Kishi government (1957–1959), which stood for a "new era in Japan-U.S. relations," and came to a head over the issue of the security treaty revision in 1960. The Sohyo-centered mobilizational organization and media-directed information campaign attracted an unprecedented mass of demonstrators around the Diet building, encouraging the Socialists and splitting the LDP. Even though the treaty was ratified, President Eisenhower's trip was canceled and the Kishi cabinet resigned. The Ikeda cabinet that followed steered away from politics, making economics the priority through the policy of income doubling. This was the start of full-fledged, high-speed economic growth.

Over the years, the switch from politics to economics has taken the wind out of both sides' sails. The LDP's desire for constitutional revision and the Socialists' desire for treaty abolition were frozen and, except for an occasional gasp, petered out. Unlike the cases of "consensus" and "convergence" between conservative and Socialist parties in the West, the two camps became bedfellows without retracting their platforms. But in the midst of rapid industrialization and social change, the bed they shared grew smaller and smaller.

Let us review the election results of this period. In 1958, in the first general election after the 1955 System was established, the LDP's party vote was 57.8 percent. Thereafter, it declined steadily: In 1967 it fell below 50 percent and reached an all-time low of 41.8 percent in 1976, showing signs of recovery thereafter. The LDP's strength in terms of Diet seats was 61.5 percent in 1958, fell below 60 percent in 1967 and below 50 percent in 1967, and reached a low of 48.5 percent in 1979.

The JSP, too, has been in a long-term decline. Starting from its all-time high of 32.9 percent of the vote in 1958, by 1960 that figure was hovering between 20 and 30 percent (after the DSP's walkout), and dipped below 20 percent in 1979. JSP Diet seats reached a high of 35.6 percent in 1958, dipped to the 20–30 percent range in 1967 and 18.5 percent in 1969, rebounded to the 20–30 percent range, but barely exceeded 20 percent by the end of the 1970s.

The sum of the LDP and the JSP vote was 90.7 percent in 1958; by 1962 it had fallen to its nadir of 62.5 percent. Their combined Diet seats totaled 97.0 percent in 1958, falling to a low of 69.4 percent in 1979. Roughly speaking, the two parties declined while maintaining a 2-to-1 ratio between them until 1969; thereafter, the JSP declined faster than the LDP.

In the February 1964 issue of *Shiso* I published a short article entitled "The Political System of 1955," which argued that the LDP-JSP oligopoly at a 2-to-1 ratio meant a long-term LDP government. In the election of 1963, the LDP garnered 60.6 percent of the Diet seats and the JSP 30.8 percent; their combined seats totaled 91.4 percent. In 1969, in the third chapter of *The Political System of Modern Japan,* "The 1955 Political System," I argued that "the party vote ratio of 2:1 will remain but the combined vote of the two parties will shrink" (p. 313). In the general election of 1967, LDP Diet seats totaled 57.0 percent, the JSP seats, 28.8 percent, and the number of combined seats, 85.8 percent. The *Asahi Shimbun* opinion poll of 1968, however, noted a decline of Socialist support, and in the following year there was a visible decline in the JSP vote.

The combined LDP-JSP Diet strength declined owing to the expansion of such third parties as the Japan Communist party (JCP), the Democratic Socialist party (DSP), and Komeito. Not until 1969 did the JCP—having lost thirty-five seats following the violent insurrection in 1950—begin to win ten seats or more. In good times, the DSP held more than thirty seats. Winning twenty-five seats in 1967, Komeito at times exceeded fifty seats. All three went through wide fluctuations in power. In 1958 their combined party vote was 2.6 percent, in 1960 more than 10 percent, in 1969 more than 25 percent, and since 1976 about 30 percent. Their combined Diet seats were 0.2 percent in 1958, more than 10 percent in 1967, and more than 20 percent since 1976, with the highest 26.8 percent in 1979. If we add the JSP vote to the total, opposition seats were in excess of 40 percent in the 1970s. This phenomenon—*yo-yato hakuchu* (government-opposition balance)—is based on multiple opposition parties.

During the period of transition from LDP-JSP oligopoly to *yo-yato hakuchu,* important changes were taking place both in social structures and in political organizations, as I explain below. Internationally, the Nixon shock of 1971 was followed by the oil shock of 1973, which ushered in a period of slow growth. On the whole, the 1955 System may have broken down at the beginning of the 1970s, depending on how one defines the system. If the 1955 System means the LDP monopoly of power, it remains in existence; in any case an important change took place in the early 1970s. The special issue of *Nenpo Seijigaku* entitled "The Formation and Decline of the 1955 System" (1977) argued that the "process of decline" was already "in progress" (introduction, p. 2). In *Modern Politics* (1985), I pointed out that *yo-yato hakuchu* amounted to a transformation of the system. Perhaps it is simpler to refer to the decline of the 1955 System or to the transformation of the long-term LDP government.

Social Change

Behind the above-mentioned election results were tremendous social changes caused by the rapid industrialization that took off in the 1950s and attained full momentum in the 1960s. This third wave of industrialization followed the first wave of economic development under Tokugawa Bakufu in the eighteenth century and the second wave of rich-country-strong-arms industrialization under the Meiji state in the nineteenth. Neither the eighteenth-century nor the nineteenth-century advances, however, entailed social change of such magnitude in so short a period. We can view these social changes from three perspectives: changes in social stratification composition (industrial and occupational), changes in social modes (urban and rural), and the impact of the mass media.

Let us look first at changes in social stratification. The total employment figure grew from 36 million in 1950 to 56 million in 1980, while the primary sector fell from 48.3 percent to 10.9 percent. Thus Japan went from a 50 percent agricultural society to a 10 percent agricultural society during those decades. The tertiary sector climbed from 29.8 percent to 55.4 percent; the secondary sector increased from 21.9 percent to 33.6 percent but hit a ceiling in the 1970s, with its highest point, 34.1 percent, in 1975. In the occupational structure, the proportion of salaried workers increased from 16 percent to 30 percent during 1955–1975 and of industrial workers from 20 percent to 33 percent. The proportion of self-employed businessmen and manufacturers remained stable at 19 percent, and that of agricultural, fishery, and forestry workers declined from 41 percent to 14 percent.

To contrast this with the picture in Europe, the first French statistics, in 1856, recorded 51.7 percent for the primary sector. Hence a 50 percent agricultural society may have existed in France between the 1840s and 1860s; yet a 10 percent agricultural society was not reached there until the 1970s. According to the first statistics of imperial Germany, in 1882, the primary sector totaled 47.3 percent; we may assume that 50 percent agricultural society existed between the 1850s and 1870s. In 1960 the figure for the agricultural sector dropped to 10 percent. Thus the changes that took a hundred years to accomplish in France and Germany took place in Japan in thirty years, and by the 1970s Japan had reached the same level as these two European countries in terms of the population working in the primary sector.

Second, let us look at changes in the social mode, or urban concentration of population. With high-speed industrialization, the rural population flowed to the cities, where workers, commuters, and migrants multiplied to make social relations more fluid and varied. During 1955–1965, the population in the Pacific coast belt, including the new industrial cities such as Fukuyama, Mizushima, Goi, and Kashima, rose from 50 percent to 55 percent of the total population of Japan. In densely populated areas such as Tokyo and Osaka, the population hit a ceiling and then began to decline, and the surrounding regions, such as Kanagawa, Saitama, Chiba, Nara, and Hyogo, began to absorb migrations. In sharp contrast, in the villages and towns of the mountainous regions, the migration of the young has left a population of aged, women, and children. In time, death rates began to exceed birth rates; whole families began to leave for cities; and branch schools, public halls, fire brigades, and irrigation systems went out of existence, along with village society.

The third perspective is the rapid growth of the mass media. First, radio gave way to television. In 1955, 73.8 percent of all households owned radios, peaking at 81.3 percent in 1958 and declining to 45.8 percent in 1961. In 1955, 0.9 percent of all households owned television sets, 33.2 percent in 1960, and 94.8 percent, or saturation, in 1970. Newspapers and other printed media are holding their own. The relative effects of the printed or linguistic symbol system and the image symbol system are unclear, but journalists situated at the fountainhead of information can influence information consumers through news collection, editing, commentaries, and suggestions. Such influence erodes the mobilizational network of men of influence in a traditional agricultural society, while mobilizing the new migrants to the cities. Industrialization thus has created and expanded the mass society through the interaction of urbanization and the mass media.

The LDP's constituency, *jiban*, which is made up of farmers and self-employed businessmen and manufacturers, gathers votes through the efforts of local men of influence. In the *Asahi Shimbun* poll of 1955, 48 percent of all voters endorsed the LDP; in 1965, 45 percent did so. In 1955, 62 percent of the self-employed and 52 percent of those working in agriculture, forestry, and fisheries (AFF) endorsed the LDP, whereas in 1965, 58 percent of the self-employed and 59 percent of the AFF gave their approval to the LDP. During these ten years, the self-employed group remained stable in size, whereas the AFF group underwent a rapid decline; hence the ratio of the self-employed among LDP supporters was 24 percent in 1955 and 26 percent in 1965, compared with the ratio of those engaged in AFF industries: 44 percent in 1955 and 33 percent in 1965. The sums of the two were 68 percent and 59 percent. In terms of regions, the LDP was endorsed by 48 percent of all registered voters in cities with under 100,000 registered voters and by 48 percent in all smaller towns and villages; in both quarters combined the LDP was endorsed by 66 percent. Thus the LDP's *jiban* at this time was among the self-employed, those in AFF industries, and those in nonurban areas.

As for the Socialists, their main *jiban* was among the industrial workers and the salaried class, who were mobilized through unions and the media. As the saying went, "organizations for the JSP, face [*kao*, personal connections] for the LDP" or "newspapers for the JSP, face for the LDP." In 1955 and 1965, respectively, the JSP's supporters numbered 31 percent and 34 percent of registered voters, 51 percent and 48 percent of industrial workers, and 50 percent and 45 percent of the salaried class. Among the LDP supporters, the industrial workers were 34 percent and 40 percent; the salaried class was 27 percent and 30 percent. The proportions of both groups among JSP supporters were as high as 61 percent and 70 percent. In terms of regional distribution, 43 percent of all registered voters in the seven major cities in 1965 endorsed the JSP; in those cities with more than 100,000 registered voters, 34 percent supported the JSP. Together they constituted 43 percent of the entire group that supported the JSP. Until the 1960s those instances where the JSP polled considerable votes in the rural district were attributable to the survival of prewar peasant union organizers.

The spread of mass society erodes the traditional *jiban* of a Dietman. To cope with this erosion, individual candidates thus began organizing their personal *koenkai* (a permanent campaign organization for nurturing *jiban*) across the country during the 1958 general election campaign. By 1963, many local assemblymen had followed suit. According to a national survey in 1967, *koenkai* members constituted 6 percent of all the registered voters: 4 percent in seven major cities, 6 percent in medium and small cities, and 6 percent in the rural areas. Of those in AFF industries, self-employed businessmen, and manufacturers, roughly 10 percent belonged to *koenkai*; of those who voted for the LDP, 8 percent belonged to one. Komeito enjoyed the highest organization rate, 16 percent. By 1967, 14 percent of registered voters belonged to *koenkai*; among LDP voters, 20 percent were members, a figure exceeded only by Komeito's 24 percent.

From its founding onward, the LDP has sought to transform itself from a parliamentary party to a mass-based one. Competing with Sohyo's organizational activism made counterpart grass-roots activities necessary. Training "organizational leaders" was one consequence. Following the treaty revision upheaval in 1960, party building was spurred by the Central Political Institute and resident local organizers. But how effective these efforts have been is doubtful. Grass-roots organizations were nothing but self-help Dietmen and local assemblymen; the party, however, has had to depend on them ever since and will probably continue to do so into the foreseeable future. Two documents show this. Miki Takeo, in an advisory opinion of October 1963, said,

> Though we cannot ban personal *koenkai* at present, they pose not a little problem for party activity by their singular concentration on personal interest. We must think of ways to absorb them into the party organization in the future. To secure mutual cooperation of the two in the interim, we ought to enlist and register the important members of the *koenkai* and at least 500 others into party locals and ask them to contribute positively to party branches.

Secretary-General Tanaka Kakuei's draft proposal of September 1965 put it this way:

> The party's local organization is in reality a loose federation of Dietmen's *koenkai* and is not functioning effectively. To overcome this defect and to vitalize the grass-roots actions and organizations under the leadership of the headquarters and branches, a system of resident local organizers should be set up to become the nucleus of party activities.

In the meantime the Socialist Dietmen began to build their own *koenkai*. Although the JSP relied heavily on union vote-getting power, its union constituency averaged only 30 percent of the party vote; where unions maintained strong agitprop activities, the vote was at most 60 percent. Thus union support had to be supplemented with *koenkai*. Candidates such as lawyers and doctors who did not belong to unions found *koenkai* indispensable. The JSP's report of March 1961 stated that "despite complaints in the past, *koenkai* proved to be effective in districts with weak party organization," but that "it is desirable to absorb them into the party organization where possible." The report of February 1964 said,

> Of late we have frequently reinforced the weakness of party organization with *koenkai*. Election struggles ought to be conducted by the party organization. *Koenkai* tend to impart a personal character to campaigns, and are undesirable from the perspective of the party organization. However, we must concede their necessity to a degree under the present circumstances.

But the JSP's *koenkai* movement is lackadaisical when compared with those of other parties. According to the national survey mentioned above, only 5 percent of those voting for the JSP in the general election of 1967 hailed from *koenkai*. The figure increased to 13 percent in the 1976 election but still lagged behind those for other parties.

Also noteworthy is the JSP's "structural reform" movement, which was initiated in the late 1950s by Eda Saburo and party center secretaries who took their cue on structural reform from Italian Communist leader Palmiro Togliacci. Seeking to switch the JSP's policy line in response to the advent of mass society, this movement addressed the same issues that were dealt with by the German SPD in 1959. Whether structural reform would have succeeded remains a moot point; before it could be attempted, the movement was drawn into fierce factional conflict. In the event, Eda left the JSP in 1977 after seventeen years of contention, leaving behind a miserable ruin. But the JSP still faces the issue: What place does a Socialist movement have in a mature society?

Meanwhile, the treaty revision upheaval of 1960 must be seen as a major contemporary social movement. The mobilizational potential of the National Congress to Stop the Security Treaty Revision, based on the Sohyo unions, was reinforced by the media to produce an enormous impact made all the greater because Japan was rapidly growing into a mass society. Huge, uncontrollable crowds congregated around the Diet building. Japan was then a 30 percent agricultural society (with the primary sector at 32.6 percent). This proportion is comparable to that of the primary sectors of Nazi Germany and France under the popular front (29.0 percent in 1933 Germany and 35.6 percent in 1936 France). There appeared, therefore, to be common structural factors in all three.

The unruly crowds in the 1960 incident stiffened the JSP's back, whereas the antimainstreamers in the LDP deserted the government, forcing Prime Minister Kishi to resign. This might have been a temporary anomaly created in the early stage of high-speed growth. Standing on the platform of income doubling in the October election, the Ikeda government polled 57.6 percent in party vote and 63.4 percent in Diet seats. Due in part to the walkout by the Democratic Socialist party (DSP), the JSP's figures were 27.6 percent and 31.0 percent, respectively.

The nationwide organizing of sundry pressure groups and lobbies was an important event for the LDP, both for *jiban* maintenance and expansion and for the policy formation process. About the time the occupation ended, all sorts of national interest groups formed to petition the Diet and relevant ministries for subsidies and licenses. For the ministries' part, husbanding and promoting interest groups went on in order to expand and secure their turf and jurisdiction. Dietmen joined and orchestrated the petition drive vis-à-vis relevant ministries, the LDP Policy and Research Committee, and Diet committees in order to expand their *jiban* and sources of funding. In this fashion, we see a multidimensional, nationwide interest-distribution structure established by fusing pressure group interests, ministerial jurisdiction, and Dietmen's *jiban*.

Although there are all sorts of interest groups, the business community (for example, Keidanren) is one of the most important. Business makes generous payoffs in money, an important political resource, but money does not translate directly into votes. For vote-getting purposes, agricultural cooperatives and small-business groups are more reliable. For husbanding one's *jiban*, however, nothing can equal local governments if one can channel public works and subsidies to them. The district will flourish and a *jiban* will expand in no time. The regional development policy of the Ikeda cabinet (1961–1964) drove this interest distribution structure at full throttle. Local governments, other interest groups, Dietmen, local assemblymen, and ministries went all out in promoting their respective interests. Because regional development meant building the infrastructure for new plant investment, big business endorsed it wholeheartedly. Politics became a matter of peddling civil engineering projects, and mass society spread. I call this the regional development–type political process.

This regional development–type political process, which mobilized the central ministries, interest groups, and electoral *jiban*, is altogether different from the treaty revision–type political process. In the treaty revision upheaval, the unions and the media manipulated the masses concerning an ideological issue in politics and diplomacy. The regional development–type political process lobbies for a material payoff. Lobbying, of course, can be a type of mass mobilization, for though the red flag–waving union men and Zengakuren may be absent, local government officials, assemblymen, and agricultural cooperative (Nokyo) leaders do descend en masse on the Nagata-cho district. The scale of mobilization in this process may be smaller than in the treaty revision upheaval, but it is persistent and repetitive. At times headbanded agricultural cooperative cadres, farmers, or textile workers may surround the ministries and the Diet.

This phenomenon of an interest distribution structure, or "corporatism," first made its appearance after World War II in highly industrialized countries. Although Japan appears to be following the trend, unlike other countries, Japan's nationwide, multidimensional lobbying structure was created with a permanent ruling party, the LDP, at the apex of the interest distribution structure. With their electoral *jiban* eroded through advanced industralization, the LDP and its Dietmen sought to defend and expand their turf by distributing subsidies to interest groups. This defensive reaction, however, only hastened the demise of the LDP's traditional *jiban*, which was based on local men of influence, while intensifying the intraparty struggle for spoils. The ruling party could not have retained its privileged position without monopolizing the distribution of interests.

Being on the outside, the JSP and Sohyo were kept out of the spoils. Sohyo, however, began to switch its focus from class struggle to labor-management cooperation in the 1960s in response to Ikeda's switch from a political priority to an economic one. The benchmark of this shift was the opposition's failure to stymie the nationalization drive at the Miike Coal Mines in the summer of 1960, for this gave the final impetus to the famed spring offensive of Sohyo, which began in 1955. Sohyo's spring offensive was institutionalized in 1964 when its leaders met with Prime Minister Ikeda, thus turning the spring offensive into an annual event bereft of class character and emphasizing sharing the pie of economic growth. Also in 1964 the International Metalworkers' Federation, Japanese Council (IMF-JC), was founded at the initiative of shipbuilding, chemical, and steelworkers' unions. The IMF-JC expressly rejected class struggle in favor of labor-management cooperation to prepare for trade liberalization and intensified international competition in the metal industries. The council's expansion triggered the movement to reorganize labor, which may be regarded as the unions' participation in the LDP's interest distribution structure.

By the early 1970s the massive social change of the previous decade reached its peak, with improved standards of living and standardizations of life-style. Electric washers, refrigerators, vacuum cleaners, color television sets, air conditioners, and private automobiles reached every segment of society. The middle stratum (*chukanso*) of society set the dominant life-style, and more than 90 percent of the people came to regard themselves as middle class (*churyu*).

Industrial workers and union members did not escape these trends. As technological innovations made their way into heavy and chemical industries, the nature and style of shop floor work changed. Team work and physical labor were replaced by the isolated, mental work of monitoring automated machinery. The difference between working and middle classes began to blur, and the union movement had to change accordingly.

At this time, the number of independent voters increased. According to a Jiji Press poll, the proportion of those who did not support any party grew from 4 percent in 1960 to more than 20 percent in 1971 and exceeded 30 percent in 1976, particularly in urban areas and among the educated and the young. This trend contrasted sharply with the political indifference frequently encountered among the rural, less-educated, and aged population in the early 1960s. Because the politically indifferent in the rural areas tended to follow the suggestion of local bosses, voter turnout was high.

The urban independents know and care about politics, but they have no permanent affiliation with any political party and are under no social pressure to go to the voting booth. These independents, whose number exceeds that of nonvoters, are not necessarily nonvoters. The rapid rise of the independent voter signifies a retreat to private life and to the enjoyment of home and hobby that generally results in political passivity and a status quo orientation. But depending on circumstances, independents may give rise to surprising activism and status quo denial. Local movements addressing the issues of pollution and environmental destruction seem to have this character.

Pollution was already an issue in the 1950s. When Sato Eisaku vied with Ikeda for the LDP presidency in 1964, he took issue with the high-speed growth policy and demanded a "correction of lopsidedness" and "social development." This was both political rhetoric and prophecy. In the late 1960s, the environmentalist movements spread nationwide, and the plant enticement campaigns of local governments turned overnight into plant rejection campaigns. In the Diet session of 1970, the Sato cabinet passed fourteen antipollution bills.

The antipollution movements were framed around issues stemming from advanced industrialization, and their modus operandi presupposed the existence of a society spawned by advanced industrialization. Industrial pollution affected a locality, not a particular class. The antipollution movement called for amateur activists with spare time and intelligence-collecting ability. The flexibility of the amateur leadership prevented professionalization and rigidity in the movement; from the core to the fringe, the movement was fluid, not institutionalized. Although a campaign was particularized in terms of time, place, and issue articulation, it could touch off a secondary explosion elsewhere and escalate into a major political movement by enlisting media support. In this respect, the antipollution movement was typical of a large society. Forging a national coalition of antipollution movements, however, would be extremely difficult, and developing such a movement into a national political party with parliamentary representation as in the case of the Greens in West Germany inconceivable.

The antipollution campaigns peaked in 1970, but the *kakushin shu-cho* (radical-liberal mayors and governors) movement that followed it was similar. By 1975, 10 governors were labeled *kakushin*-leaning independents; in the following year, one quarter of the country's 640 mayors were *kakushin*, with the majority independents elected with varied combinations of endorsements by four opposition parties. All candidates called for service to or dialogue with the citizenry, assailing the existing local administrations for a bias toward the LDP and big business and against environmental and life-quality concerns. Improved election campaigns directed at "floating" votes were successful, as several victories were chalked up to irate inhabitants opposed to the construction of petrochemical refineries in their communities. Corruption and division among the conservatives helped the opposition as well.

On the whole, however, *kakushin* mayors and governors stood on flimsy ground. Within the elective mayoral and governorship system, they garnered independent votes, thanks to conservative mistakes, but they landed in the middle of conservative local governments. *Kakushin* parties in local assemblies were usually in the extreme minority, and local administration machineries were conservative by nature. The *kakushin* challengers, it appeared, had parachuted alone into enemy strongholds. Perforce they fell back on participatory politics to cope with conservative local bureaucracies and assemblies. But the institutionalization of participatory politics was not only difficult but also generated extra friction with local governments. When the period of slow growth arrived in 1973, *kakushin* local governments faced fiscal problems and were retaken by their conservative adversaries. By 1979, twenty out of forty-seven governors were so-called local administration professionals who hailed from among the former officials of the Ministry of Home Affairs, even though most styled themselves as conservative-leaning independents and paid lip service to increased welfare and citizen participation.

Thus we may classify postwar social movements into three categories: mass mobilization by labor unions, as happened in the treaty revision upheaval; lobbying campaigns by interest groups involved in regional development; and local citizen groups in the antipollution movement.

The Political System

The foregoing has dealt with the massive social changes caused by advanced industrialization and their impact on politics. We now move to the political system that has promoted advanced industrialization.

What role did the political system play in industrialization? What was the feedback on this system?

The prime mover behind advanced industrialization was the three-in-one combination of the LDP, the economic ministries, and big business. The Home Ministry had been liquidated, its officials purged, and governorships made elective by democratization in the early occupation period. In contrast, the economic ministries were vital limbs of the occupation rule. Although occupation policy fluctuated widely from liberal reforms to remilitarizing Japan, the ministries' role kept expanding. The Ministry of International Trade and Industry (MITI) was created in 1949 to implement the so-called Dodge Line, which called for balanced budgets, a single exchange rate, export promotion, rationalization of industries, and economic independence. Using foreign exchange quotas as a weapon, MITI channeled technology, money, and resources to promising industries. If excessive investment or production resulted, MITI had recourse to administrative guidance to adjust the output. As Chalmers Johnson points out, a powerful trade and industrial policy was put together.[1]

At the same time, the *zaibatsu* conglomerates, which had been thoroughly broken up in the early occupation, came back to life, albeit with a younger generation of business leaders. Because the family holding companies, the core of *zaibatsu*, were not resurrected, the recombinations of former *zaibatsu*-affiliated enterprises were looser and joined by new enterprises that came into being during the recovery and growth periods. Competition was fierce indeed, but the risks of excessive competition and bankruptcy were lessened by government assistance. Secured by the lifeline of government industrial policy, an enterprise could be launched as an adventure. By the time a government White Paper pronounced in 1956 that "it is no longer [the era of] postwar," steel, machine tool, chemical, and other older industries had expanded; synthetic fiber, plastic, electronics, and other industries were emerging; technological innovation and productivity increase were much-touted watchwords; and petrochemical complexes were rising one after the other on Japan's Pacific coast.

What role did the LDP play in Japan's industrialization? At the upper reaches, the LDP consisted of two things: (1) the administrative talents of a limited number of former bureaucrats turned politicians and (2) the huge political funds provided by *zaikai* (the business community). The party could not survive politically, however, without professional pol-

---

[1]See Chalmers Johnson, Introduction to *MITI and the Japanese Miracle: The Growth of Industrial Policy, 1925–1975* (Stanford: Stanford University Press, 1982).

itician Dietmen, who constituted the majority. Thus the LDP depended on bureaucratic talent, business funds, and professional politicians' votes. The self-appointed task of the LDP government was to maintain its Diet majority, to keep out the Socialists, and to ensure freedom of action to the bureaucracies and the business community in their pursuit of industrialization. In this sense the LDP's role was a supportive one. This view is less than accurate, however; in reality intraparty factionalism produced surprisingly disruptive effects, despite which industrialization proceeded. Therefore, the LDP at once encouraged and disrupted industrialization.

The conservatives have been combining and recombining since prewar days. From the outset the LDP was a coalition of factions, but factionalism began to be institutionalized after the party's presidential election of 1956 (in which MITI minister Ishibashi defeated Secretary General Kishi by seven votes). Selecting the LDP president, whether by ballots or in a smoke-filled caucus room, generates heated factional conflicts in which promises of ministerial posts and money flow freely. Appointments to cabinet, Diet, and party posts are made partly on the basis of political merits and partly on factional balance.

The faction is the operational unit that secures and distributes the LDP presidency and other posts. Generally speaking, the more posts a faction can secure for its members, the faster and stronger it will grow. The faction also distributes political funds, and the larger factions have increased fund-raising abilities. A faction can also intercede with a bureaucracy to get a subsidy on behalf of a member and his *jiban*; thus the faction's purpose is securing appointments, funds, and *jiban*. Factions were more firmly institutionalized during the Kishi government; since then, all LDP Dietmen have been enlisted in one. Faction membership lists are printed in newspapers, factions maintain headquarters offices, factions hold regular meetings, and faction newspapers have become a matter of course.

In the late 1950s, there were eight factions called the "eight divisions," the bureaucratic factions of Kishi, Sato, Ikeda, and Ishii and the party politicians' factions of Ono, Kono, Matsumura-Miki, and Ishibashi. The bureaucratic–party politician distinction depended on the leader's background. A faction leader, be he bureaucrat or politician, tended to have his kind under him, but every faction was a mixture of both.

A government is maintained in power by factions, called the mainstream,[2] that cooperate with the prime minister. The nonmainstream always exists and, if circumstances permit, becomes antimainstream, revolting against the prime minister. At times, even the mainstream factions revolt. During the treaty revision, the antimainstream factions conspired with the JSP to arrange for Kishi's retirement, and only his brother Sato remained loyal.

The dynamics of factionalism were standard in the Nagata-cho district, although the media and public opinion had been unsparing in their criticism. Having had to pour money into the bottomless pit of politics, the business community, too, felt for some time that enough was enough. Thus Prime Minister Ikeda, proclaiming faction liquidation and income doubling as his goals, established the Party Organization Commission and appointed Miki Takeo its chairman. As the 1963 Miki proposal pointed out, "Clearly, what the people want most of the LDP is faction liquidation." Ending factions, he was convinced, was "the way to restore public confidence in the LDP and lay the foundation for building a modern political party." Thereupon all the factions complied reluctantly.

Ono and Kono, who defended factions as a bulwark against bureaucratic dictatorship and as a school for political apprenticeship, had to follow suit. Trying to liquidate factions—the first principle of the LDP—however, was like defying Newton's law of gravity. In several months, all factions were back in business, and no one took seriously subsequent calls to disband. Because the factions could not be destroyed, the business community again joined them. Funds were once again channeled through factions. Bureaucracies, interest groups, and the voters all contributed to turning factions back into the linchpins of the political system.

In the second half of the 1960s, which was the decade of industrialization, one can detect changes in the three-in-one combination of economic ministries, big business, and the LDP. First, heavy and chemical industries had acquired adequate strength and international competitiveness and were thus no longer in need of MITI's protective guidance. Initiative in industrial policy passed from the public to the private sector. Second, the key ministries, particularly Finance, lost their ability to control the political process; consequently, the LDP, which had hitherto depended on their expertise, had to cultivate its own. This is

---

[2]The term *mainstream* is used in two senses. One is purely formal, referring simply to those who are "in" with a cabinet. The other is substantive, referring to the Yoshida faction or its subdivisions.

not to say that business could dispense with government assistance. International trade cannot be divorced from politics and foreign relations. The LDP, too, still needed the bureaucracy's know-how, experience, and law- and budget-drafting abilities. The three-in-one combination continued, with an internal shift, as external pressure mounted.

By external pressure, I mean that exerted by the interest distribution structure. The local combination of interest group, ministerial jurisdiction, and *zoku jiban* created a structure that defied the control of the Finance Ministry. (*Zoku*, or tribe, refers to a grouping of Dietmen united by the particular interest they are lobbying for, as in "defense *zoku*.") When Finance lost some of its budgeting power, the buck was first passed to the LDP's Policy Affairs Research Council (PARC), then on to the LDP's three officers (secretary general, chairman of PARC, and chairman of the executive council), or the cabinet. Strangely enough, political supremacy over the bureaucracies expanded when the ruling party lost its commanding majority. As government policy began to meet increased resistance in the Diet, it became imperative for the LDP to cut deals with the opposition and make them stick.

As decision-making power passed from the bureaucracy to the party, LDP politicians with bureaucratic backgrounds seemed to lose their edge in the party. Bureaucrats owed their privileged position to their administrative knowledge and experience, but within a decade of Diet incumbency, party professionals could acquire such experience on their own. At the same time, the bureaucrats had to become party politicians, so that the difference between the two types became less relevant. The political factions disappeared with the death of Ono and Kono in 1964 and 1965; the bureaucratic factions' rule came to an end with Sato's retirement in 1972, as Tanaka rose to power.

Tanaka represented a blend of the bureaucrat and the politician. Ever since his first electoral victory in 1947, he has devoted himself to administering public works and civil engineering projects, and he owed his power base to these activities. This background might seem to place him in the political faction, and indeed he possessed uncanny political insights and courage; but he was also endowed with an unparalleled memory, number-crunching abilities, and administrative skills, whence his epithet, "Computerized Bulldozer." Tanaka did not share Ono's or Kono's congenital dislike of bureaucrats. Rather, he did well by them, listened to their advice, and gained their trust. He was a party politician who knew how to have bureaucrats minister to his needs. Tanaka's counterpart in this regard was Ohira Masayoshi.

Tanaka was also a product of the fast growth and the regional development boom of the 1960s. Adapting himself to the boom with unsurpassed skill, he pushed it vigorously and climbed to the apex of politics by doling out funds derived from land speculation, dummy companies, and construction businesses. The political arena was fueled by the construction boom and corrupted by money. Tanaka extended his network to every part of the interest distribution structure and boasted that his faction was a "general hospital" capable of taking care of every need. When in 1972 he wrested power from Fukuda Takeo, Sato's heir apparent, on the platform of "remaking the Japanese archipelago," LDP rule had reached a turning point.

After the 1955 System

In the latter half of the 1970s, Japan was close to being a 10 percent agricultural society, with the tertiary sector exceeding 50 percent in the first half of the decade. Mass society was spreading; the LDP's solid *jiban*, based on local men of influence, was disintegrating; and the JSP's labor unions were fast losing their vote-getting power.

According to *Asahi Shimbun*'s surveys of 1965 and 1975, the proportion of those who supported the LDP held steady at 45 percent. Among the salaried class, they were 39 percent (1965) and 41 percent (1975); among industrial workers, 28 percent (1965) and 34 percent (1975); among self-employed businessmen and manufacturers, 58 percent (1965) and 59 percent (1975); and among AFF workers, 59 percent (1965) and 62 percent (1975). Every category increased but the shift among industrial workers was significant.

Next, we will look at the occupational composition of LDP supporters in 1965 and 1975. Among the salaried class, we find 20 percent (1965) and 27 percent (1975); among self-employed businessmen and manufacturers, 26 percent (1965) and 25 percent (1975); among industrial workers, 18 percent (1965) and 25 percent (1975); and among AFF workers, 33 percent (1965) and 19 percent (1975). This meant that although the LDP retained the loyalty of about 60 percent of AFF workers and self-employed businessmen, more than 50 percent of its supporters were among the salaried class and industrial workers. In terms of regional distribution, in major cities with more than 100,000 registered voters, LDP supporters represented 34 percent (1965) and 42 percent (1975); in cities with fewer than 100,000 registered voters, 66 percent (1965) and 57 percent (1975). The LDP's increasing support in urban areas is apparent in these statistics.

Support for the JSP declined from 34 percent to 24 percent between 1965 and 1975. Among the salaried class, support for the JSP measured 45 percent (1965) and 30 percent (1975); among industrial workers, 48 percent (1965) and 30 percent (1975); among self-employed business-men and manufacturers, 26 percent (1965) and 11 percent (1975); and among AFF workers, 19 percent (1965) and 18 percent (1975). The occupational composition of JSP supporters was as follows: among the salaried class, 30 percent in 1965 and 37 percent in 1975; among indus-trial workers, 40 percent (1965) and 41 percent (1975); among self-employed businessmen, 15 percent (1965) and 9 percent (1975); and among AFF workers, 14 percent (1965) and 11 percent (1975). That is to say, although JSP supporters decreased on the whole, the sum of salaried and industrial workers increased from 70 percent in 1965 to 78 percent in 1975. In terms of regional distribution, the JSP lost support in major cities and rural areas (declining from 53 percent in 1965 to 42 percent in 1975) but gained in the small and medium-size cities (47 percent in 1965 to 58 percent in 1975).

LDP support expanded among the salaried class, industrial workers, and in major and medium-size cities. The JSP contracted, but with other parties cultivating voters in the major and medium-size cities, the opposition as a whole was not far behind the LDP in Diet seats. Because of the increase in floating votes, it is difficult to predict how Diet seats will swing between the government and the opposition. There is more instability to the LDP's tenure than meets the eye, but the demise of the LDP government is difficult to imagine. Should the LDP poll less than half the Diet seats, it could remain in power in coalition with a minor party; if the opposition parties were to poll a majority of seats, forming a coalition would be extremely difficult. Thus unless the LDP splits, it can remain in power into the foreseeable future. Change in government will continue to take place among LDP factions.

Finally, two points interest me about LDP rule in the period of government-opposition equilibrium. First, the LDP has nurtured and maintained its electoral *jiban* through the interest distribution struc-ture. Because the vote-getting ability of business associations and agricultural cooperatives was critical in the context of equilibrium, massive subsidies were injected into these sectors. Sixty percent of self-employed businessmen and agriculturalists support the party. The question is, is it possible to continue this lopsided political subsidy?

The interest distribution structure is a mechanism for bloating the budget. As noted above, the pressure to bloat the budget has transferred the budget-making power from the Finance Ministry to the LDP. The pressure continued into the slow-growth period following the 1973 oil shock, and the sale of government bonds has increased since 1975. To stop the growth of government debt, in 1981 the Suzuki government set the goal of "administrative reform without a tax increase." The Second Ad Hoc Committee on Investigation into Government Administration and its successor, the Administrative Reform Council, were established at the initiative of *zaikai* and the bureaucracies.

One should expect an enormous reaction to an attempt to cut back on payoffs to interest groups, as the recent sales tax fiasco testifies. Even the association of small and medium-size enterprises, by far the staunchest and most solid foundation of LDP support, can be alienated at least temporarily if its interests are violated. That is how an interest group behaves. Then how could the salaried class with its status quo orientation revolt against the sales tax? But it did, apparently as a slap at the prime minister for going back on his campaign promise not to institute a sales tax. That is how independent voters behave.

Second, I would like to state my thoughts on the media as a political weapon. One can mobilize the voters in a mass society by manipulating policy symbols and leadership images. "A new era in U.S.-Japan relations," "doubling income," "social development," and "remaking the Japanese archipelago" are all grandstanding policy symbols. Nowadays politicians go out of their way to project an appealing personal image. If media manipulation can outmaneuver the interest distribution structure, the LDP will be forced to transform itself. But how effective will such manipulation be? It is not possible to measure or to predict the floating votes among the status quo–oriented independents. It seems certain, however, that in the double election of 1986 (in which the elections of the upper and lower houses coincided), the prime minister's personal popularity among the independents added extra votes to the bedrock support of the interest groups. But this victory, dependent on floating votes, was wobbly. After proclaiming the "1986 System" in August, Nakasone had to confess ruefully six months later, "The masses are shifting like sands."

The media are weapons not only in electioneering but in party and Diet management. Miki and Nakasone seem to have been conscious of this. Miki had the task of "clearing the mess" following the Tanaka graft scandal, and Nakasone spoke of "settling accounts with postwar politics." For a collateral or minority factional leader (such as Nakasone or Miki) to survive in the rough-and-tumble world of politics, he has to be a "Balkan politician" or a "weather vane." When one is suddenly thrust into the prime minister's office with the Shiina mandate, as in Miki's case, or at Tanaka's behest, as in Nakasone's, his greatest weapon has to be the media. Miki showed a keen interest in media management, and he always wrote his own briefing memos for press conferences and television appearances. With media and opposition support, he held off the intraparty opposition. In his handling of the Lockheed scandal and the revision of the antimonopoly law, moreover, he managed to tip the equilibrium in his (and the opposition's) favor.

Nakasone knew how to exploit the media even better than Miki. With international media playing up the Ron-Yasu entente, Nakasone manipulated the LDP and the opposition. There were differences, of course. Miki alienated business with the political funds control law and the antimonopoly law revision, but Nakasone played up to business with his administrative reform. The Balkan politician and the weather vane were the opposite of each other in this regard.

3 | Rearmament Controversies and Cultural Conflicts in Japan: The Case of the Conservatives and the Socialists

Otake Hideo

FROM THE SUMMER OF 1950 WHEN THE POLICE RESERVE FORCES WERE founded, to the mid-1980s, rearmament has given rise to acute conflict in postwar Japan's politics. Involving questions of constitutionality, rearmament has been debated as a political issue of democracy and liberalism. Concealed underneath has been the cultural tension between tradition and modernity: Should the prewar political culture that supported the emperor system continue? For this reason, rearmament triggered a serious ideological schism that transcended differences over defense policies and left a decisive impact on the birth and development of the 1955 System.

Heretofore, academic discussions of this subject have concentrated on the former Seiyukai government and Prime Minister Yoshida, the protagonists of the rearmament by installment, and the left-wing Japan Socialist party (JSP), which opposed the government on the platform of disarmed neutrality. The rearmament controversy, however, went beyond the two contenders. It seems indispensable to extend our analysis to the conservatives who opposed Yoshida on the one hand and to those

Socialists who objected to disarmed neutrality on the other. This chapter seeks, first, to shed light on the multifaceted conflict by analyzing these two hitherto neglected groups. Second, it seeks to point out the characteristics of Japan's liberalism and social democracy that were the ideological underpinnings of the two groups.

Ashida Hitoshi and Nishio Suehiro, the subjects of this chapter, were the leaders of the prorearmament movement among conservatives and right-wing Socialists, respectively. Together they were the linchpins of the Katayama and Ashida governments. The Ashida-Nishhio axis was the only realistic alternative to the 1955 System of LPD domination, as Kataoka concedes in his discussion. In this author's judgment, the rearmament controversy cut the ground from under their "bipartisan" cooperation, thereby making the 1955 System inevitable. A third aim of this chapter is to understand the 1955 System by looking at what might have been.[1]

Following the outbreak of the Korean War, the Yoshida government was forced into incremental rearmament under U.S. pressure. In late 1950, Ashida Hitoshi began to argue for full-fledged rearmament. He was joined in February 1952 by Hatoyama Ichiro, Ishibashi Tanzan, and former admiral Nomura Kichisaburo, who seized the occasion of their imminent depurge and John Foster Dulles's second visit to Japan. These leaders of the anti-Yoshida forces put rearmament on the agenda of postoccupation Japanese politics, thereby injecting controversy into conservative-*kakushin*, intraconservative, and intra-*kakushin* politics. Interestingly enough, these advocates of positive rearmament were called "liberalists" and were isolated in politics and persecuted by the military before and during the war. Why did such men unite with the right wing and former military men to be the cutting edge in the confrontation against the left? This is an important question when examining postwar liberalism and conservatism. In this section, I will focus on Ashida and explore his arguments for full-fledged rearmament in the context of liberalism and nationalism in postwar Japan.

At least until he organized the government in June 1948, Ashida's political beliefs contained the liberal creed that was absent in self-styled

---

[1]Among English-language books, the following are the best balanced: Martin E. Weinstein, *Japan's Postwar Defense Policy, 1947–1968* (New York: Columbia University Press, 1971); J.A.A. Stockwin, *The Japanese Socialist Party and Neutralism* (Melbourne: Melbourne University Press, 1968). For more recent works, see Otake Hideo, "Defense Controversies and One-Party Dominance: The Opposition in West Germany and Japan," in T. J. Pempel, ed., *Uncommon Democracies: One-Party Regimes* (Ithaca, N.Y.: Cornell University Press, 1989).

Japanese liberalists such as Yoshida. As Professor Shindo Eiichi, the editor of the Ashida diary, points out, Ashida was heir to the Meiji tradition of Ichiko (a prewar prep school) liberalism and humanism. A stint in Europe as a diplomat acquainted Ashida with the workings of parliamentary democracy, and his subsequent posting in Moscow gave him firsthand knowledge of the Russian revolution, confirming his belief in Western-type democracy and his stand on the liberal left. When prewar social contradictions erupted in tenant-landlord and labor-management disputes, his solution was to increase popular participation—including women—in politics and to expand the role of political parties and parliament. His change of career to professional politician in 1932 at the age of forty-four stemmed from his political convictions. Ashida consistently stood for internationalist diplomacy before and during the war, remained critical of the military, ran for the Diet without being endorsed by the government party, and was elected after a painful fight against officialdom. He did not hesitate to welcome the emergence of James Ramsey McDonald's cabinet in wartime Britain. (Together, the JSP and the JCP were called the democratic forces while they were favored by SCAP in the first half of the occupation, that is, before the U.S. policy reversal in 1948. Thereafter, they were called *kakushin*, which translates into radical liberals, because of their opposition to the government and the United States.)

As a middle-school student, however, he once dreamt of "devoting myself to the task of 'Asian hegemony,'" a dream that led him to choose a diplomatic career. There is an undeniable strain of Meiji nationalism in him, which was an important precursor to his activism on behalf of rearmament. Yet Ashida's nationalism was hidden and did not become manifest until the 1950s. Perhaps it is more accurate to call him a national-liberalist.[2]

After the war, he endorsed the occupation reforms promoted by the New Dealers at SCAP GHQ, became a strong advocate of constitutional reform in the Shidehara cabinet, actively lobbied as welfare minister on behalf of three major labor bills, performed a central role as the chairman of the constitution revision commission, and established the center-left coalition government with the help of the JSP's Katayama and Nishio. By criticizing the postwar imperial family and the system of imperial sanctions (see his diary), he contrasted with the "old liberalists" of Yoshida's stripe. Ashida was different from most conservative politicians, who acceded to postwar changes out of political opportunism.

---

[2]Shindo Eiichi, Preface, in Shindo Eiichi, ed., *Ashida Hitoshi nikki* (Ashida Hitoshi diary) (Tokyo: Iwanami Shoten, 1986), 20, 29.

Undoubtedly, there was a strain of strong elitism in Ashida's disposition as well. His personal history, which took him through Ichiko and Tokyo University, included his fondness for literature, his diplomatic career, and his long sojourns abroad. Although he was moved by the audience support he encountered on the campaign trail, he had strong contempt for the educational level of the Japanese masses. The following is from his letter of thanks when elected prime minister:

> The only thought in my mind is to devote myself to righteous public service. Neither popularity nor fame interests me. . . . After all, I have decided to sacrifice myself on behalf of the masses with such little education. Why should I expect any return?[3]

In contrast, see his January 1949 diary entry concerning the crowds that appeared on his tour through Fukuchiyama to test his standing in the first election since his indictment in the Show Denko (Shoden) bribery scandal:

> Overflowing audience said to be two thousand strong. . . . There were some 200 women, children, middle-school students, but they were all ears. Moved by indescribable emotion. In closing, I said "So many of you have come to hear me speak tonight even though this is a personal gathering [Ashida, being under indictment, was not running under a party label]. I do not know how to thank you." I was choking and crying. Some in the audience were crying, too. Afterward, they cheered me with *banzai* and Godspeed from the balcony, the floor, and everywhere. It was a tearful sight. What could be more moving in life?[4]

Ashida differed from Yoshida in having chosen the life of professional politics. But he was also different from ordinary politicians in the Hatoyama camp, who were short on ethics, principles, and ideas. At times, Ashida's elitism stood him in good stead. He was his own man, neither bureaucrat nor politician in factional affiliation or personality type.

Ashida's liberalism, it must be noted, was antipacifist and anti-Communist. Throughout his life, he distinguished himself from the pacifism, neutralism, and disarmamentism that characterized the postwar liberal left as might have been expected of a career diplomat. As the author of the so-called Ashida Memorandum,[5] which was addressed

---

[3]Ibid., II, 152.

[4]Ibid., III, 30.

[5]Hata Ikuhiko, *Shiroku Nihon saiguntri* [History of Japan's rearmament] (Tokyo: Bungei Shunju, 1967).

to General Robert Eichelberger, commander of the Eighth Army, and which first outlined what came to be the Japan-U.S. security system under Yoshida, Ashida repudiated the all-around peace formula (demanding peace both with Moscow and Washington) and strongly lobbied for placing Japan's security under U.S. military protection. After the doves carried the Minshuto party with a call for all-around peace just before the upper-house election of June 1950, Ashida struggled successfully to reverse the party decision. Such a foreign policy stance would naturally extend to his later advocacy of rearmament.

As a left-wing liberal, Ashida took a middle-of-the-road stance after the war. Before heading his own government, he vied with the extreme right ("feudalistic, conservative, reactionary forces such as the Kono faction and the obscurantist, bureaucractic Yoshida group"); after he resigned he contended with the extreme left—the Japan Communist party (JCP). Following the start of the Dodge Line and the Korean War, when the JCP adopted violent tactics, Ashida's anticommunism became pronounced. Although he preferred public opinion formation and mobilization to authoritarian repression, his stance led him to mingle with the prewar right-wingers, particularly Akao Bin. In the event, the line between Ashida and the right wing became blurred.

The immediate antecedent to Ashida's advocacy of full-scale rearmament was the start of the Korean War. At that time, he was lying low, having been driven from government, arrested, and indicted in connection with the Shoden scandal; it was the rearmament issue that gave him a chance at a political comeback. His December 1950 rearmament proposal transformed him overnight into its chief spokesman. He then went on a nationwide lecture tour. In his February 9, 1952, diary entry, he said,

> I must ride this wave and devote myself to opinion formation. Admiral Nomura Kichisaburo saw me at a lecture and said, "Give up the ambition to be prime minister, and dedicate yourself to this campaign. If the prime ministership comes your way that's a different story." I said repeatedly to myself, "That's right. I must remember."

Although Ashida was acquitted in the lower courts, the prosecution appealed. The ensuing legal battle prevented his taking the Minshuto party presidency and prime ministership, driving him to the public lecture circuit and to public service. Even so, Ashida did not seem to be driven by political ambition or to be conscious of the partisan implications of his campaigns. His sense of urgency in the face of a national crisis made him feel that the Japanese, divorced from international politics by the occupation, were in a stupor. His alarm at the outbreak of the Korean War comes through in his diary.

> 6/28 [1950] [Three days after the war commenced.] The U.S. has shown its determination by dispatching the Air Force to Korea and a fleet to Hong Kong and Taiwan. I am a bit relieved. The American move is well done. The swiftness is striking.
>
> 7/19 [I told an old Jiyuto friend that] the world conflict manifested in the Korean incident has the potential to turn into a major war. There is no salvation for those who stand aside and intone neutrality. The Japanese people should make their stand clear.
>
> 7/20 The evening paper reports on Truman's radio speech. The U.S. has declared a state of emergency because of the Korean War, and decided on military expansion and market control. Japan remains indecisive.
>
> 7/25 I think the Japanese today are really silly and cowardly. . . . There are fools who think the [Korean] incident is a conflict that concerns third parties but not them. They pass themselves off as journalists and mislead people.

At one point, Ashida argued for expanding the Police Reserve, feeling that World War III was near. He came up with a scheme for allowing Japanese citizens to volunteer for service in the United Nations forces and presented it to William J. Sebald, political adviser to SCAP (the equivalent of U.S. ambassador to occupied Japan), for transmission to General Douglas MacArthur.[6] Neither MacArthur nor Yoshida was interested. At the same time, Ashida insisted on the need for a "bipartisan" foreign policy and probed for ways of persuading Yoshida and the JSP to cooperate with each other. Again, Yoshida was uninterested.

Thereafter, Ashida changed his strategy and began to criticize Yoshida openly in the hope of mobilizing public opinion in favor of defense. At the request of SCAP GHQ, he wrote and made public an advisory opinion on December 7, 1950, that began as follows:

> The situation in the Far East harbors a great crisis. The design of the communist countries against us can no longer be concealed. A strong possibility exists now for World War III to break out in the next few years. When the United States, Britain, and France are all busy making ready for that event, it is impermissible for Japan alone to remain on the sidelines. Present-day Japan is in urgent need of unifying its national will, without which we cannot ride out the crisis. . . . The task of the government is to take the initiative to tell the people that Japan is on the brink

---

[6]Shindo, *Ashida Hitoshi Nikki*, VII, 412.

of danger, to remind them that we must defend the country by our own efforts.

Ashida thought that shaping public opinion was the most important immediate task and saw defense buildup as a long-range goal; thus he was not seeking rapid military expansion. He thought of his mission as ideological propagandizing, a task befitting a party politician in a democracy. Expecting the JSP to educate the working class, he cast himself in the role of a progressive leader, acting as a bridge between the conservatives and the Socialists so as to form a national unity front:

> To cope with the unprecedented difficulty facing the country, we must have solid popular support. No government can conduct itself boldly without it. This is especially true in regard to national defense. The violent uprisings and labor offensives masterminded by the communists can only be countered if we have the support of moderate workingmen. I think it is impossible for the government to make headway in its anti-communist measures if it treats the working class with hostility. The JSP's cooperation is most necessary at this juncture.[7]

At the same time, Ashida tried to swing Minshuto's foreign policy around to his position. On December 26, 1950, Minshuto's foreign affairs committee held a meeting to discuss basic policies toward the impending peace treaty. Ashida persuaded it "that depending on the development of the international situation, it may be necessary to move from an expansion of the police force to rearmament." The committee agreed to a new foreign policy plank aimed at "expansion and preparation of autonomous defense power" and agreed that the plank would be proposed to the party congress slated for the following January. Ashida ran into opposition, however; the left wing in Minshuto, consisting of Kitamura Tokutaro and Kawasaki Shuji, insisted on keeping within the constitutional limit (expansion of the Police Reserve) and criticized the committee's "excess." The left wing was mindful of the fact that the Ashida Memorandum was controversial. Rearmament was identified with war by the masses, and Minshuto feared losing popular support.

At the January 20, 1951, congress, Minshuto adopted a declaration saying,

> We definitely denounce aggressions, and offer unstinting assistance to the defense of freedom and justice. The Japanese are not a cowardly nation

---

[7]*Asahi Shimbun*, December 28, 1950; Shindo, *Ashida Hitoshi nikki*, III, 408–9, 450–55.

that seeks security at the expense of the occupation powers while standing with arms folded and without shedding a drop of blood. . . . We resolve to smash the do-nothing coalition on the right as well as the traitorous international communist forces on the left. We resolve to restore honor to the Japanese nation as quickly as possible, to adopt bold and innovative national-salvation policies, and to place the motherland on a lasting foundation."

Besides using right-wing-like rhetoric ("restore honor to the Japanese nation"), this declaration is noteworthy for its abstract description of defense and rearmament. This vagueness, due in part to the internal opposition on the left, also reflected the fact that Ashida and other Minshuto leaders lacked expertise in defense policy, which gave the defense debate an ideological, spiritual character. Ashida's column, "The Spirit of National Defense," in the mid-February *Yomiuri Shimbun* is similarly vague on defense plans. "The defense forces Japan is planning," he said, "must be entirely different in character from the Police Reserve in existence. The armed forces need to be based on a greater spirit of devotion and patriotism both in the officer corps and in training."

Minshuto's policy toward the peace treaty was similarly vague. On defense policy, the party said, "We will take measures for national defense through the establishment of self-defense forces that uphold the principles of the United Nations Charter, and that are adequate to preserve the dignity and security of an independent Japan." Such forces were to be separate from the Police Reserve. Ashida seems to have had in mind a 200,000-man contingent enlisted under U.N. auspices.[8]

Before long, Ashida became a single-issue politician, standing solely on a defense plank. In the process, he isolated himself in Minshuto (soon to be Kaishinto). *Tokyo Shimbun* described the circumstances as follows:

Minshuto is supposed to be the rearmament party, since its February congress set forth the plank calling for "the establishment of self-defense forces." But upon closer examination, the party is a bystander to Ashida's personal efforts in founding the New Rearmament Promotion League and in recruiting supporters across the country. If anything, a majority is . . . saying, "Don't rock the boat.[9]

[8]Ibid., IV, 14; *Asahhi Shimbun*, March 4, 1951, evening edition.
[9]*Tokyo Shimbun*, August 5, 1952.

His rearmament thesis did touch off frenzied support in a small sector but ran the risk of alienating the general public. In addition, his pending trial prevented his running for the party presidency, which went to the recently depurged Shigemitsu.

Why was it that Ashida, who stood for progressive liberalism, wound up being more hawkish than Yoshida, whom he regarded as a conservative reactionary? First, unlike most conservative politicians, Ashida was impelled by a strong sense of international crisis following the Korean War. Yoshida always brushed aside suggestions of an impending third world war, and for other party politicians, who became impervious to the implications of the cold war, rearmament was primarily an issue of spiritual values and nationalism. Ashida resorted to that same rhetoric but combined it with his analysis of international circumstances.

Second, Ashida's rearmament thesis was significant in the context of party politics. As a means of attacking Yoshida, the hard-line regarding external affairs was ideal. Third, after the purge was lifted, Ashida did not hesitate to join forces with returning former military officers and right-wingers and can thus be credited with having put together the conservatives' "autonomous defense thesis" by fusing native nationalism with cold war rhetoric.

Despite his erstwhile aim of enlisting the support of the "working class," Ashida increasingly relied on right-wing rhetoric and right-wing connections, unnerving the workers and intellectuals even more than Yoshida had and antagonizing the moderates. Ashida's anti–Dodge Line, anticonservative economic policies, the denominator of his coalition with the Socialists, were canceled out by his rearmament policy.

The case for defense against external threat is not by itself antiliberal; it may be the common sense of the "free" world, as Ashida used to avow. It was a dangerous policy, however—particularly in the contemporary Japanese context—to appeal to native nationalism as a vehicle of rearmament. Instead of saying, "We must defend the achievements of the occupation policy from totalitarianism," Ashida argued that "we must defend the nation with our blood" or "it is national humiliation to depend on foreigners for defense." These rationales not only undermined his collaboration with the moderate left but confused and weakened the liberal-left among the conservatives. His Korean War–induced return to traditional nationalism meant the bankruptcy of his left-liberalism. All the same, Ashida, an expert on international relations, dressed native nationalism in the garb of cold war and postwar rhetoric, thus paving the way for the rise of the "self-defense thesis" among conservatives.

Ashida's, Hatoyama's, and Ishibashi's reliance on the restorationist subleaders and the traditional culture–bound masses rested on their pessimism toward Japan's political culture. They never expected their own liberalist philosophy to be accepted at the mass level. This negative judgment about the autonomy of liberalism as a political force stemmed from the bitter experience of having been suppressed by the government and alienated from the people. What sustained them in their isolation was not their liberalism but their constituents' traditional support, "dating back to the days of the fathers" and resting on patron-client ties. As they faced the need to argue for rearmament in defense of liberalism, they were bound to seek political support in the traditional culture.

Having been educated in the West, Ashida and his fellow liberalists were the elite of the elite. Ashida, Hatoyama, and Ishibashi all read European-language literature with ease and subscribed to foreign magazines. Thus they did not have a language in which to address the common man and had to rely on subleaders who did, which is why the liberalists fell back on traditional symbols and rhetoric rather than on liberal arguments to cope with communism.

In its logical construction, the foregoing thesis is the obverse side of the liberal-left's thesis, which is that Japan needs communism and socialism to cope with the arrested (or premodern) state of its political culture. Japanese liberalists, both on the right and on the left, were pessimistic about the mass acceptance of their liberal values, at least in the short run. Hence they concluded that a pragmatic coalition with a political force, of right or left, harboring a basically totalitarian tendency was unavoidable. Lacking in political autonomy, Japan's liberalists, the authors of the rearmament policy, ended up self-destructing as a political force.

The Socialists and Rearmament

We must examine the JSP if we are to understand fully how Japan dealt with the rearmament issue. The JSP's response to rearmament was the product of a complicated process with a complex political and social background. We will confine ourselves to only two aspects of the subject: (1) The political cultural conflict between the modern and the traditional that existed not only between the radical liberals and the conservatives but also within the ranks of the radical liberals themselves. The traditional political culture within the JSP right wing was a serious impediment to winning support among intellectuals, white-collar workers, and unionized workers (especially the young ones), leading those constituencies overwhelmingly to the left wing. (2) In

Japan, internal conflict in the Socialist camp was framed in terms not of Socialist economic policy but of defense policy. As a result, a fissure developed within the right wing, specifically, among the Social Democrats. This rift in turn made the left wing dominant.

These two factors weakened the Realists, who were expected to lead an economic conversion away from Marxism. In Japan, the turn toward realism came some twenty-five years later than in most West European Social Democratic parties.

In the New Manifesto of January 1986, the JSP declared its decision to abandon Marxism-Leninism. This conversion was similar to those carried out by Socialist parties in Western Europe (West Germany, Austria, Switzerland, Denmark, the Netherlands, and Belgium) around 1960.[10] In this section, we will examine the reasons for the JSP's delayed conversion in light of the Western European experience.

The JSP's New Manifesto carefully avoids any reference to defense issues, and there is no prospect that a clear-cut conversion on defense will take place in the near future. Although a conversion in economic policy is a departure from the tradition of Marxism and the labor movement, a conversion in defense policy is a departure from the peace movement, which is essentially a movement of intellectuals and the upper middle class. One conversion may be as necessary as the other for an ideologically based movement to become the party in power, but each develops along a different path. In the case of the West German Social Democratic party (SPD), the two conversions did not proceed in tandem. Moreover, the SPD showed a renewed inclination toward pacifism in the 1980s.

All the same, a political party's defense policy can decisively affect its political economic stance. The JSP provides a typical example of a defense controversy overwhelming all other issues, yielding a strong coalition of Marxist-Leninists and pacifists (who are moderately reformist) and isolating the defense Realists. The resultant split among the Socialists aborted conversions not only in defense policy but in economic policy as well.

From its founding in November 1945 until the fall of the Katayama (Socialist) government in 1947, the JSP was controlled by Katayama Tetsu, Nishio Suehiro, Mizutani Chozaburo, and other leaders of the Socialist right wing, especially those of the former Shakai Minshuuto (Socialist People's party) group, the so-called Shaminkei. The early JSP hewed to the ideology of the latter-day Minshato (Democratic Socialist party); Katayama translated this ideology into political principles. He

---

[10]Otake, "Defense Controversies and One-Party Dominance."

introduced Socialist doctrine into economic policy and "bourgeois," or parliamentary, democracy into politics. Naturally, he was opposed to violent revolution and communism.

But the JSP right wing's modernity in matters of principle was spoiled by its traditional life-style and saddled by the legacy of prewar leadership experience. Nishio Suehiro, the pillar of the Katayama cabinet, represented those traditional elements. Because they distrusted intellectuals, Suehiro and men like him belittled abstract ideas and principles. This was natural for workingmen.

An episode from Nishio's handling of a strike settlement with Sumitomo Steel Casting in the Taisho period is revealing. When collective bargaining with management was about to be wrapped up successfully, Nishio secured management's assurance that his "face would be respected" before he spoke to an assembly of workers with the company officers present:

> For the sake of Sumitomo's honor, I cannot disclose the content of our negotiation, but I am convinced that our demands will be by and large met in the near future. I want you to trust Nishio's word and get back to work starting tomorrow, without asking further questions. If my promise is not realized in the near future, you may take it that I was bought off and betrayed you. You would then be free to kill me or do whatever you please. Also, if you cannot trust me, you should change your agent.

The workers endorsed him with a round of applause. Nishio heaps praise on this performance in his memoir as a case of a "well-done deal."[11]

Steeped in a *yakuza*-like culture, prewar labor leaders were wont to demand and get carte blanche, a style that carried over to the postwar period and was introduced into party politics. Its practitioners took the system of representative democracy as an extension of love-it-or-leave-it, boss-type leadership, and they had a high regard for prewar experience in Diet negotiations and compromises using *haragei* as an instrument. In all respects, they shared common traits with the prewar political conservatives. Both were anti-Communist, but the Socialists' skepticism was based not so much on a critique of Communist political doctrine as on the suspicion that the Communists were not worthy of their personal trust. Here one can see an extension of authoritarian anticommunism under the emperor system.

---

[11]Nishio Suehiro, *Taishu to tomo ni* (With the masses) (Tokyo: Nihon Rodo Kyokai, 1971), pp. 42–43.

The traditional thought that Nishio represented was not confined to the boss-type leaders but was a reflection of the political culture that held sway over unorganized workers with little education. Several analyses of early postwar political culture show that the constituency of the Socialist right wing strongly adhered to traditional values. These values, also held by the conservative constituency, sharply conflicted with the "modern consciousness" among organized labor and the intellectuals. Consequently, the left-right division in the JSP reflected a division in political culture that was even deeper than the doctrinal schism.[12] (The right wing did accommodate a modern intellectual like Katayama, but he was an exception.) The problem was that social democracy in Japan manifested itself in ideological commitment to liberal democracy, but it was too traditional to appeal to organized labor, white-collar workers, or intellectuals.

The division in the JSP has serious implications. Japan's traditional political culture was based on the emperor-in-the-state system, and history shows that Japan's fascism and militarism were built on an extension of that system. The traditionalists, such as Nishio, were oblivious of this structural relationship, as demonstrated by their attitude toward the prewar political system. Nishio states in his memoir that at the time of the Manchurian Incident, he was inclined to approve it on the ground that a small country like Japan needed lebensraum.[13] He does not say that he changed his mind after the war.

In 1938, Nishio delivered a speech on the Diet floor, in support of the national mobilization law, in which he cheered Prime Minister Konoye by saying "Be bold like Hitler, Mussolini, and Stalin" and for which he was censured. Nishio recalls the incident without regret. When defeat became inevitable, he says he was "chagrined to no end as a Japanese." Moreover, he held fast to the belief that the emperor was a vital "spiritual prop" for Japan; to the end of his life he remained personally loyal to the emperor.[14]

Much the same can be said of Asanuma Inejiro, a middle-faction leader of Japan Workers' and Peasants' party origin: "As a Meiji-generation man, he had always respected the emperor. He had a Shinto shrine in his living room to which he bowed every morning, a custom he

---

[12]Kido Kotaro and Sugi Masataka, "Shakai ishiki no kozo" (Structures of social consciousness), *Shakaigaku Hyoron*, 1954.

[13]Nishio Suehiro, *Shinto eno michi* (The road to a new party) (Tokyo: Ronshosha, 1960), p. 32.

[14]Ibid., pp. 46, 49.

observed to his dying day.[15] Thus, the right-wing Socialist leaders never bade farewell to the emperor ideology but, on the contrary, lived under its shadow. From their vantage point, it was incomprehensible that the left wing should be so provoked by the prewar emperor system or by the conservatives' revival of fascism. They viewed the left wing's concern as ideological, unrealistic, or a Communist conspiracy. From the vantage point of the left wing, Nishio's traditionalism placed him in the conservative pale and was incipient fascism, thus harboring a grave threat.

Collisions of the two views took place not over Socialist economic policy but over foreign and defense policy. First, for the JSP left wing, national defense was a revival of militarism, and the choice was between the absolutist emperor system and democracy, between premodern and modern. Second, for the right wing, the defense and foreign policy issues in early postwar Japan offered little real choice; well-defined choices existed only in the minds of intellectuals, and it was the "excessive" idealism of the left that was at issue. Third, those conservative leaders who demanded rearmament—mainly Yoshida's critics—showed less interest in defense itself than in using it as leverage to restore traditional values (Ashida was an exception). The defense controversy was of a piece with the conflict between modernity and tradition.

The prewar legacy of Nishio and his friends provoked not only the orthodox left in the JSP—the Rono faction—but also the so-called middle faction, leading ultimately to the split among Social Democrats. The foreign and defense policy issues that triggered the split were more properly the domain of the peace movement, not necessarily linked with socialism. Ironically, the split strengthened the hand of Marxist-Leninists in the party. The case of Wada Hiroo shows how this came about.

A *kakushin* bureaucrat at the Agriculture-Forestry Ministry during the war, Wada was elevated to director of the Economic Stabilization Board in the Katayama government, an important policy-making post and a pivot around which the programs of the Socialist cabinet revolved. After the JSP's grave setback in the 1949 poll, involving the defeat of Katayama and Nishio, Wada joined the party and was regarded as its savior. Wada did not disappoint his friends when he vowed, "I want to do my small share from inside in order to rid the JSP of the heavy

---

[15]Tsurusaki Tomokame, *Asanuma Inejiro shoden* (A biography of Asanuma Inejiro) (Tokyo: Taimatsusha, 1979), p. 111.

ideological coloration of the past and bring in more realism."[16] The right wing thought of him as a strong counterweight to the expanding left; but Wada drew closer not to the right wing, the mainstay of the Katayama government, but to the left, which dug the administration's grave. When the two wings formally split, he stayed with the left, becoming a member of its Central Executive Committee. The bureaucrats, doctors, and journalists who later joined the party and chose the left wing were policy-oriented and "urban stylish"; their siding with the left against the Shaminkei had serious implications for the future of the Socialist party.

Why did Wada veer to the left after entering the party with realistic economic policy proposals? The major reason is said to have been his "physiological revulsion" at the right wing or, to be precise, its "coyness with those in power, lack of principles, accommodationist character," and old-fashioned anticommunism. Behind this revulsion lurked Wada's *intellectual* idealism. A gifted child and the son of a prewar middle-school instructor, Wada went through the elite course of prep school and Tokyo Imperial University to become an Agriculture-Forestry Ministry official. During his prep school days, he fell in love with tennis and poetry. The tension between Nishio and Wada reflected the social chasm between a prewar union steward and a postwar intellectual cum politician.

Even so, Wada positioned himself as a former official with a realistic economic policy against the Marxists within the left wing. As the left-wing policy committee chairman in the fall of 1953, for instance, he put together a long-term economic plan with the help of progressive scholars and bureaucratic economists entitled "A Challenge against the Mutual Security Act: The Economic Construction Five-Year Plan" that was hailed as a "realistic policy of the loyal opposition." In short, he was closer to the right wing with regard to economic policy and positioned to vie with the Marxists should the two wings be united.

As the peace treaty and rearmament issues surfaced, however, Wada became an adamant spokesman for the left-wing platform. In the JSP foreign policy committee in late 1950, for instance, he squared off against Sone Eki and Nishimura Eiichi of the Nishio faction, "insisting that the party take an unequivocal stand against rearmament, resting the case not only on Article 9 of the constitution but on socialist peace

---

[16]In writing this section, the author depended on Otake Keisuke, *Maboroshi no hana: Wada Hiroo no shogai* (A flower of illusion: The life of Wada Hiroo) (Tokyo: Gakuyu Shobo, 1981).

in Japan."[17] At the crucial Seventh Party Congress of January 1951, he spearheaded the opposition to rearmament by drafting the Three Principles of Peace. He went on to become the most uncompromising opponent of the peace and security treaties in the controversy of 1951 and masterminded Suzuki Mosaburo's move to split the party on the issue. In this controversy, a coalition of Marxist-Leninists and left-leaning Social Democrats was pitted against right-leaning Social Democrats.

As Wada saw it, the problem with the Shaminkei leadership was that, behind its rhetoric of "realism" in foreign and defense policy, it persisted in excessively rigid and doctrinaire positions. Indeed, Nishio did not (and could not) convincingly explain the nature of the *military* threat against Japan; he rested his case on the principle (*tatemae*) that an independent nation ought to have armed forces. Or, projecting abroad his dislike of Communists at home, he would dwell on the danger of communism and the Communist states, but he lacked any flexible analysis of the reality of the Sino-Soviet threat in the context of the complicated Asian situation.

Wada's disarmed neutrality thesis, however, also tended to be fundamentalist and doctrinaire, despite his intention to the contrary. His neutralism was an echo of the idealism and impracticality of academics and pundits (*bunkajin*) clustered around the Peace Problem Discussion Forum on the one hand and the unvarnished and innocent antiwar sentiment of the general public on the other. There was also a current of left-wing nationalist sentiment that yearned for true independence from the United States and an honorable reinstatement in the international community, a sentiment that transcended the calculations of national interests.

In the end, for the JSP, disarmed neutrality ceased being a policy or a means of national security that was constantly being reviewed, revised, and abandoned as international circumstances shifted; instead it became a permanent ideal. Nishio was justified in calling the disarmed neutrality plank ideological and demanding its revision. But the JSP's split and Nishio's subsequent walkout from the unified JSP undermined the social democratic force vis-à-vis the left. The JSP leaned further and further to the left, isolating Wada.

The major assumption of Wada's conduct, as revealed in his 1954 booklet entitled *Democracy on the Defensive*, was that Japan was in

---

[17]Nihon Shakaito, *Shakaito no sanjunen* (Thirty years of the JSP) (Tokyo: Japan Socialist Party Headquarters, Education and Propaganda Department, 1963), p. 140.

danger of becoming a fascist nation and that the right-wing Socialists were so far from being reliable allies that they were likely to boost fascism. Antifascism as a desideratum led to the choice of the Marxist-Leninists as allies, even if they ultimately rejected parliamentary democracy in favor of proletarian dictatorship.

When the JSP broke over the peace and security treaties in 1951, the two wings were in a rough balance, although the right had an edge of sixty to forty-six in the number of Diet members. The social democratic group—though ousted from party control—was almost half the party. A new conflict, however, began to appear between the Shamin and Nichiro factions over rearmament and the security treaty question. In the event, Nishio's "realism" failed to carry even the right wing.

Internal conflicts of the right-wing JSP were not simply over ideology but over appointments. About the time of the 1951 split, former Nichiro leaders, such as Kawakami Jotaro, returned to the party upon being depurged and captured many posts in the right-wing executive departments while Katayama and Nishio (a defendant in the Shoden trial) were out of power or in disgrace. The demotion of the orthodox Shamin leaders intensified the conflict, and the middle faction made matters worse by its independence. The resulting complications meant that who was to be chairman of the right-wing JSP—Kawakami, Matsuoka, Katayama, or Asanuma—was not decided until August 1952, just before the general election. Further problems arose over the reinstatement of Nishio, who had been expelled for his part in the Shoden bribery scandal, and that of Hirano Rikizo, who had left the party before Nishio. Nishio returned in August and Hirano in October 1952. The Nichiro and middle factions, the left wing of the right-wing JSP (so to speak), objected to their return on the grounds that they would advocate rearmament. Their fears were well founded.

Little information exists on Nishio's views on rearmament for the period beginning with his expulsion and ending with his reinstatement. Occasionally, however, he appears in the diary of former Prime Minister Ashida, with whom he shared complete confidence. Ashida, for instance, says,

> 7/18/50 Told Nishio how equivocal Japanese attitude was toward the Korean situation. Explained the Soviet trend and the inevitability of World War III. Nishio also thinks "the world war is already on." Says the JSP's responsibility is large and he wants to unify it but can't get a handle on it. Says he can do it if given a chance. First, he would talk to Wada on the left, then Asanuma and Miyake Shoichi in the middle, and Katayama. But complains he's got no chance while on the out. Says, "Morning and

noon I am thinking about this problem only." When all is said and done, Nishio is the first among the Socialists.

12/7/50 Called at Takeda Giichi's home to talk with Nishio, three of us. Gave Nishio a frank briefing of events since June 23. Read him my letter of advice to [SCAP] GHQ [a letter in which Ashida pointed to the acute need for educating the Japanese on national defense]. Says, "I am in wholehearted agreement, but why doesn't Yoshida do that? He can do good for both Japan and the JSP."

1/12/51 Went to see Takeda at 4 p.m. Had a three-way discussion with Miki Takeo, who just returned from the U.S. and Nishio. I said Japan should take the initiative in rearmament. They are opposed to Japanese initiative on rearmament.

2/6/51 Visited Nishio high up in the Yomiuri Building because he wanted to talk to me about internal JSP situation. Here is what he said: ... he will fight the Three Principles of Peace in the January party congress. Expects to lose the vote and retreat. But as international tension mounts, public opinion will change. The right wing hopes to challenge the Three Principles in the foreign-affairs committee by June. By then he would also move to call an extraordinary congress. For that purpose, he is already talking to Tanahashi and X of the middle faction, designating the latter as the leader. Wada Hiroo may wish to convert later rather than commit himself now. Suzuki Mosaburo has been agitating among the youth. Now he's happy currying their favor. We need not worry because he's got no guts. The good news put my mind at ease.

Being on the outside, Nishio sought to influence party policy decisions behind the scenes using his liaison with Sone and Nishimura. He also appealed to the public through interviews and lectures. In his January 1951 lecture in the Osaka City Hall, he is quoted as saying,

On Japan's rearmament, what I want to stress is that, first, "There has been no independent state without arms." Switzerland and Sweden, which are peace-loving beyond anyone's doubt, are armed for self-defense. If Japan wants to be independent, we must also rearm. Second, to those who say, "The existing constitution should not be changed for frivolous reasons," I say, we must absolutely change it. The existing constitution was not chosen by our free will. At that time, the Japanese nation was steeped in militarism. It was first necessary to wipe this out and get off to a peaceful and independent start. That's why that constitution was made. Following the peace conference, the end of occupation, and our regaining freedom, it is only natural that we take a new look at the constitution. As for the content of rearmament, we must listen to experts rather than to politicians. But here is an outline. The right of command should belong to the prime minister, and the defense minister must be a civilian. Whether

the force-level should be 150,000 or 200,000 is now debated. The important thing is to have a force that cannot go on offensive but can defend.[18]

Nishio repeated the message on March 1 and added,

Because the goal of rearmament is to defend the peace for both Japan and
the world, our insufficient capabilities must be supplemented by a Japan-
U.S. defense pact or regional collective-defense arrangement. Some people
suggest that we upgrade the Police Reserve to a national defense force. It
cannot live up to the task.[19]

The foregoing demonstrates that Nishio shared a virtually identical
view with all of Yoshida's conservative opponents, including Ashida,
Hatoyama, and Ishibashi (though Nishio was critical of Ashida's liaison
with Akao Bin, a right-winger).[20] The Socialist left wing was justified
in criticizing Nishio for being no different from the conservatives. Even
some JSP right-wing and middle-faction leaders like Katayama and
Mizutani were strongly opposed to all-out rearmament.

After the founding of the right-wing JSP in the fall of 1951, the party
leadership carefully formulated the platform so as to prevent internal
conflict.[21] In the January 1952 congress, the party executives adopted a
directive that criticized the left-wing JSP's "no-defense neutralism"
and that endorsed a limited self-defense capability while rejecting total
rearmament and stressing economic stability. The party likewise endorsed a system of regional collective security but rejected the existing
security treaty with the United States. Moreover, the congress left
standing the parallel, conflicting interpretations of the directive. The
August congress just before the general election repeated the practice
by avoiding a debate on rearmament.

But Nishio did not remain silent. Having been reinstated in August,
he moved for the adoption of a revised directive in congress the following January, calling for rearmament. Said he, "It is inevitable that Japan

---

[18]*Sangyo Keizai Shimbun*, February 26, 1951.

[19]*Yomiusi Shimbun*, March 2, 1951.

[20]Shindo, *Ashida Hitoshi Nikki*, IV, 76.

[21]The analysis of the right-wing JSP rearmament debate that follows is based
mostly on Asahi, Mainichi, and Yomiuri newspapers. Also useful was Horie
Jin and Kusunoki Seiichiro, "Nihon Shakaito no anzen hosho seisaku," in Horie
Jin and Ikei Yu, eds., *Nihon no seito to gaiko seisaku* (Japan's political parties
and their foreign policy) (Tokyo: Keio Tsushin, 1980). The Diet library holds a
vast collection in its Asanuma Inejiro Archives, on which I have drawn. The
archives await more intensive research.

will rearm sooner or later. If we want to be a ruling party, we should not oppose rearmament or constitutional revision for transient reasons." Not to be outdone, Nishio's critics submitted a counterdraft that was more negative toward rearmament and the security treaty and demanded its adoption by the party. Thus the debate in congress centered on rearmament. Surprised by Nishio's proposal as well as by its consequences, the party center tried its utmost to talk him into withdrawing it in favor of the center's draft.

He remained silent for a while. But after he attended the world congress of the Socialist International in July where he became convinced of his correctness by observing the defense debate among Western Social Democrats, Nishio renewed his uninhibited criticism of the party's opposition to receiving Mutual Security Act (MSA) assistance, thus rekindling the defense controversy. Sone Eki, a former Foreign Ministry official and the Nishio faction's authority on foreign and defense policy, reportedly went so far as to say, "I would rather join with the conservative advocates of rearmament than with the left wing." The dispute also pitched the Shamin faction against the Nichiro-dominated center over party control. Nishio blamed the right-wing JSP's two successive election defeats on the center's handling of the defense issue. The right-wing JSP, sure of overtaking the left wing at the polls, was highly agitated about the opposite outcome. In contrast, the doves, consisting mostly of the middle faction, became alarmed over a possible rightward shift and began to look for ways to isolate Nishio through a coalition with the left-wing JSP. Nishio sought to frustrate this move, while the center—with increasing difficulty—continued to straddle the fence.

Things came to a head again over the directive for 1954. In the previous fall, Sone, as director of the International Bureau, drafted a foreign policy directive stating that "the communist camp's peace offensive based on the large military and economic powers of the Chinese communists goes hand in hand with the threat of direct and indirect aggressions." Accordingly, Sone recommended that "(1) While the security treaty must be fundamentally altered, an interim Japan-U.S. regional collective-security system based on equality must be endorsed. The U.S. military presence in Japan must be superseded by Japan's self-defense efforts. (2) If the United Nations police force is established, Japan should take part." The party leaders in the policy deliberation committee, the senior cadre conference, and the Central Executive Committee (CEC) intensely debated the hawks who supported the Sone draft. On November 27, 1953, the CEC, after a heated late-night debate, accepted Chairman Kawakami's motion to delete Sone's two recommendations, whereupon Sone resigned as chief of the International Bureau and as a member of the CEC, in protest.

In the party congress that opened on January 17, 1954, the Tokyo branch of the Seamen's Union submitted a revised draft, which stated that "the MSA assistance will go through whether one likes it or not. Based on this assumption, we ought to work out pragmatic measures to use it for the improvement of national life and self-defense apparatuses" and that "if a majority of the nation should demand a constitutional revision, we will not stand in the way, provided that consolidation of democratic socialism goes forward." The prefectural delegates from Osaka and Kanagawa, from which Nishio, Nishimura, Sone, and other hawks hailed, supported the draft. Their opposite numbers from Ishikawa, Fukui, and Yamaguchi countered, calling for "all-out efforts to defend the constitution and oppose rearmament." Throughout, the congress was enveloped in unprecedented tension.

Said an Osaka delegate, "If we persist with such a purely negative attitude toward the military as we exhibit today, [the military] will become reactionary. To defend the nation and state, we need to have an army that understands socialism." Nishio's efforts notwithstanding, the opposition was in the overwhelming majority. The Nichiro-controlled center was sympathetic to the draft revision of the middle-faction doves, and Nishio isolated himself further. In the end, all revised drafts were withdrawn and the center's proposed draft, written by Sone, passed. For the time being, realism seemed to prevail, but Nishio's offensive pushed the Nichiro and middle factions toward the left-wing JSP in the long run.

The democratic-socialist line could not carry even the right-wing JSP, not because of the Marxist left but because of the Nichiro faction, the self-styled moderate Social Democrats and heirs of Nihon Ronoto (Japan Workers' and Peasants' party). What kind of pacifism did the Nichiro group, which dominated the right wing of the JSP, advocate?

As opposed to the union background of the Shamin cadres, the Nichiro faction's leaders—Kawakami, Asanuma, Miwa Juso, Kono Mitsu, Miyake Shoichi, and the rest—were intellectuals and college graduates. Plunging from campus life into the social movement among peasants and workers in response to the call, "To the masses!" (Shamin's Katayama had a similar background, which seems to account for his falling-out with Nishio), these men, in contrast to Nishio's down-to-earth pragmatism, carried a heavy dose of humanism and idealism. Small wonder that their heartstrings were tugged by the pacifism in vogue at the time. Interestingly enough, the carte blanche leadership of Shamin kept them at a distance from the masses, whereas the Nichiro type tended to overidentify with the masses. The latter were easily moved and swept away by the current of the moment.

The Nichiro leaders were also tainted by having "driven the people into war" in cooperation with the military. Whereas the right-leaning Shamin leaders maintained their honor by defending Saito Takao, a Dietman threatened with expulsion for his antimilitarist speech, Nichiro not only denounced Shamin but played an active role in wartime mobilization as a coalition partner in the Unity party (Taisei Yokusan-kai). With the exception of Asanuma, who did not run for the Diet during the war, the Nichiro cadres took part in the coalition and thus were purged during the occupation.

That taint weighed heavily on their conscience, and without exception they carried out self-criticism before returning to public life when the purge was lifted. In contrast, Nishio's wartime fracas with the military gave him safe conduct thereafter. Nichiro leaders had to be extremely sensitive to the charge that the call to rearm signified a militarist revival.

Even more important, there was widespread support for disarmed neutrality among labor, white-collar workers, intellectuals, and housewives, a sharp contrast with the situation in Europe—particularly in West Germany, on the front line of the cold war—where the Soviet threat stymied neutralism and pacifism. In Japan, the cold war was translated into a domestic context: Rearmament was taken as the cutting edge of domestic reaction. Even after the outbreak of the war in Korea, debate on the security issue gave way to antimilitarist ideology at all levels—among the grass roots, intellectuals, and party politicians.

Nishio's policy seems far removed from the realism of electoral politics at a time when even Prime Minister Yoshida was having second thoughts owing to public opinion and economic conditions about full-scale rearmament. Moreover, the Yoshida government was busy enacting antilabor legislation, such as the Labor Act Revision, the Strike Restraint Act, and the Anti-Subversion Act. To speak out in favor of rearmament under those circumstances amounted to support for those "reactionary" bills.

As Nishio went on the offensive he may have been trying to revive the Katayama-Ashida coalition of 1947–1949 by adopting Ashida's stance on rearmament. Such a center-left coalition would have created a workable challenge to Yoshida's Liberal party. Nishio and Ashida appear at least to have probed such a possibility. As an alternative to the Dodge Line's disinflationary economic policy, it had a sound footing. A major obstacle to restoring a center-left coalition was the chasm between foreign and defense policy issues, which Nishio may have been trying in vain to eliminate. In any case, his setback meant that instead of an alternating two-party system consisting of a conservative and a center-left party, Japan would have an LDP permanently in power, opposed by a radical Socialist party.

I would like to reevaluate the rearmament issue in the context of the birth of the 1955 System, which rearranged Japan's postwar political parties. If we set aside the JSP as an antisystem party, Japan's political arena was divided three ways by parties that stood for classical liberalism, revised capitalism (or left-wing liberalism), and social democracy. No party was able to control a stable majority, and a government had to be based on a coalition of any two. Thus, in 1947 Minseito entered a coalition with the JSP. After its demise, Seiyukai—having temporarily won a strong majority—ran the government alone, championing the turnaround toward liberal economic policies called the Dodge Line. During this time, Minseito and Ashida, in particular, inveighed against the government's "anachronistic" liberal policies and sought to revive the coalition with the Socialists. For the JSP's part, Nishio and the right wing, responding to Ashida's feelers, converged to produce the abortive attempts at bipartisan foreign policy over the peace treaty and at organizing the Shigemitsu cabinet. All that came to naught, however, with the founding of the LDP. The merger of the liberals and the democrats excluded the chances for a democratic-socialist coalition.

In the realignment of political parties, rearmament played a catalytic role. At Ashida's initiative, Minseito took the most hawkish stance, enlisting the cooperation of the right-wing groups. That in turn confused and split the liberal left and made a coalition with the Socialists impossible. Hatoyama and Ishibashi, who led the anti-Yoshida forces in conjunction with Minseito, had a similar impact. At the same time, the conservative government's rearmament and right-wing policies reinforced the left wing in the JSP, isolated the right-wing JSP, and split the party. In driving out the right wing (the latter-day Democratic Socialist party), the JSP rejected the chances for another coalition with the progressive wing of the conservatives, consigning itself to the status of a third party. This basic alignment persists to this date. Since the onset of the even balance between the conservatives and *kakushin* in the Diet that began in the mid-seventies, several attempts at centrist coalition have been made, without any success in drawing out the LDP left.

The rearmament issue had aborted the Minseito-Socialist coalition, split the JSP, driven out the proponents of coalition from the JSP, and closed the chances for *kakushin*-centrist cooperation. The LDP's one-party dominance rests on the absence of a bridge between left liberalism and democratic socialism. This chapter has pointed out that behind the dynamism of political alignments in postwar Japan there lurks a void of ideological self-discipline among liberals and Social Democrats.

4 | The Japan Socialist Party before the Mid-1960s: An Analysis of Its Stagnation

Tani Satomi

THE JAPAN SOCIALIST PARTY (JSP) WAS FOUNDED IN OCTOBER 1945, thereby unifying various prewar Socialist factions. Owing to the Supreme Commander for the Allied Powers' (SCAP) policy of fostering new political forces to the left of the prewar Japanese political parties, the JSP won a plurality in the 1947 election and went on to lead a coalition government with Shimpoto, a conservative party. After that U.S. policy was reversed by George Kennan's containment policy, the JSP suffered a devastating defeat in the 1949 election, plummeting from 143 to 48 seats in the Diet. Following the Korean War, however, the JSP found its calling as a critic of U.S. efforts to rearm Japan and began to expand rapidly in the early 1950s, securing about a third of the Diet seats (167 in the lower house and 78 in the upper house). Given that the Socialists had never won more than 42 seats in the lower house before the war, it was a remarkable success.[1]

But the JSP's fortune did not last. In 1955, the high-speed growth of the Japanese economy began, giving people a taste of the consumer society. The social structure of the country began to change, and the

---

[1] Thirty-seven seats were won by Shakai Taishuto, the rest by independents.

JSP failed to adapt to those changes. In the first half of the 1960s, the party was on a plateau; in the latter half, it experienced a sudden decline. The year 1960, when Japan underwent a great upheaval over the revision of the U.S.-Japan security treaty, was a watershed for the JSP. This chapter will trace the party's history before the mid-1960s and try to explain why it failed to grow into a party capable of alternating with the Liberal Democratic party (LDP) in government. Politics is the art of the possible. In the inevitable flow of history, was there an alternative path for the JSP? I analyze the causes of the JSP's stagnation using five issues: (1) the failure of the Katayama cabinet, the only cabinet led by Socialists, (2) left-wing dominance and electoral strategies of the JSP, (3) the JSP's local government activities, (4) the shortcomings of the JSP's rural policies, and (5) Japanese political culture.

Failure in Power

One of the best ways for a party to gain the trust of voters is to be in power and demonstrate governing ability. In Japan, the JSP's chairman, Katayama Tetsu, led a government in coalition with two conservative parties in 1947. When the Katayama government collapsed, the JSP participated in another coalition government but made such fatal mistakes that it was thoroughly defeated in the 1949 general election. If the Socialists had better administered the two governments, the JSP could have become the loyal opposition, ready to take over the government when the conservatives failed, much as the German Social Democratic party (SPD) has learned to do. Why did the JSP fail?

First, we must deal with the policy of SCAP GHQ, the nerve center of the U.S. occupation of Japan. As the supreme force, GHQ often wielded absolute influence on Japanese politics. Without the decisive intervention of SCAP, democratization and demilitarization of Japan could not have been realized; Japan was *forced* to institutionalize complete political freedom. The leftist forces in Japan greatly benefited from this democratization policy. At first, SCAP even supported the Japan Communist party (JCP) in order to overturn the ancien régime. After a short honeymoon, however, SCAP and the JCP began to quarrel; within a year of Japan's surrender, they were divorced. In place of the Communists, the Socialists became the object of SCAP's solicitude and preference. Early in the occupation period, the occupation authority thought of the JSP as the liberal, middle-of-the-road force between the Communists and the conservatives and hoped it would play a leading role in democratizing party politics.[2] The occupation policy was directly responsible for the JSP's ascent to power.

The results of the 1947 election alone did not warrant the formation of the Katayama government, for the JSP merely won a plurality of seats in the Diet. A coalition government was inevitable, but early in the negotiations the largest conservative party, the Liberal party, led by Yoshida Shigeru, refused to participate in the Socialist-led government. If the Democratic party, the second-largest conservative party, had refused to join the coalition, the Katayama government would not have been realized. When the Democratic party sought to head the coalition by naming its own prime minister, SCAP intervened in favor of Katayama, thus forcing the Democratic party to accept the Socialist premiership.[3]

This meant, however, that the Katayama government depended on SCAP's will and that withdrawal of SCAP support could wreck the JSP. For example, GHQ's decision to purge Hirano Rikizo, minister of agriculture and forestry, because he had been too sympathetic to the militarists, damaged the Katayama government. Hirano, one of the founders of the JSP, had played a conspicuous role in the election campaign in 1946. His purge in 1947 was one reason sixteen Diet members seceded from the JSP to form the new but short-lived Social Progressivist party.[4]

The Katayama government was succeeded by another coalition headed by Ashida Hitoshi, president of Minshuto. Before long, however, the new cabinet including the prime minister, Vice–Prime Minister Nishio Suehiro, and several other politicians—all in the middle-of-the-road camp endorsed by GHQ's all-powerful Government Section (GS)—came under fire for allegedly taking bribes from Showa Denko, Inc.

G-2, under MacArthur's command, was headed by a hard-line anti-Communist general, Charles Willoughby, who showed an unusual interest in prosecuting the alleged miscreants, going so far as to investi-

---

[2]Takahashi Hirohiko, "Shakaito shuhan naikaku no seiritsu to zasetsu" (The rise and fall of the Socialist-led cabinet), in Asao Naohiro et al., eds., *Koza Nihon rekishi* (Tokyo: Iwanami Shoten, 1977), pp. 269–70. On the early occupation policies toward the JCP and the JSP, see Takemae Eiji, "Early Postwar Reformist Party," in Robert E. Ward and Sakamoto Yoshikazu, eds., *Democratizing Japan: The Allied Occupation* (Honolulu: University of Hawaii Press, 1987), pp. 339–65.

[3]Takahashi, "Shakaito Shuhan naikaku no seiritsu to zasetsu," pp. 270–71.

[4]Iizuka Shigetaro, Uji Toshihiko, and Habara Kiyomasa, *Ketto 40-nen: Nihon Shakaito* (The 40 years since the founding: The Japan Socialist party) (Tokyo: Gyosei Mondai Kenkyusho, 1985), pp. 96–97.

gate some GS officials also suspected of taking bribes. Clearly, an intra-GHQ power struggle was behind the affair. Today, some assert that the whole scandal was manufactured by G-2.[5] Indeed, most politicians, including Ashida and Nishio, were later acquitted but too late to clear the JSP's name. The Shoden scandal, as it was called, was catastrophic for the JSP: The party was reduced in 1949 to 48 Dietmen from 143. With Yoshida's liberals winning a stunning majority of 264, the mandate was unambiguous.

To make matters worse, however, the change of government coincided with the 1948 shift in U.S. occupation policy brought about by containment. In Japan, the shift's breathtaking sea change altered all the basic assumptions of U.S. foreign policy. NSC 13/2, a major directive of the National Security Council drafted by George F. Kennan, director of the policy planning staff at the State Department, ordered a halt to further democratization and placed a priority on economic recovery. This was the beginning of the so-called reverse course, which was accompanied in Tokyo by a shift in the balance of power within MacArthur's staff. Until then, the New Deal reformers in the GS kept rightists like Yoshida at bay; henceforward, Yoshida's conservatives took the Socialists' place.[6] The conjunction of the ruinous coalition and the U.S. policy shift polarized Japan's politics. With the middle-of-the-road leaders on trial for bribery, the left-wing Socialists began to blame JSP's misfortune on unprincipled collaboration with "monopoly capital" and "American imperialism." The political center fell out and could not be revived.

In retrospect, a Socialist government was premature in 1947–1948, less than two years after the JSP's formation. Consisting of labor leaders and humanist intellectuals in its right wing, the JSP's leadership was not ready to run the government when it was thrust into power by the vagaries of occupation policy.[7] The JSP needed more time to settle its organizational problems and to learn to put its act together in the Diet. Besides, the JSP obtained only 17.6 percent of the electoral vote and

[5]Shukan Shincho, ed. *Makkasa no Nihon* (MacArthhur's Japan) (Tokyo: Shinchosha, 1970), pp. 321–24; Iizuka et al., *Ketto 40-nen*, p. 109; Junnosuke Masumi, *Sengo seiji* (Postwar politics) (Tokyo: Tokyo University Press, 1983), I. 255–58.

[6]On the change of occupation policy, see Sakai Ryuji, "Reisen no gekika to senryo seisaku no tenkan" (The intensification of the cold war and the shift in occupation policy), in Asao et al., *Koza Nihon rekishi*.

[7]When Professor Takahashi Masao of Kyushu University advised Katayama not to head the government, Katayama replied, "I agree with you in principle, Masao. But we have no choice as long as the JSP is the leading party." Takahashi, *Shakaito no himitsu* (The JSP's secrets) (Tokyo: Chobunsha, 1981), p. 34.

less than 33.0 percent of the lower house in 1947, in contrast with the 34.1 percent the German SPD gained in 1965. The JSP's initiative in the coalition government was thus heavily constrained by the overwhelming power of the conservatives.

Yoshida, knowing that the Socialists were not ready to manage the government, thrust them into power with the hope that they would discredit themselves. Insisting that the "rule of constitutional government" demanded the leading party to take power, he rejected a role for his Liberal party in a coalition government.[8]

The JSP also lacked a decisive and skilled leader. Prime Minister Katayama neither refused the move to install him in power nor took a leading role in the coalition and persisted in being indecisive and reluctant to act. When faced with pressure from SCAP to purge Hirano, his own minister, Katayama wavered about dismissing him and instead resorted to a subterfuge, complicating the matter unnecessarily. Some right-wing Socialist Dietmen and friends of Hirano bolted the JSP in anger; among them was Suzuki Zenko, who later switched to the LDP and became a prime minister. When the left wing of the JSP rebelled against the cabinet over the supplementary budget of 1948, Katayama's lack of strong leadership accelerated the centrifugal trends in the party and encouraged attacks from both inside and outside. But the JSP did not have anyone to take Katayama's place, partly because the party's most influential leaders had been purged.

Finally, the Socialists lacked the will to maintain the cabinet. In general, political parties hold government control as long as possible. But the Socialists in the Katayama government seemed glad to pass the power to Ashida's coalition, even though the lower house neither voted no-confidence nor rejected the government budget. The cabinet could have survived a little longer had Katayama possessed the will to power; if his government had survived longer, the Shoden scandal might have been stillborn.

The failure of the Katayama government led to a serious setback in the 1949 general election, spoiling the political careers of those who had entered politics after the war.[9] The JSP did not regain its lost

---

[8]Yoshida also obstructed the Katayama cabinet's efforts to develop Socialist policies. Kinoshita Takeshi, *Katayama naikaku shiron* (History of the Katayama cabinet) (Kyoto: Horitsu Bunkasha, 1982), pp. 88–97. Yoshida took seriously the differences between his party and the JSP, a fact that did not endear him to SCAP until the reverse course came. See Inoki Masamichi, *Hyoden Yoshida Shigeru* (Yoshida Shigeru: A biography) (Tokyo: Yomiuri Shimbunsha, 1981), pp. 300–301.

[9]Among the defeated candidates were Katayama, Vice–Prime Minister Nishio Suehiro, and fourteen out of twenty-six members of the central executive

momentum until the 1952 general election. Many JSP politicians, damaged before they fully established their credentials, were not reelected. This was serious for the JSP because, as a semicadre party, it depended on votes cast for personal reasons.[10] Moreover, the failure of the coalition governments presaged the decline of the party's right wing, which was blamed for the decision to enter the coalitions with the two conservative parties over the objections of the left wing.

The JSP had at least one more chance to share power. Holding roughly a third of the Diet seats, the party could have come to power when the conservatives were divided and no one party controlled a majority. The first such chance came in 1947; the second chance came in 1953, when Yoshida's liberals lost their majority and no single party could form a government without a coalition. At the time, the JSP had 138 seats but was divided over the peace and security treaties. Seeing the struggle among the conservatives, Takano Minoru, secretary general of Sohyo and left-wing leader of the Socialist movement, proposed that the JSP vote for Shigemitsu, the leader of the Progressive party, to form an anti-Yoshida coalition. Takano was rejected by the party.[11]

The official reason for rejecting Takano—that it was unacceptable to blur the distinction between *kakushin* and the conservatives[12]—was probably a cover for other reasons: (1) The left wing of the JSP, influenced by anarcho-syndicalism, was apt to look down on the government.[13] Indeed, it opposed the formation of the Katayama government. (2) Many Socialists feared that another coalition would impair their so-called *shutaisei* (a word originating in German idealism that means something like "the self-identification that earnest and genuine Socialists were supposed to hold"). (3) Not least, their bitter experience during the coalition days discouraged them from making another attempt. In the last analysis, most Socialists were naive enough to believe that a political party that avoided political power could retain both its vigor and the electorate's respect. In 1955 the conservatives united in the LDP

---

committee. Nihon Shakaito Secretariat, *Nihon Shakaito no 30-nen* (The 30 years of the JSP) (Tokyo: JSP Secretariat, 1976), I, 105.

[10]On the concept of the cadre party, see Maurice Duverger, *Les Partis Politiques* (Paris: Librairie Armand Colin, 1976), pp. 118–29.

[11]The question of a coalition government that included the JSP remains moot. See Tominomori Eiji, *Sengo hoshuto shi* (History of postwar conservative parties) (Tokyo: Nihon Hyoronsha, 1977), p. 53.

[12]Secretariat, *Nihon Shakaito no 30-nen*, I, 200–202.

[13]Gerald L. Curtis, *The Japanese Way of Politics* (New York: Columbia University Press, 1988), pp. 131–33.

and, though still divided on critical issues, never allowed the JSP to govern.

Left-Wing Dominance and Organizational Fallacy

When the JSP was founded, the right wing led the party. In the 1940s, right-wing Diet members, who outnumbered left-wing members, formed the Katayama government despite the skeptical left. Right-wing dominance in the party did not last long. Although the left wing was in the minority at the national level, it soon began to expand at the local level. Before long, local activists dissatisfied with the right-wing leadership strove to send their delegates to national conventions. The JSP also became excessively dependent on Sohyo's militant leadership. Sohyo, another creation of SCAP GHQ (the Labor Section), was to vie with the JCP-dominated Sanbetsu and provide the middle-of-the-road JSP with a union constituency. In fact, Sohyo members joined the JSP en masse but became the backbone of the left wing. In the meantime, the right wing lost influential leaders: In 1948, Hirano and Kawakami were purged and Nishio was expelled from the party over the Shoden affair. The left wing lost only one to the purge.

The left-wing advance intensified the conflict within the JSP as the left succeeded in defeating the right in the election for secretary general in 1950, though a right-wing leader was reelected chairman of the Central Executive Committee (CEC) at the same time. At the Seventh Congress in January 1951, the left-wing delegates clearly outnumbered the right wing, and the left overwhelmed the right in the lower house. Thus the left wing dominated the JSP till Ishibashi Masatsugu was elected chairman of the CEC in 1983.

The right-wing Socialist leaders came from three major groups: leftist intellectuals, leaders of the prewar labor movement, and leaders of the prewar tenant farmers' movement.[14] With the exception of the intellectuals, they tended to be small inner circles in which they behaved like patriarchs. The leader-follower relationship resembled the so-called *oyabun-kobun* (boss-henchman, or patron-client) relationship. The leaders, who were inclined to uphold the seniority system as all-important, thus alienated the younger generation, especially in the postwar movement. That is why left-minded activists such as Takano Minoru, whose alleged self-restraint and intellect seemed to attract many

---

[14]Ishikawa Masumi, *Sengo seiji kozoshi* (History of postwar Japanese political structure) (Tokyo: Nihon Hyoronsha, 1978), p. 27.

younger activists,[15] were able to take control of Sohyo, the largest federation in the labor movement.

In a sense the Japanese Communists radicalized the JSP. Until the defeat of Japan, the Communists had been almost the only force to resist militarism. Some Communists were murdered by the police, and others were under detention for more than ten years. Moreover, they anticipated Japan's defeat in World War II with "scientific" analysis; after the defeat they were free of the guilt with which Japan was charged. Bolstered by the SCAP's early policies, the JCP and its constituency expanded and by 1949 had thirty-five seats in the lower house. It lost all of them in the 1952 election because of shifts in both the JCP's policy and SCAP's, but apparently its supporters then shifted to the left-wing JSP, part of which was a collateral faction of the Communists called Ronoha.[16] The JSP's right-wing leaders, feeling vulnerable to the charge of "collaboration with the militarists," supported "peace" issues as the cold war intensified, placing the JSP squarely in opposition to Japan's foreign policy of military cooperation with the United States.

With the left wing leading the outnumbered right wing, the JSP merged again in 1955, simultaneously with the conservatives' merger. But the left wing's control of the party did not help the Socialists. Most left-wing Socialists were sympathetic with the Marxism of the Ronoha faction, which had vied with the Kozaha faction, a predecessor of the JCP, and harbored anarcho-syndicalist yearnings for political crisis, general strikes, and national mobilization. The JSP frowned on the workaday politics of policy debate and compromises and concentrated on adamant class struggle against "monopoly capitalism." Policy debates and the search for realistic alternatives were, the militants often insisted, a form of concession to monopoly capital. Curiously, the left-wingers—with the exception of dedicated Ronoha theorists—did not reject parliamentarism as a cover for bourgeois domination; on the contrary, they regarded the European political system as indispensable to Japan's modernization. For them, socialism was an expression of their admiration for modern Europe; thus they chose to walk both the parliamentary and the extraparliamentary paths. The 1960 riots against the revision of the Japan-U.S. security treaty were perhaps the best example and the high point of the JSP's modus operandi. The JSP left

---

[15]Tamura Yuzo, *Sengo Shakaito no ninaite-tachin* (Those who were in charge of the postwar Socialist party) (Tokyo: Nihon Hyoronsha, 1984), p. 270.

[16]For a history of Ronoha, see Curtis, *Japanese Way of Politics*, pp. 133–38; Ishikawa, *Sengo seiji Kozoshi*, p. 131.

wing's peculiar approach is illustrated by Suzuki Mosaburo, chairman of the CEC of the JSP between 1955 and 1960:

> Whenever the possibility of the JSP participating in a coalition becomes a significant political issue, that is not simply because the JSP is one of the major parties in the Diet, but also because any government, without the participation of the JSP, cannot enjoy enough support among all the working people, who constitute 95 percent of the whole nation: Most people will always find the party indispensable to a stable cabinet. The weight of the JSP in any coalition government will always be heavy, whether the number of the seats in the Diet be big or small; in other words, the JSP always has a kind of qualitative significance.[17]

In his opinion, the Socialists represent all the working classes. Objectively, 95 percent of the people supported the revolution. When Diet support did not measure up to this expectation, the JSP looked for support from the masses. Such a mobilizational strategy sometimes gave the JSP considerable veto power but made the party look unconstructive, and people began to see the JSP as opposed to everything. Moreover, left-wing activists and Diet members often considered it a concession to monopoly capital to search for realistic alternatives to governmental policies through Diet activities.

When all is said and done, however, the JSP, radical left wing and all, did manage to hold roughly a third of the Diet seats throughout these years. What accounts for its longevity in the minority position? One answer, stressed in Kataoka's introduction, is the JSP's peculiar foreign policy function; the other is Sohyo's organizational support. After being radicalized by the reverse course, the JSP set forth the Four Principles of Peace, its foreign policy plank, to which it has rigidly adhered to date. The principles are as follows: support for an all-around peace, that is, opposition to a separate peace with the United States; opposition to foreign military bases; and neutrality. (We should also add the JSP's adamant defense of the no-war constitution.) This plank, established on the eve of the San Francisco peace conference, undoubtedly contributed to the recovery of the JSP in the 1952 election and thereafter from the devastation of 1949. During the 1950s the left wing's rate of expansion always exceeded that of the right wing. The right wing, comparatively strong in the metropolitan areas, was weak in rural areas, but the

---

[17]Suzuki Mosaburo, "Shakaito no ayumubeki michi" (The road the JSP ought to take), *Shakai Shimbun*, March 10, 1948.

left wing, advancing in both areas,[18] owed its rapid increase to its success in rural areas.

The strength of the one-third minority in the opposition after San Francisco enabled Yoshida to achieve two contradictory goals: On the one hand, he managed to hitch Japan's fortune to that of the United States in the cold war; on the other, he enlisted the Socialists' help in resisting U.S. demands for contributions to fighting the cold war. Thus Japan could concentrate its efforts on economic reconstruction.

Both ideologically and organizationally, Sohyo was the backbone of the JSP after San Francisco. The JSP has never had a mass organization to conduct effective election campaigns. Party members have numbered about forty or fifty thousand, except for a short period just after the war when they numbered around a hundred thousand, and there were no JSP branches in two-thirds of all municipalities in the 1950s.[19] With such a weak organization, it seemed impossible that the party should obtain the more than ten million votes it managed to garner. Only Sohyo's organizational muscle could have filled the gap.

Sohyo's strength was in giant industrial unions—collectively labeled Kankoro (government and public)—in the public sector such as the railway workers' unions and the postal union that are ubiquitous in the land. The local branches of Sohyo, consisting mainly of Kankoro workers, campaigned actively for the JSP, especially for the left wing. A journalist reported on a campaign, circa 1953, as follows:

> The local campaign headquarters of the JSP are established in the local branches of Sohyo. . . . In most cases, both are the same organizations. The Sohyo branches financially back up the left-wing candidates and mobilize volunteer workers for the campaign. At a branch of the National Railway Workers' Union, they have a list of all the member workers. The names of the workers are classified according to their addresses. And their addresses are, in turn, grouped systematically into their districts. . . . That list is crucially useful in election campaign activities.[20]

Besides money and campaign organizations, Sohyo provided party members and candidates. For instance, in 1958, workers made up 52.7

---

[18]Kyogoku Jun'ichi, "Sengo sosenkyo ni okeru tohyo kodo" [Voting behavior in postwar elections], *Shiso*, September 1960, part 2, pp. 50–53.

[19]Hisayoshi Takeo, "Kakushin seito no soshiki-ryoku" (The organizational power of *kakushin* parties), *Shiso*, June 1959, p. 83.

[20]Hirose Ken'ichi, *Saha Shakaito no jittai* (Truth about the left-wing JSP) (Tokyo: Sekkasha, 1955), pp. 99–100.

percent of the JSP.[21] In the same year, 29 percent of the JSP's Dietmen in the lower house were from trade unions.[22] The number of Diet members from the trade unions continued to increase gradually throughout the 1950s and 1960s until the so-called Sohyo-JSP block appeared. The left wing's advance in rural areas relied on the same human networking on which the conservatives depended, but did not necessarily entail the ideological transformation of the rural voters.[23]

The JSP's dependence on Sohyo has been incessantly criticized,[24] with numerous critics arguing that that dependence is one of the JSP's major obstacles to breaking the "one-third barrier." There is some substance to this charge, for dependence on Sohyo dictated a doctrinal orthodoxy of sorts and adherence to the Sohyo line did not endear the Socialists to the general voters, who became disenchanted by the ideology as Japan entered the consumer age. Unlike the JSP, the LDP was capable of drawing a large number of voters without party membership and with but fleeting party identification. The JSP had to choose between the Sohyo constituency and the general public, and it stayed with the former.

It was not out of the question, however, for the JSP to develop a non-Sohyo constituency of the progressive variety; indeed, such a constituency would capture many local governments in the 1960s, as shown below. Possible alternatives were consumers' cooperatives, farmers' cooperatives, environmental groups, small-entrepreneurs' organizations, and so forth. The Socialist politicians could also have developed their own *koenkai* organizations, but not enough Socialists penetrated local communities or other social networks.

In the 1963 general election, twenty-six incumbent Diet members of the JSP, including about ten leading figures, lost their seats. With long tenures in office, most of them had relied mainly on personal reputation, not on labor organizations. They were supplanted by candidates supported by Sohyo, although the JSP's collective strength hardly changed. The shift in the party's organizational character that had

---

[21]Hisayoshi, "Sengo sosenkyo ni okeru tohyo kodo," p. 90.
[22]Ishikawa, *Sengo seiji kozoshi*, p. 27; Taguchi Fukuji, *Nihon no kakushin seiryoku* (Japan's *kakushin* forces) (Tokyo: Tobundo, 1961), p. 13.
[23]Hirose, *Saha Shakaito no jittai*, p. 101.
[24]See, for example, Robert A. Scalapino and Masumi Junnosuke, *Parties and Politics in Contemporary Japan* (Berkeley: University of California Press, 1962), p. 97.

begun in the 1950s was completed.[25] The plateau on which the JSP stayed during the 1960s reflected the equilibrium between the exit of the old-type Socialists and the advance of the newcomers who relied mainly on Sohyo. This election also marked the final decline of the right-wing remnants who had not followed the DSP's walkout in 1960. Because that old right wing was comparatively popular in the metropolitan areas, that decline deprived the JSP of its urban character. The JSP's share of the electorate in the metropolitan areas was 28 percent in 1955; in 1963, 20 percent, eaten away by the JCP and Komeito.[26] Besides its own small but militant mass organization, the JCP succeeded in organizing various social groups, such as women, young people, and small entrepreneurs and merchants. Komeito was backed by a strong religious organization, mainly in the metropolitan areas.

The JSP's share of the electorate and the absolute number of votes at the general elections changed in three different areas. Two are typically metropolitan (one comprises Tokyo and Kanagawa prefectures and the other consists of Kyoto, Osaka, and Hyogo prefectures), and one is a typical rural area (the Shikoku district). The figures suggest that although the number of voters increased rapidly in the metropolitan areas during the 1960s, the JSP was unable to capture these new voters and only maintained those it had secured by the end of the 1950s. In metropolitan Tokyo, some of the nonorganized voters who had formerly voted JSP on broad ideological issues fell away, and the gap between the total number of registered voters and the JSP party vote widened. In the rural areas, the party kept the electorate it had obtained in the 1950s, which was sufficient.

Local Government Activities

In most industrialized countries, local government is another arena where political parties vying for power at the national level can prove their ability to rule. When a party is out of power at the center, it can impress voters with an alternative political course in local governments under its control. The postwar local government system in Japan gives parties plenty of chances to try their policies, despite the centralization of administrative power and the weak financial basis of most local governments. In Britain, in contrast, local governments can do only what the law permits them to do under the doctrine of ultra vires; if

[25]Fukui Taguchi, "Nihon Shakaito ron" (A discourse on the JSP), *Chuo Koron,* September 1957, p. 126.
[26]Ishikawa, *Sengo seiji kozoshi,* p. 118.

they want to do something that is not legally authorized, they must ask the Parliament to pass a local bill authorizing it, a lengthy and expensive procedure. In the United States, Dilon's rule functions in much the same way as does Britain's doctrine of ultra vires. Japanese local governments, however, can in principle do anything the law does not prohibit.[27]

Thus, Ninagawa Torazo, the famous leftist governor of Kyoto Prefecture, offered his subsidy program to the farmers when the central government cut one of its agricultural subsidies, thereby gaining support for himself. Offering many other programs different from the national government's in such fields as education, welfare, and the protection of small enterprises, Ninagawa was in office continuously for twenty-eight years. Originally backed by the JSP, that party's ineptitude made him a pro-JCP politician,[28] and the JCP in Kyoto Prefecture succeeded in raising its share of votes under the umbrella of a sympathetic prefectural government.

Another example is that of Fukazawa Masao from the village in the Iwate Prefecture in northern Japan, who was born in the village and became mayor in 1957. In the 1950s, Sawauchi was a poor village; infants and old people were in bad health, but most villagers were too poor to see a doctor as often as necessary, and the health administration was not functioning well. When Fukazawa took office, the infant mortality rate in the village was 6.96 percent, that is, seven out of one hundred babies died before their first birthday. (Today the average rate in Japan is about 0.6 percent, less than one out of a hundred.)

Fukazawa endeavored to improve this state of affairs by instituting free medicine for infants and people over sixty through subsidizing the health insurance system, though the village's financial margin was narrow. Sawauchi was the first local government in Japan to exempt the poor from medical expenses. At the same time, he improved the public health nursing system, introduced preventive care organizations into the local communities, and added more equipment to the only

---

[27]On the Japanese local government system, see Kurt Steiner, *Local Government in Japan* (Stanford: Stanford University Press, 1965); Nagata Naohisa, "The Development of Japanese Local Government and Its Current Issues," in Eropa Local Government Center, ed., *Comparative Study on Local Public Administration in Asian and Pacific Countries* (Tokyo: Eropa Local Government Center, 1984), pp. 114–30.

[28]See Ellis S. Krauss, "Opposition in Power," in Kurt Steiner, Ellis S. Krauss, and Scott C. Flanagan, eds., *Political Opposition and Local Politics in Japan* (Princeton, N.J.: Princeton University Press, 1980).

hospital. Following his campaign, the infant mortality rate had dropped to zero by 1962. All this was done without bankrupting the village.[29]

Fukazawa's remarkable achievements in Sawauchi impressed many Socialist politicians, though he was neither pro-Socialist nor proconservative. When the Socialists came to power locally in the late 1960s and early 1970s, they began adopting policies exempting the needy from medical fees, which won them considerable popularity. The leftist success in the field of welfare policy forced the national LDP government to reconsider its policies of economic growth. Fukazawa presented an alternative to Japanese politics in an age when economic values overwhelmed other considerations.

Several prefectures have been governed by JSP-backed or pro-JSP governors, though most did not stay in office for long, whereas many municipal governments have been ruled by Socialists or pro-Socialists. Had the JSP learned the lessons of Ninagawa and Fukazawa and creatively managed the local governments under its control, it could have enjoyed greater success; however, the JSP has been rather indifferent to local government activities apart from getting control over them.

Rural Strategy

Despite difficulties, the Socialists enjoyed considerable support in rural areas where they developed an appropriate strategy and were more active than the conservatives. For example, the JSP obtained more than a third of the seats in seven rural prefectures in the 1947 general election. In two of them, the party won half the seats because the Socialists had struggled there on behalf of tenant farmers before the war, which suggests something about the JSP's rural strategy.

Agrarian reform is perhaps one of the most important political events in Japan's postwar history. More than five million acres of farmland previously owned by landlords, many of them absentee, have been expropriated and distributed to the tenants. The success of this reform was due in part to some Japanese government bureaucrats' endorsing the drastic measure; they had long sought a similar reform but never had the political power to carry it out. The Socialists were stupefied by the windfall.[30]

---

[29]Kikuchi Takeo, *Jibun-tachi de inochi o mamotta mura* (A village that protected the villagers' health by itself) (Tokyo: Iwanami Shoten, 1968).

[30]See Owada Keiki, *Hishi Nihon no nochi kaikakaku* (The secret history of Japan's agrarian reform) (Tokyo: Nihon Keizai Shimbunsha, 1981), chap. 1. Certainly the Socialists and the Communists resumed the farmers' movement

In addition to land redistribution, various bills were introduced to democratize and improve rural society. For example, the Land Improvement Act was enacted in 1949 to help cultivators exchange their paddies and enlarge their lots for convenience. Each local government was ordered to establish an elected agricultural committee, one of the newly introduced administrative committees. More important was the Agricultural Cooperative Act, passed in 1947. These acts enlarged the scope of governmental services in the rural areas, and, together with the liquidation of the old class system and the birth of a new order, they opened up fertile fields for electoral politics.

The JSP in the 1940s, however, did virtually nothing regarding rural matters except air some proposals to nationalize fertilizer companies. In 1949 the action program of the party pointed out the necessity of immediately formulating an agricultural policy to lead the farmers' movements.[31] The Socialists then engaged in vain debates over the modalities of the Socialist revolution they anticipated. The conservatives did not have a monopoly on substantive ideas about agricultural policy, but they could at least rely on the bureaucrats.

Later, the JSP started to formulate more practical policies. Its basic idea was to modernize farming by joint management and to protect Japanese agriculture against international free trade. Fixed on the idea of cooperatives, the party tried to isolate the agricultural sector from the structural changes taking place in the Japanese economy.[32]

The Socialists who had participated in the prewar tenant movements formed the Japan Farmers' Union (JFU) in February 1946, struggling fiercely for land redistribution. The JFU rapidly grew in size, but having no program for the postreform period, it shrank rapidly thereafter. The Socialists were thinking only in terms of class struggle at a time when

---

soon after the distribution, but they did so simply to fight the landlords with the help of SCAP's power. They did not have pragmatic policies. See the case of Okayama Prefecture in Mizuno Aki, *Okayama-ken shakai undoshi* (History of the social movement in Okayama Prefecture) (Tokyo: Rodo kyoiku senta, 1979), vol. 7, 249–65.

[31]The only policy devised by the JSP was a subsidy for farmers, regardless of the deficit. Note the typical triad of JSP slogans: "Raise the producers' prices," "Lower the consumers' prices," and "No rearmament." See, for instance, Nihon Shakaito soshiki iinkai nominbu, seisaku shingikai, *Nogyo kiki taisaku zenkoku noson katsudoka kaigi no sokatsu* [The conclusion of the conference of national village activists to cope with the agricultural crisis] (mimeo) (JSP, 1958).

[32]See Allan B. Cole, George O. Totten, and Cecil H. Uyehara, *Socialist Parties in Japan* (New Haven, Conn.: Yale University Press, 1966), pp. 401–7, for a more detailed analysis of the JSP's agricultural policy.

class distinctions were disappearing. From the 1950s on, Socialist farmers' movements weakened except in those areas where farmers were threatened with expropriation of their newly acquired lands to make way for U.S. military bases.[33]

In the meantime, agricultural cooperatives established by the 1947 act enlisted nearly all farmers. The purpose of the co-ops was not to promote joint farming, as Socialist theoreticians had hoped, but to improve the economic conditions of members through the collective purchase of equipment, loans on favorable terms, and the like. This purely economic organization banned political activities by members. Which political force took control of them was important, however, for the leaders of the co-ops could garner the votes of the rural districts; but there is little mention of the agricultural cooperatives in the JSP's major documents, and the LDP moved into the vacuum with gusto.

Another profitable rural strategy for a political party is to dole out public works and case works not related to macroeconomic policies. Neglected by the prewar regime, the rural population lived in poverty in the early postwar years. Thus a Dietman from these backward districts could greatly improve both his and his constituency's lot. Former Prime Minister Tanaka Kakuei, for example, obtained many public works projects for his constituency in Niigata Prefecture and secured overwhelming voter support. In contrast, Miyake Shoichi, a former leader of the tenant movement in Niigata and later the vice-speaker of the lower house, proved either ineffective or reluctant to engage in pork barrel politics. Whenever his constituents asked him to influence the central bureaucracy to do something for their villages and towns, they were disappointed; many voters who had once supported the JSP switched to Tanaka and the LDP. Even low-level Socialists in the Niigata area deserted the JSP and became part of Tanaka's political machine.[34] To be sure, access to the pork barrel is easier at the center of power, but the JSP remained above it all and clung blindly to collective agriculture and class struggle.[35]

---

[33]Mizuno Aki wrote a sixteen-volume history of Socialist movement in Okayama Prefecture. But he could not make any mention of the farmers' movement after 1947: Because of the absence of U.S. bases in Okayama, the farmers' movement disappeared after 1947. See Mizuno, Vols. 13–16.

[34]Takabatake Michitoshi, *Chiho no okoku* (Local political powers) (Tokyo: Ushio Shuppansha, 1986), p. 35.

[35]Wada Hiroo, a left-wing leader, talented bureaucrat, and minister of agriculture in the Yoshida cabinet in 1946, proposed a dazzling array of agricultural policies. But the JSP showed no interest. Nihon Shakaito seisaku shingikai,

Japanese Political Culture

The JSP failed to break the so-called one-third barrier in the Diet, a barrier originally erected by the JSP to frustrate the conservatives' scheme to revise the constitution; a two-thirds majority in both houses is required to initiate an amendment. In no time, however, the tables were turned on the JSP, and it found itself incapable of expanding beyond one-third of the Diet seats. In contrast, the LDP—though falling just below a two-thirds majority—has been in power permanently. Why has the JSP failed to break the barrier? Why have the conservatives been so successful?

Sato and Matsuzaki say it is the highly homogeneous character of Japanese society. According to them, Japanese conservatives can easily integrate themselves because few political conflicts or cleavages stem from religious or ethnic divisions (the only exception might be Soka Gakkai, which provides votes for Komeito). Ethnic minorities in Japan, such as the Ainu, Uilta, Korean, and Chinese, are so small that they can hardly be influential in politics. Class consciousness has weakened since the early 1960s, and even industrial workers are apt to be more loyal to their company than to their class.[36] But the homogeneous-society hypothesis explains neither how homogeneity is linked with conservative dominance nor why the LDP lost votes during the 1950s and the 1960s.[37]

A more popular explanation associates Japanese political culture with the LDP's electoral success. Classes and other social cleavages do in fact exist in Japan; but as Flanagan and Richardson have pointed out the effect of these on political behavior, especially on voting, is often canceled by cultural factors, such as respect for human relations and the social network.[38] Japanese political culture is also thought to favor

---

"MSA ni chosen shite" (Let us challenge the Mutual Security Act), in JSP, ed., *Shiryo Nihon Shakaito 40-nen shi* (Documents of the JSP's 40-year history) (Tokyo: JSP, 1985), pp. 252–70.

[36]Sato Seizaburo and Matsuzaki Tetsuhisa, *Jiminto seiken* (The LDP regime) (Tokyo: Chuo Koronsha, 1986), pp. 13–14.

[37]Contrary to most Japanologists, Scott C. Flanagan and Bradley M. Richardson argue that Japan has deeper cultural and value cleavages than Germany does. See their *Politics in Japan* (Boston: Little, Brown, 1984), p. 79.

[38]Scott C. Flanagan and Bradley M. Richardson, *Japanese Electoral Behavior* (London: Sage Publications, 1977), chap. 7.

the conservatives. For example, Hrebner attributes the LDP's longevity in office to the conservative, passive electorate and the ineptitude of the opposition parties, especially the JSP.[39]

It is dangerous, of course, to exaggerate the importance of the political culture. Some recent studies on voting behavior and party support reveal that occupational interest, policy preference, and other social factors help form a voter's political attitude.[40] But the political culture underlying those factors cannot be ignored, especially in examining Japanese politics early in the postwar period. Japanese people are often said to be passive in the political sphere, though it remains questionable whether they are more so than the citizens of some European nations such as Italy. Whenever researchers ask Japanese citizens if they are willing to participate in politics to realize their own interests and ideas, less than a fifth answer yes. Most people prefer to depend on either their representatives or politicians to realize their interests and policy preferences.[41] This passivity toward political activities leads to accepting present authorities and orders and indirectly helps the conservatives.

Japanese political culture helps the conservatives in a more direct fashion as well. Hayashi's statistical analyses of the relationship between the Japanese way of thinking in daily life and their party support find that they tend to support the LDP not necessarily because of its policies but because they like its flexible style of behavior and traditional way of thinking. They are apt to dislike those who insist on principles or ideologies and deny the importance of traditional elements. The Japanese also dislike incessant progressive criticism of the present state of the society because of the psychological strain of such criticism.[42] There is also a propensity to defer to superiors and to suspect as immoral those who challenge the existing authority.[43]

Social conservatism is stronger in rural areas. In the 1940s and the 1950s, Japanese society was predominantly rural, and agriculture was

---

[39]Ronald J. Hrebner, *The Japanese Party System* (Boulder, Colo.: Westview Press, 1986), p. 28.

[40]Miyake Ichiro, *Seito shiji no bunseki* (Analyses of party support) (Tokyo: Sobunsha, 1985); Inoguchi Takashi, "Senkyo to kokyo seisaku" (Elections and public policy), *Leviathan*, October 1987, pp. 92–112.

[41]NHK Hoso Yoronchosa-sho, ed., *Gendai Nihon-jin no ishiki kozo* (The ideological structure of today's Japanese) (Tokyo: NHK, 1979), pp. 174–80.

[42]Hayashi Chikio, *Nihon-jin no seiji kankaku* (The political sense of the Japanese) (Tokyo: Idemitsu Shoten, 1982), chaps. 5, 6; see also Flanagan and Richardson, *Politics in Japan*, chap. 4.

[43]See Matsushita Keiichi, *Shin seiji ko* (New thoughts on politics) (Tokyo: Asahi Shimbunsha, 1977), pp. 60–63.

the largest industry in terms of employment. Even in 1960, 44 percent of the Japanese lived outside administratively defined cities. Moreover, after a 1958 law prompted the merger of municipalities, Japanese cities came to contain many rural areas within their boundaries. In those days, it was crucial for all parties to gain the support of farmers and other rural dwellers.

The conservative atmosphere, more prominent in the rural areas, crystallized in the *jiban* (literally "foundation," but "turf" is a close approximation). An analogue of *jiban* is the political machine that enlisted illiterate and helpless immigrants in urban areas in the United States in the early part of this century; a precinct captain and ward heelers offered small services or material favors in exchange for their constituents' votes. A *jiban* then is a network of sorts between the local influential and his clients. A *jiban* with a fixed number of votes is an asset that can be transferred from one political candidate to another, depending on the say-so of the boss. The archetype of the *jiban* was the relationship between a wealthy landlord and his tenants; acting as subleaders, landlords were linked to professional politicians.

The *jiban* became popular in the 1920s.[44] The landlord class disappeared in the occupation reforms, but the *jiban* lingered on because the cooperatives and other public agencies were soon organized into the old political machines and because the voters, including newly enfranchised women, remained obedient to their local notables.[45] In national and local elections, the *jiban* garnered votes for conservative candidates in rural areas. Robert Ward, who conducted research in a village in the outskirts of Okayama in the 1950s, found that prewar *jiban* remained more or less intact.[46] Ward concludes his report as follows:

---

[44]Kitaoka Shin'ichi, "Jiyu Minshuto," in Kamishima Jiro, ed., *Gendai Nihon no seiji kozo* (Contemporary Japan's political structure) (Tokyo: Horitsu Bunkasha, 1985), pp. 50–51. The landlords' influence was already declining in the Taisho era, 1911–1925, but they were not powerless either. See Masumi Junnosuke, *Nihon seito shiron* (History of Japan's political parties) (Tokyo: Tokyo University Press, 1979), vol. 5, pp. 344–45.

[45]On localism among Japanese voters, see Bradley M. Richardson, *The Political Culture of Japan* (Berkeley: University of California Press, 1974), pp. 56–59; Matsushita Keiichi, *Gendai Nihon no seiji-teki kosei* [Contemporary Japan's political structure] (Tokyo: Tokyo University Press, 1962), chapter 6; Ishida Takeshi, "Sengo minshu kaikaku to kokumin no taio (Postwar democratic reforms and the people's reactions), in Asao Naohiro et al., eds., *Nihon rekishi* (Japan's history) (Tokyo: Iwanami Shoten, 1977), volume 12, p. 148; Kitaoka, "Jiyu Minshuto," pp. 50–51.

[46]Richard K. Beardsley, John W. Hall, and Robert E. Ward, *Village Japan* (Chicago: University of Chicago Press, 1959), pp. 435–36.

An appreciable decrease in conservative strength in one of Japan's staunchest conservative areas and the gradual emergence of a left-wing opposition are long-term and slow-moving trends which are subject to future
interruption, diversion, or distortion in terms of their political
consequences.

As a matter of fact, considering the enormous stresses to which postwar
Japanese society has been subjected, the continued strength, resiliency,
and adaptability of the traditional sociopolitical order and processes are
most impressive. Politically, as otherwise, Niiike [the village being in-
vestigated] remains an essentially conservative community.[47]

In the late 1950s *jiban* was partially supplanted by a new type of
vote-getting organization called *koenkai*,[48] a private organization of a
Dietman, with no link to the party or intermediaries.[49] During the early
postwar period, however, *jiban* was a major obstacle for the JSP because
it offset the favorable effects of the occupation reforms and made it
difficult for the Socialists to link up with rural voters through their
own intermediaries.

Conclusion

The Japanese Socialists were not ready to assume power when it was
foisted on them in the 1940s; rather, as pawns in the hands of larger
forces, they soon abandoned power in disgrace. A major dispute then
flared in the party over how to vindicate itself. Once again, the party
was sucked into the vortex of a storm, this time the cold war; by the
time the Socialists found their identity, the leadership was in the hands
of radical ideologues. With hindsight, the optimal course for the JSP
might have been to revive the center-left coalition of 1947–1948 to give
the party political skill, organization, and expertise. A center-left coalition would also have preserved the strength of the right wing and
checked the left wing; above all, it would have been possible for the
JSP to become a viable opposition, ready to reenter the government.
Instead, the JSP was frozen into the 1955 System as a permanent minority, though an indispensable component, of that system.

---

[47]Ibid., pp. 405–7.

[48]Masumi Junnosuke, *Gendai Nihon no seiji taisei* (The political system of
contemporary Japan) (Tokyo: Iwanami Shoten, 1966), p. 224.

[49]On the early phase of *koenkai* development, see Nathaniel Thayer, *How the
Conservatives Rule Japan* (Princeton, N.J.: Princeton University Press, 1969),
chap. 4.

But permanent minority status is corrupting. The JSP's future is not bright unless it can break out of the system. To invigorate and cleanse the system, Japan needs an occasional change in government. Because that is impossible under the existing order, both the LDP and the JSP are victims.

5 | Shigemitsu Mamoru and the 1955 System

Ito Takashi

SHIGEMITSU MAMORU (1887–1957), ALONG WITH HATOYAMA ICHIRO and Ogata Taketora, played an important role in the 1955 System of Japanese politics, including the founding of Jiyu Minshuto (the Liberal Democratic party). His role may not have been the most significant, but it cannot be ignored.[1]

In 1985, I received Shigemitsu's papers from his son and copublished part of them with Watanabe Yukio under the title *Shigemitsu Mamoru shuki* (1986),[2] records Shigemitsu had kept from the second half of the

---

[1]At this time, there is only one biography of Shigemitsu: Toyoda Kunio, *Shigemitsu koyo shoden* (Oita: Niho no bunkakai, 1957). There are three memoirs by him: *Showa no doran* (The turbulent Showa) (Tokyo: Chuo Koronsha, 1952); *Shigemitsu Mamoru gaiko kaisoroku* (Diplomatic memoirs of Shigemitsu Mamoru) (Tokyo: Mainichi Shumbunsha, 1953); and *Sugamo nikki* (Sugamo diary) and *Zoku Sugamo nikki* (Sugamo diary, a sequel) (Tokyo: Bungei Shunjusha, 1953). *Shigemitsu Mamoru shuki* (Shigemitsu Mamoru notes) and *Zoku Shigemitsu Mamoru shuki* (Shigemitsu Mamoru notes, a sequel), which I have recently published, contain materials that are contemporaneous with his earlier memoirs. The latter contains notes that were written soon after the events covered and hence are valuable historically. The post-Sugamo portion has never before been published.

[2]My comments at the end of that volume give the circumstances that led to that document's publication.

1930s, when he was a diplomat, to the time when he was imprisoned as a war criminal in 1947. In 1988, I coedited, with Watanabe, *Zoku Shigemitsu Mamoru shuki* (hereinafter *Zoku*). Included in the sequel are recently discovered records for the period covered in the first volume, as well as the diary he kept after being released from Sugamo Prison.

This diary, which contains much information on the conservative merger, has been donated to the Kensei Kinenkan and can be read by the public. Professor Mikuriya Takashi of Tokyo Metropolitan University used it to publish "The Activities of the Second Conservative Party, 1945–1954: Ashia, Shigemitsu, and Miki in the Ashida and Shigemitsu Diaries."[3] In this article, Professor Mikuriya clarifies the process involved in the merger of the conservative parties. In this chapter I analyze the groups that were close to Shigemitsu and the flow of political intelligence and information to him from these groups. I touch briefly on the interesting question of continuity and change in Shigemitsu's perceptions of Japan and its place in the world order, leaving a fuller discussion for another occasion.

Shigemitsu graduated from Tokyo Imperial University in 1901 and, on passing diplomatic and consular examinations, became a career diplomat. Having been a member of the Japanese delegation to the Paris peace conference in 1920 and feeling the need to upgrade Japan's diplomacy, he joined forces with Arita Hachiro, Saito Hiroshi, Horiuchi Kensuke, and other young ministry officials to organize Kakushin Doshikai (the Innovation Comradeship Society). Although the goals of Kakushin were ambiguous, the range of the Kakushin trend in public opinion in Japan of the post–World War I period contained a good deal of criticism of capitalism and Western imperialism in Asia.

Shigemitsu's Kakushin group dissolved when a pro-German, pro-Italy group led by Shiratori Toshio emerged in the wake of the Manchurian Incident. A traditional diplomat, Shigemitsu began to part company with Shiratori after Shigemitsu's ambassadorial appointments (1936–1941) in Moscow and London. His anti-Communist leanings had begun shortly before but grew stronger during those years. Because Germany and Italy were equally totalitarian, he adamantly opposed Japan's alliance with them, favoring instead cooperation with the Anglo-American powers. On returning home in 1941, Shigemitsu was appointed ambassador to China during the Wang Ching-wei regime. In 1943 he became the foreign minister in the Tojo cabinet and orchestrated the Greater East Asian Conference, where he advocated Asia's

---

[3]*Journal of Modern Japanese Studies* 9 (1987): 94–122.

liberation. At about this time, in close liaison with Privy Seal Kido Koichi, he began undercover moves to end the war. Immediately after Japan's surrender, he was made the foreign minister in the Higashikuni cabinet in charge of delicate negotiations with the Allies.

Baron Shidehara Kijuro, Yoshida Shigeru, and Ashida Hitoshi, prime ministers in the early postwar years, were all former diplomats, as was Shigemitsu. They were deeply involved in Japan's postwar politics because Japan was at that time occupied by a foreign power. As distinguished from the other three, Shigemitsu was incarcerated as a class A war criminal in Sugamo Prison for a seven-year sentence. He wrote that he owed this experience to the strong pressure exerted by the Soviet Union, rather than the United States, which did not press his prosecution. According to Shigemitsu's diary, Joseph Keenan, chief prosecutor in the Far Eastern Military Tribunal, visited him in 1953 and said that "I did everything I could to get you off the indictment at the Tokyo Trial" and that "MacArthur believed you were innocent"[4]; nor did the United States oppose his later political resurrection. Shigemitsu did not seem to harbor a trace of anti-American resentment.

He was sentenced in December 1948 and paroled in November 1950. In November 1951, his sentence was reduced; because he had already served his term, the parole was ended. Because he was concurrently purged, however, he could not take part in politics until he was depurged in March 1952. He spent most of those one-and-a-half years putting in order the memoirs he had written in prison, publishing the result under the title *Showa no doran*, which attracted much popular interest. In 1953, he published *Shigemitsu Mamaru gaiko kaisoroku*.

In 1945–1946, he began writing his thoughts on the postwar international situation and Japan's role in it. He stated that, although the United States and the Soviet Union might cooperate in war, they would ultimately diverge because their societies differed in fundamental ways and that each was engaged in the construction of a postwar international order under its hegemony.[5] Being an anti-Soviet hard-liner, he left no doubt as to which side Japan should align itself with. That anticommunism is the one unchanging, basic premise underlying all of Shigemitsu's thinking.[6]

---

[4]*Zoku*, p. 589.

[5]Ibid., p. 339, dated December 20, 1945.

[6]As a wartime foreign minister, Shigemitsu maintained that his policy design was to "adopt nationalism to liberate east Asia and rebuild Asia" because the

In 1946, Shigemitsu wrote that Japan must correct its erroneous ways, maintained since the Meiji Restoration, and adjust to existing world conditions. He added that the need for this change had existed before the Pacific War and that the Pacific War was itself part of the process of change. Moreover, he felt that MacArthur's strong reform efforts were part of the necessary stimuli for change.[7] Note that in this connection those who have been labeled conservatives strongly supported changes in Japan. This phenomenon is part of a consistent pattern in modern Japanese history, although most Americans continue to rest their hopes for change on the liberals (i.e., the Socialists).[8]

It is difficult to determine when Shigemitsu decided to put his anti-Communist and reformist ideas into political action. Kishi Nobusuke, a latter-day LDP prime minister, wrote that he and Shigemitsu had pledged in Sugamo Prison to strive for the reconstruction of Japan.[9] When Shigemitsu was depurged, he became an adviser to Nihon Saiken Renmei, which Kishi had formed and whose platform included anti-communism, support for the U.S.-Japan alliance, and the revision of the constitution.

Visiting Shigemitsu before the depurge were his former subordinates in the Foreign Ministry such as Tani Masayuki, Kase Toshikazu, and Ota Saburo. Kase was personally close to Shigemitsu; as Tojo's foreign minister, Shigemitsu had requested that Kase serve as ministerial secretary and director of the North American division. When Shigemitsu was the first postwar foreign minister, he requested that Kase accompany the delegation that signed the surrender documents aboard the *Missouri*. After Shigemitsu's arrest as a war crimes suspect, Kase did his utmost to protect him and other Foreign Ministry colleagues in the same predicament. When Shigemitsu's family became destitute, Kase's

---

design was in keeping with the world trend that "destined nationalism to win out." *Zoku*, pp. 317, 339. He noted that although the United States found it impossible to ignore this trend, Britain and other European powers were still persisting in "imperialist policy." He was also concerned about the Soviet Union's "communist-democratic assistance for nationalist movements." *Zoku*, pp. 316–17.

[7]*Zoku*, p. 391, dated January 20, 1946.

[8]As above, Shigemitsu was Kakushin in a broader sense. Those who opposed the Nazi-like Kakushin before 1945 and communism and socialism after 1945 were labeled conservative.

[9]Kishi Nobusuke, Yatsugi Kazuo, and Ito Takashi, *Kishi Nobusuke no kaiso* [Memoirs of Kishi Nobusuke] (Tokyo: Bungei Shunjusha, 1981), pp. 89–90, 99.

wife (without Kase's knowledge) sold an expensive wedding dress to raise money for them.[10]

These men were the initial supporters of Shigemitsu's reentry into politics. As Kase wrote,

> It was Oasa (a Kaishinto leader and a good friend of Kase's) who recommended the Shigemitsu appointment [as party president]. The decision was made in my house in Nishigomon, where three of us met. After this, Japan's politics were to see Yoshida and Shigemitsu square off and cooperate with each other as heads of two major parties. Because I was a friend of both of them, my situation was delicate. . . . But my sense of chivalry bound me to the role of helping Shigemitsu make a comeback. The fact was, he was helpless without me. Naturally, Oasa, with his political connections, became a senior leader of Kaishinto, but he got along better with Yoshida. This meant Oasa could be a conduit between Yoshida and Shigemitsu. In time Yoshida tacitly accepted my siding with Shigemitsu.[11]

The second group of men to approach Shigemitsu just before his depurge were Kaishinto executives. At that time, Kaishinto did not have a president, and the segment of the party composed of depurged politicians, such as Matsumura Kenzo and Oasa Tadao, sought out Shigemitsu.[12] On Shigemitsu's release from Sugamo Prison, Matsumura wrote,

> Public sympathy made him popular. While in retirement in Kamakura, his *Doran no Nihon* [should be *Showa no doran*], written during his incarceration, was published to achieve wide acclaim. With so much going for him, he became a presence in the public mind.
>
> Shigemitsu's retirement in Kamakura lasted for a year and a half. I

---

[10]Kase Toshikaze, *Kase Toshikazu kaiso roku* (Kase Toshikazu memoir) (Tokyo: Yamate Shobo, 1986), p. 104. Kase continued to help Shigemitsu after his release and arranged to publish *Showa no doran* (Ibid., p. 110).

[11]Kase, *Kase Toshikazu kaiso roku*, p. 111.

[12]In Matsumura Kenzo, *Sandai kaikoruku* (Three generational memoirs) (Tokyo: Toyo Keizai Shinposha, 1964), p. 298, Matsumura states that he got to know Shigemitsu when the latter was held over as foreign minister from the Tojo cabinet to the Koiso cabinet. Matsumura, who was chairman of the policy research committee and secretary general of Yokusankai at the time, wrote, "Foreign Minister Shigemitsu would visit Dai-Nihon seijikai whenever he had a chance to brief us on the diplomatic situation. His briefings were excellent summaries that made intelligible the development of diplomatic events and policies, no matter how sensitive. I thought to myself, 'This is quite a guy,' and became a good friend of his." Matsumura and Shigemitsu were both appointed ministers in the Higashikuni government, the first postwar cabinet.

organized Kaishinto with like-minded friends and was looking for a suitable leader. After debating the merits of several candidates, I said, "How about Shigemitsu? Isn't he best qualified?" And that settled it. Ashida supported him, having been his college mate and a fellow career diplomat. Oasa was impressed by his background and knowledge. A few holdouts were overruled in our choice of party president.[13]

The left wing of the party, represented by Miki Takeo, was not enthusiastic about Shigemitsu.

Ashida Hitoshi also approached Shigemitsu at this time. Ashida had passed the diplomatic service examination in 1910 with Shigemitsu and began his career in Gaimusho. Ashida switched to politics and ran successfully for the Diet in 1932. A progressive conservative, he was prime minister of the Minshuto-Socialist coalition in 1948 but by the close of that year was arrested for his alleged part in the Shoden bribery scandal. In 1952, Ashida was still on trial, and though there were moves to appoint him president of the new party, he declined in favor of Shigemitsu, although the two men appear not to have been personal friends.[14]

Shigemitsu, however, hesitated to accept the call to be Kaishinto president because the party was split and because he was well aware of the difficulty in getting political funds. His connection with Nihon Saiken Renmei (Kishi's group) was another reason for his hesitation because he was expected to become *its* president. In May 1952, however, he accepted the Kaishinto invitation and was elected president at the party convention the following month.

Shigemitsu served as Kaishinto president for two-and-a-half years, to November 1954, and during this period aimed at becoming prime minister. In November 1954, Nihon Minshuto was formed by anti-Yoshida politicians; the Kishi and Hatoyama factions of Yoshida's Jiyuto merged with Shigemitsu's Kaishinto. Hatoyama became president and Shigemitsu its vice-president. At this time, Oasa Tadao and Kase Toshikazu, who had been endeavoring to establish Shigemitsu as prime minister, visited him at home to express their "regrets that having drawn [you] into politics, we could not consummate our wish," thus abandoning the hope for a Shigemitsu government.

In his diary covering his two-and-a-half years as Kaishinto president,

---

[13]Matsumara, *Sandai kaikoroku*, p. 299.

[14]When Shigemitsu was paroled, or depurged, Ashida left no entry in his diary. Shigemitsu appears in Ashida's diary for the first time on March 18, 1952.

Shigemitsu recorded that four groups provided him with political intelligence and information. The first of these groups was composed of those former diplomats who had first expressed support for him, among them Suma Yakichiro, a former diplomat and a Kaishinto Diet member since 1953.[15] The second group was composed of Oasa and Matsumura, who had to balance two goals: They wanted Shigemitsu to become party president but did not want to alienate the left wing of the party. That this group of professional politicians chose Shigemitsu, who had never had any real political experience, is noteworthy; deep down, however, Shigemitsu never trusted them, and they in turn had doubts about his bureaucratic background. Having pushed Shigemitsu's presidential bid, Matsumura sounded a bit embarrassed when he wrote, "Shigemitsu has had no experience in party politics. In addition, he [is] taciturn to the point of appearing brusque at times." Later those professional politicians would feel vindicated.[16] Ashida, too, frequently expressed unhappiness about Shigemitsu.[17]

The third group, made up of men such as Hayashi Hikosaburo, Kato Takeo, and Akiyama Konosuke,[18] were from *zaikai* (the business community), but few personal details on them are available, although they provided much political information because of their closeness to Yoshida Shigeru. The fourth group had Kishi as its principal member. Ayabe Kentaro of this group was from the same prefecture (Oita) as Shigemitsu

---

[15]Suma was a former diplomat, but he does not appear often in the prewar portion of *Shigemitsu Mamoru shuki*. Presumably he was removed from the diplomat group around Shigemitsu, mentioned above. Suma ran as a depurged Kaishinto candidate in 1953, and Shigemitsu stumped for him (*Zoku*, p. 591). From here on, he appears in the Shigemitsu diary, often as a purveyor of important intelligence.

[16]Matsumura, *Sandai kaikoroku*, p. 300.

[17]See, for instance, *Ashida Hitoshi nikki*, vol. 5, p. 87, for a February 28, 1953, entry.

[18]Hayashi Hikosaburo was providing Shigemitsu with subsistence at the end of 1951, on the eve of the latter's entry into politics (*Zoku*, p. 514). According to the eighteenth edition of *Jinji Koshinroku* (Who's Who) of 1955, Hayashi was born in 1890 and in the early 1950s was president of Sanshin Construction and Suiso Trading Company. He lived in Zaimokuza, in Kamakura, close to Shigemitsu. Like Kato and Akiyama, he as a Keio graduate. How the three were connected to Shigemitsu remains obscure.

Kato Takeo was born in 1877, graduated from Keio University, joined Mitsubishi, and was chief executive officer of Mitsubishi Bank in 1943–1945. He was an adviser to Keidanren after 1952. Akiyama Konosuke was born in 1884, studied at Keio University, joined Dai-Nihon Seito, and was president of the Monopoly Corporation in 1949. At this time he was on the board of directors of Mitsubishi Bank. He, too, lived in Kamakura's Zaimokuza.

and provided funds. Miyoshi Hideyuki and Kishi, who had been elected to the House of Representatives in 1953 from Jiyuto, met with Shigemitsu from time to time, providing him with information and trying to influence him.

At first Shigemitsu hoped to restore a two-party system made up of moderates and conservatives. On May 7, 1952, on accepting the party presidency, he wrote, "It is the urgent task of the moment to make a wide appeal to men sharing our concern, to rally the progressive elements, to consolidate the foundation for a two-party system, to make certain that democratic politics will go forward without a lapse, and to establish a patriotic party." Here he contrasted progressive elements to the conservative Jiyuto and patriotic party to the treasonous Communists. Two days later he wrote to Yoshida thanking him for his friendship over the years and denying any ill will in accepting the presidency without consulting him. "Rather," Shigemitsu said, "at a time when the communizing of Japan is in full swing, I want to dedicate myself to the task of building two parties to ensure the functioning of democratic politics, and to avoid the fatal confusion that beset Germany after World War I. . . . There is no other way," he went on, "than nurturing the growth of your Liberal party on the one hand and founding a second party that rallies all the progressive forces other than the communists."[19] In seeking an alternative between Yoshida's conservatives and the Socialists, Shigemitsu was charting a course parallel to that of Ashida.

Shigemitsu had to change his plans, however, as political realignments began in the two general elections in the early 1950s. In the October 1952 election, Kaishinto increased in strength from sixty-seven to eighty-nine but in the April 1953 election dropped to seventy-seven. Yoshida's Jiyuto fell steadily, from 285 to 242 to 202. Following the 1953 election, Yoshida not only lost the majority but faced an internal revolt from the Hatoyama faction, which demanded rearmament. The left wing of the Socialist party climbed from sixteen to fifty-six to seventy-two, while the right wing climbed more gradually: from thirty to sixty to sixty-six. Against the backdrop of war in Korea and U.S. pressure on Japan to rearm, two parallel developments were taking place. On the one hand, Japan was being polarized by the rapid expansion of the radical Socialists; on the other hand, Yoshida's refusal to rearm was beginning to isolate him. Politics was divided three ways among the Socialists and two groups of conservatives.

---

[19]*Zoku*, pp. 539, 541–42.

The business group approached Shigemitsu in 1953. On February 5, 1953, Hayashi told Shigemitsu that Yoshida would not reject a meeting with him.[20] On February 12, Okazaki Katsuo, foreign minister under Yoshida and his trusted lieutenant, asked Shigemitsu for cooperation in the Diet. Shigemitsu agreed, with one condition: forming a political party that could confront the "destructive" Communist party.[21] It is not clear, however, whether Shigemitsu had abandoned the two-party system.

In March 1953, one month before the election, Shigemitsu began surreptitious negotiations with Ikeda Hayato, the pillar of the Yoshida faction, by going through a third party, Oasa; however, Shigemitsu was unable to obtain satisfactory promises and conditions. The Yoshida faction's feelers, motivated by its desire to counter the Hatoyama faction in Jiyuto,[22] were disrupted by the sudden dissolution of the House of Representatives and the general election of April 1953.

The left wing of Kaishinto hoped to topple the Yoshida government by combining with the two Socialist parties, but the remainder of Kaishinto wanted to wrest power from Yoshida through negotiation. In April 1954, the Jiyuto vice-president, Ogata, publicly announced his hopes for a merger of the conservative parties. The four groups close to Shigemitsu wanted him to maintain contact and negotiate with the mainstream of Jiyuto, but Shigemitsu was wary of these political feelers. He was concerned that the left-wing Kaishinto would bolt the party if he embraced Jiyuto. Yet Shigemitsu knew that his own chances of succeeding as prime minister were based on the cooperation of the conservatives.

The efforts of the business group continued after the election, though Shigemitsu did not record them in his diary during the postelection period. But the results of the 1953 election, which weakened Kaishinto, smashed his hopes, and that year he began speaking of "rallying constructive forces."[23] This move was paralleled by Ashida's drift toward rearmament in disregard of the Socialists. On September 27, 1953, a period of huge lacunae in Shigemitsu's records, a Yoshida-Shigemitsu talk took place; we do, however have the recollections of Miyazawa

---

[20]Ibid., p. 568.

[21]Ibid., p. 571.

[22]Ibid.; March 2, 1953, pp. 577–78, and March 8, pp. 581–82, contain fairly detailed information.

[23]*Zoku*, pp. 539, 541–42.

Kiichi,[24] who was close to Ikeda Hayato, Yoshida's faithful follower. From these recollections we learn that the three mediators' initials were H, K, and A, that is, the members of the business group. Yoshida agreed to this talk to get Kaishinto to endorse entering into military cooperation with Washington under the terms of the Mutual Security Act (MSA). Miyazawa records that Oasa said, "Shigemitsu will not go along unless he is assured of being the next prime minister." An agreement was reached, however. Masumi Junnosuke, using other sources, also concludes that Yoshida hinted strongly that he would yield to Shigemitsu.[25]

Earlier, during the 1953 election campaign, Shigemitsu met with Kishi of Jiyuto and discussed the question of a postelection coalition.[26] On May 6, 1953, after Kaishinto had lost a number of seats, Ayabe told Shigemitsu that the parties should combine with Yoshida as president. After a while, Yoshida would step aside, and Kishi, Ogata, or Shigemitsu would become president. All this should be decided on in a Yoshida-Shigemitsu talk, said Ayabe. Shigemitsu opposed the suggestion, but Ayabe told him that because Jiyuto outnumbered Kaishinto by a large margin, Kaishinto had no choice.

On the same day, Hayashi (of the business group) told Shigemitsu that he had told Ikeda Hayato (through Kato Takeo) that he would propose the following to Yoshida: Yoshida would work for the merger of the two parties, and when the new party had been formed, Yoshida would retire and Shigemitsu succeed him. But until this new party was formed, Shigemitsu would unconditionally support the Yoshida cabinet. Ikeda said that a similar proposal had been made to Yoshida by Miyoshi; Yoshida, however, had not gone along. When Hayashi asked Shigemitsu what he should do, Shigemitsu told him to go ahead and approach Yoshida.[27]

On the same day, Tani Masayuki (of the diplomats' group) urged Shigemitsu to talk to Yoshida. On May 13, Sawada Renzo (of the diplomats' group) and Tani saw Shigemitsu to report on Sawada's meeting with Yoshida. Sawada said he asked about Yoshida's yielding later to Shigemitsu, who understood international politics. Yoshida replied that

---

[24]Miyazawa Kiichi, *Tokyo-Washington no mitsudan* (Tokyo-Washington secret talks) (Tokyo: Jitsugyo no Nihonsha, 1956).

[25]Masumi Junnosuke, *Sengo seiji* (Postwar politics) (Tokyo: Tokyo University Press, 1983), p. 425.

[26]*Zoku*, p. 590.

[27]Ibid., pp. 600–602.

he agreed in principle but could not promise anything.[28] On the 14th, Kishi and Miyoshi met Shigemitsu at Hayashi's residence, where Kishi and Miyoshi urged a Yoshida-Shigemitsu talk.[29] On the 16th, Sato Eisaku, Jiyuto's secretary general, arrived with a letter from Yoshida asking for a talk.[30]

This solicitude from Jiyuto was prompted by its loss of a majority and the possibility of the opposition parties' (the Hatoyama faction of Jiyuto, Kaishinto, and the two wings of the JSP) voting in their candidates for speaker and vice-speaker of the lower house. There was also the possibility that this combination would vote Shigemitsu in as prime minister.

The opposition succeeded in electing its choices for the two posts; Shigemitsu, however, did not care for support from the left-wing Socialist party,[31] and Yoshida was ultimately elected prime minister. On the day before the formation of the fifth Yoshida cabinet, the Yoshida-Shigemitsu talk was finally held. Yoshida expressed his hope for a coalition cabinet.[32] Shigemitsu, however, said that Kaishinto would remain in opposition. In September, the Hatoyama faction, which had bolted earlier, returned to the Jiyuto fold.

The next round of contacts between Jiyuto and Kaishinto began in February 1954. According to Ashida, he, Ogata, and Ishibashi began discussing the formation of a new conservative party in late 1953. The lacunae in Shigemitsu's diary ended February 12, 1954, when Shigemitsu recorded that, through Okazaki, Suma received Yoshida's interpretation of the political situation:

> In order to resolve the problems the government is facing in the Diet, the two conservative parties, Jiyuto and Kaishinto, must cooperate. Jiyuto's top leaders have all agreed that both Jiyuto and Kaishinto must dissolve, the Yoshida cabinet give up its power, and a new party be formed. The political problems will then be resolved on the basis of this new party.[33]

Unfortunately, the diary is silent on how far this proposal went.

On February 18, Ashida began consulting with Ishibashi; when joined

---

[28]Ibid., pp. 605–6.

[29]Ibid., p. 606.

[30]Ibid., p. 607.

[31]Shigemitsu told Ashida that "this speaker election is also a Red maneuver." *Ashida Hitoshi nikki*, vol. 4, p. 340.

[32]*Zoku*, p. 609.

[33]Ibid., pp. 617–18.

by Ogata, they discussed what kind of political party should be organized after the Yoshida cabinet's fall.[34] The Yoshida proposal and the
Ashida-Ishibashi-Ogata consultation should be seen in the context of
the new problems afflicting the Yoshida cabinet: his ministers and party
secretary general were being implicated in a shipbuilding scandal that
threatened to undermine the government. Shigemitsu's diary recorded
proposals from many sources on forming a new party based on the
merger of Jiyuto and Kaishinto; the stumbling block was that Yoshida
would not step down and yield to Shigemitsu.

According to Ashida's diary, Ashida and Shigemitsu met on March
22 to discuss the formation of a new party. Although Shigemitsu's diary
is silent on this point, Ashida told Ogata on March 23 that Shigemitsu
had said that he was willing to serve as a "mere soldier."[35]

On March 28, Ogata gave the following statement to the press:
"Yoshida favors a new conservative party. The president shall be elected
by democratic means. Kaishinto appears to be willing to go along with
this." This statement shocked the political world. Shigemitsu wrote in
his diary that he had received information from various sources to the
effect that Yoshida had not said what Ogata claimed and that Ogata
had misunderstood Yoshida's position.[36]

In April, those in the second and third groups (i.e., professional
politicians and businessmen) told Shigemitsu that thinking differed
about the new party among those closest to Yoshida (i.e., Ikeda and
Ogata), that Shigemitsu should reject any suggestion from Ogata, and
that he should instead wait for the next opportunity or opening.[37] On
April 9, Shigemitsu told a newsman that the precondition for the formation of the new party was Yoshida's yielding his position. Shigemitsu
consequently turned down the overture from Yoshida.[38]

In the meantime, the danger to Jiyuto showed no signs of ebbing,

---

[34]*Ashida Hitoshi nikki*, vol. 5, pp. 118, 135–37. To a proposal by lower-house
speaker Tsutsumi Yasujiro that a conservative merger be based on Yoshida's
promise of a future transfer of the presidency from him to Shigemitsu, Ashida
replied that the president should be chosen by "the democratic method." Ashida
implied that a merger under Yoshida as prime minister was objectionable to
Kaishinto, and that Shigemitsu in Jiyuto would lose popularity.

[35]Ibid., pp. 140–41.

[36]*Zoku*, pp. 626–29, 638. Furthermore, Ayabe strongly urged Shigemitsu to
follow Ogata's advice and become foreign minister. Finally he "publicly dis-
owned" Shigemitsu for not acting on the advice.

[37]*Zoku*, pp. 628–29.

[38]Ibid., pp. 629–30.

with the procurator calling for the arrest of Sato Eisaku, secretary general, for his role in the scandal. This threat was defused when Justice Minister Inukai Ken intervened. Jiyuto, however, was still not out of the woods, for it faced no-confidence motions in the Diet. Three options available to Yoshida were to (1) secure Kaishinto's help in voting down the no-confidence vote with a promise to yield the government to Shigemitsu; (2) lose the no-confidence vote and dissolve the Diet for a new election to be fought under Yoshida's leadership; or (3) resign. Kaishinto was tempted by the first option because an election might mean a further loss of strength. With a good chance that the two wings of the JSP would soon capture a majority, Kaishinto split on how to cope with the dilemma. At this juncture Yoshida sent a secret letter to Shigemitsu requesting a meeting.[39]

What impact, if any, did this letter have? Kaishinto ambivalently said it would submit a no-confidence motion but without support from the Socialist parties. In the public's view, this step at once undermined and saved the Yoshida cabinet.

On April 28, the Hatoyama and Kishi factions of Jiyuto, the Ashida faction of Kaishinto, and Nihon Jiyuto (Miki Bukichi and Kono Ichiro, followers of Hatoyama who had refused to return to Jiyuto) held a plenary session of the Dietmen's Conference to Promote the Organization of a New Party (Shinto Kessei Sokushin Kyogikai Giin Taikai). By this time, it was accepted that a merger of conservative parties would take place in the near future. On May 7, Shigemitsu announced that Kaishinto was also aiming toward this end and said at a press conference that a new party was not on the agenda during the current session and that when the procurator's investigation into corruption was over, Kaishinto wanted to rally patriotic forces on the basis of five principles: (1) defense of democracy, (2) establishment of self-defense forces, (3) building of a self-reliant economy, (4) a review of occupation policy and

---

[39]Arriving in Yugawara on April 25, Shigemitsu heard from home that a letter had come from Yoshida and returned home the next day to read it. That letter is now in the Kensei Kinenkan archives, along with other documents collected by the Shigemitsu family. These documents have been catalogued in *Shigemitsu Mamoru kankei monjo mokuroku* (The Shigemitsu Mamoru archives catalogue) (Tokyo: Kensei Kinenkan, 1987). In the letter, Yoshida asked for a secret meeting to discuss several things and suggested that foreign Minister Okazaki would be glad to arrange one. Shigemitsu met Okazaki that night and talked with Secretary General Matsumura and Oasa (*Zoku*, pp. 637–39). No record of the meeting exists.

occupation-bequeathed laws, including the constitution, and (5) reno-vation of politics through the introduction of a responsible party system.[40]

This announcement represented a fundamental departure from his earlier stance because he did not stipulate how the next prime minister would be chosen. Shigemitsu's diary is silent on what motivated this change in attitude, but Shigemitsu may have finally realized that he could not get any kind of promise from Yoshida. From here on, there is no mention of any approach from the Yoshida group or of any intelligence received from anyone relating to any aspect of a possible Yoshida-Shigemitsu rapprochement.

The discussions between Jiyuto and Kaishinto proceeded on the basis of Shigemitsu's announcement. On June 14, the tumultuous Diet session ended, thanks to a compromise between the two parties. On June 23, Jiyuto unilaterally ended its talks with Kaishinto. On the same day, Shigemitsu announced his intention to form a new party:[41]

We have been making as many concessions as possible. Our offer not to make "transfer of leadership" a condition for an open election of a new party leader meant our willingness to meet them more than halfway. Now that Jiyuto has issued an ultimatum in rejecting our offer, we have no recourse. In view of Japan's predicament in the blind alley, however, we cannot do otherwise than reaffirm the need to mobilize a strong patriotic force.[42]

Shigemitsu then wrote, "Ashida disappointed by rupture. Can't understand his reason." It appears that while Ashida was prepared to live with Yoshida's being elected the new party leader, Shigemitsu could not.

On June 25, 1954, Shigemitsu received a request for a meeting from Hatoyama.[43] That summer, Shinto Kessei Sokushin Kyogikai held successful political rallies throughout the country. Ashida, who wanted to

---

[40]*Asahi Shimbun*, May 7, 1954. Ashida says he heard from Ayabe on May 12 that the reason was that "Tani Masayuki gave Shigemitsu tearful advice the other day, asking him to join the new party." *Ashida Hitoshi nikki*, vol. 5, p. 179.

[41]*Zoku*, p. 655.

[42]*Asahi Shimbun*, June 24, 1954.

[43]*Zoku*, p. 656. Having received Hatoyama's request through Miki Bukichi, Matsumura called Shigemitsu in Yugawara to ask him to return immediately to Tokyo. After consulting senior leaders, he asked Shigemitsu to "put off the meeting to see the attitude of Kishi, Ishibashi, etc."

see the merger of all conservative parties, met with Yoshida on September 14.[44] According to *Asahi Shimbun*, Ashida asked Yoshida to make up his mind for the sake of stability, and Yoshida replied, "I have been giving it some thought. I am not interested in keeping power for its own sake. Indeed, I want to retire as soon as the circumstances permit." Ashida told the press, "I have received a strong impression that Prime Minister Yoshida has decided to transfer power to a suitable person soon after his return from the trip abroad."[45]

About this time, there is a month-long blank in Shigemitsu's diary; when the record resumed on September 18, 1954, Shigemitsu wrote that he sent Matsumura Kanzo to see Hatoyama. On the following day, Shigemitsu proposed to Hatoyama that they form a new party and bring about Yoshida's downfall; there was no longer a possibility of Yoshida's yielding to them voluntarily.[46] This was the first mention in his diary that he had changed his position on the matter. On September 21, Shinto Kessei Sokushin Kyogikai changed its name to Shinto Kessei Jumbikai (Preparations Committee for Organizing the New Party). Hatoyama belonged to it, but Shigemitsu did not because the left wing of Kaishinto was dragging its feet. On November 10, Shigemitsu and Hatoyama met and agreed to form a new party;[47] on the 24th, they formed Nihon Minshuto with Hatoyama as president and Shigemitsu as vice-president. This represented Shigemitsu's final abandonment of any hope to become prime minister.

On November 30, 1954, an extraordinary session of the Diet was convened. Nihon Minshuto controlled 120 seats in the lower house, whereas Jiyuto was reduced to 185. Although Yoshida called for a dissolution (to fight a new election), even his closest adherents disagreed. The cabinet resigned. Minshuto and the two wings of the JSP voted Hatoyama prime minister. On December 10, the Hatoyama cabinet was formed with Shigemitsu as vice–prime minister and foreign min-

---

[44]*Ashida Hitoshi nikki*, vol. 5, p. 256. Ashida wrote, "The content of the conversation is as enclosed," but added no enclosure. But because the story soon leaked to the press, he held a press conference.

[45]*Asahi Shimbun*, July 13, 1954.

[46]*Zoku*, pp. 664–65.

[47]Ibid., p. 669. But until the plenary session of the New Party Organizing Committee, Kishi schemed to cut out the Kaishinto progressives, such as Miki Takeo. The progressives in turn joined Shigemitsu to fight back. A final compromise was arrived at just before the opening session (*Zoku*, pp. 670–72).

ister, concurrently. His diary after this records only his activities as foreign minister.

Beginning in April 1955, discussions to merge Jiyuto with Minshuto commenced. Shigemitsu's diary mentions these events without any comment. The four advisory groups that had earlier been so prominent no longer were mentioned. This is not to say that he was not a possible candidate for prime minister in this period but that he no longer seemed to have the strong backing of any group. In short, Shigemitsu had reverted to his old bureaucratic persona as diplomat.

The conservative merger was completed with the formation of the LDP on November 15. Instead of a party president, the LDP chose an acting presidential committee consisting of Hatoyama, Ogata, Miki Bukichi, and Ono Banboku. Shigemitsu was not named.

In his diary he expressed dissatisfaction with Hatoyama's policy vis-à-vis the United States on the grounds that it might cause a split between the two countries.[48] Shigemitsu was also among those who were extremely apprehensive about Hatoyama's diplomatic approach to the Soviet Union. (In January 1955, Japanese-Soviet negotiations began in response to a Soviet overture. The government appointed Matsumoto Shun'ichi ambassador plenipotentiary for the talks, slated to be held in London. Shigemitsu, Tani, Kase, and the Gaimusho bureaucracy had been cool toward the Soviet initiative, and Moscow's representatives had gotten in direct touch with Hatoyama, who—along with Kono—was very interested.) Shigemitsu "warned Hatoyama against talking to the Socialists first and insisted on talking to Jiyuto first." On Hatoyama's briefing for the Socialists, Shigemitsu commented, "Hatoyama acted as if he were dealing with a brother, an attitude entirely different from that toward Jiyuto." In the debate on the floor of the lower house that day, he said, "The JSP acted like a party in power, and Jiyuto like a party out of power. We have trouble ahead."[49]

Meanwhile, Shigemitsu visited the United States between August 24 and September 4 to talk to the secretary of state. One of his aims was to get the Americans to understand the Japanese-Soviet rapproche-

---

[48]In April 1955, Foreign Minister Shigemitsu negotiated with U.S. Ambassador Allison and General Taylor, commander in chief of the Far East, over the defense budget. Some in the cabinet were hard-nosed toward the U.S. demand. Shigemitsu wrote, "The Hatoyama cabinet undermines Japan-U.S. relations" (*Zoku*, p. 695).

[49]Matsumoto Shun'ichi, *Mosukuwa ni kakeru niji* (The rainbow over Moscow) (Tokyo: Mainichi Shimbunsha, 1955), pp. 24–25; *Zoku*, pp. 702, 710.

ment; another was to broach the subject of revising the security treaty.[50] Secretary Dulles, fearing Hatoyama's neutralism, was brusque and rough. Secretary General Kishi and Kono, who accompanied Shigemitsu, got to know each other well on this trip and took an oath of mutual help in the future. The London negotiations between Matsumoto and Jakob Malik stalemated over the territorial issue and were suspended on September 21, 1955. They were reopened in 1956 but once again deadlocked on March 25. On March 22, the Japanese government had Matsumoto advise the Soviets of its desire to begin negotiation on the fisheries question. Shigemitsu's entry on March 23 showed that the internal conflict was still intense: "Cabinet meeting today. Interrogated Agro Minister Kono on his questionable policy. Tension in the meeting. PM incompetent."[51] The Kono-Ichikov meeting on fisheries was concluded on May 15 but did nothing to abort the heated debate on how to proceed with the peace treaty.

On July 13, 1956, Shigemitsu was appointed plenipotentiary for the final Moscow talks. Shigemitsu, who had up to then maintained a rigid antitreaty stand and demanded the return of all four disputed islands, did an incredible about-face in Moscow. He agreed to the treaty in exchange for only two islands and asked for a go-ahead from his government. But the Japanese government opposed Shigemitsu's position and recalled him on August 13. Why Shigemitsu suddenly changed his position is a mystery. His diary during this period casts no light on this question.[52]

Prime Minister Hatoyama went to Moscow, and in 1956, Japan and the Soviet Union formally ended the state of war between their two countries and agreed to exchange ambassadors while postponing the peace treaty indefinitely. The Soviet Union agreed not to veto Japan's admission to the United Nations. Shigemitsu gave Japan's maiden speech in the U.N. General Assembly as Japan's chief representative. On December 23, 1956, the Hatoyama cabinet resigned; after a bitter struggle between Ishibashi and Kishi, Ishibashi became president of the LDP and prime minister. Shigemitsu, who was not even a candidate, died on January 26, 1957.

To understand Shigemitsu's conduct, I have devised figure 5.1 to show where he stood in relation to other leaders and parties. Shigemitsu was never far from Yoshida on major issues, but as president of Kaishin-

---

[50]Kishi et al., p. 130.

[51]*Zoku*, p. 774.

[52]Matsumoto, pp. 114–15.

FIGURE 5.1

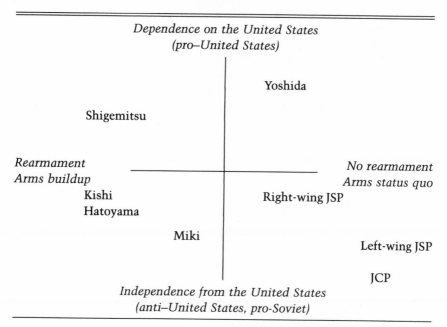

Dependence on the United States
(pro–United States)

Yoshida

Shigemitsu

Rearmament   No rearmament
Arms buildup   Arms status quo
        Kishi   Right-wing JSP
        Hatoyama

            Miki
                                                    Left-wing JSP

                                                    JCP
        Independence from the United States
        (anti–United States, pro-Soviet)

to, he had to concern himself with the overall management of a two-party system. He seems to have planned to rally to his party conservatives who were not under Yoshida's control, conservatives on the Kakushin fringe of Kaishinto, such as Miki Takeo, and the anti-Communist Socialist right wing.

But Kaishinto was not as successful in expanding as Shigemitsu had hoped. The conservative camp as a whole was confronted by the stunning rise of communism in East Asia—the founding of the People's Republic of China, the military offensive in Korea, and the activities of the Japanese left. Thus uniting the conservatives overrode the need for a second conservative party, a line of thinking propounded by Hatoyama and Yoshida since the end of war.

If all conservatives were to belong to one party, which group would dominate it? Shigemitsu seemed to feel that a peaceful transfer of power from Yoshida to himself was the best plan. He would discover, however, as did Hatoyama, that Yoshida could only be driven out of power and that Yoshida would only use Shigemitsu for his own ends. To drive out

Yoshida, the entire opposition, including Communist forces (represented in the Diet by the left wing JSP) had to be enlisted. The opportunity presented itself when the Shigemitsu cabinet was put on the agenda in 1953; but Shigemitsu could not go through with it and chose instead to support Hatoyama's anti-Yoshida drive through Nihon Minshuto. In Minshuto, however, Shigemitsu was outshone by Hatoyama, a popular politician. Hatoyama's prime ministership depended on Socialist votes and his policies for bipartisanship with the JSP, which agitated Shigemitsu, who continued to hope for cooperation with Jiyuto. Eventually, Jiyuto and Minshuto would merge, but by then Shigemitsu had lost his political connections with former Kaishinto members and was too old to take the leadership. His ambitions were never fulfilled.

6 | Toward the Liberal Democratic Party Merger: Conservative Policies and Politics

Tsutsui Kiyotada

THE LIBERAL DEMOCRATIC PARTY (LDP) WAS FORMED BY A MERGER between the Liberal party and the Japan Democratic party in 1955. Many works exist dealing with the events immediately antecedent to the conservative merger,[1] but there is a dearth of works documenting the history of postwar conservative parties in the years before the merger. For instance, little research exists on Kaishinto, the Democratic party's precursor and a major protagonist of the merger,[2] which makes it difficult to grasp the origins of the LDP's policy, ideology, and personalities. The purpose of this chapter is to survey the history of the postwar conservative parties before 1955. Because it is difficult to detail

[1]For instance, see the detailed memoir by Kishi Nobusuke, who sponsored the merger, in *Kishi Nobusuke kaiko roku* (Memoirs of Kishi Nobusuke) (Tokyo: Kosaido, 1983).

[2]See the recent work by Mikuriya Tadashi, "Showa niju-nendai ni okeru daini-hoshuto no kiseki: Ashida nikki, Shigemitsu nikki ni miru Ashida, Shigemitsu, Miki" (The track of the second conservative party in Showa 20s: Ashida, Shigemitsu, and Miki as seen in the Ashida memoir and the Shigemitsu diary), *Nenpo kindai Nihon kenkyu*, No. 9 (Tokyo: Yamakawa Shuppan, 1987), pp. 289–316.

the immediate postwar period, in which many small parties kept merging and splitting, we will focus mainly on the post-1952 period, when many purged politicians returned to public life on the signing of the peace treaty.

In 1952, there were three major conservative groups in Japan. One was Kaishinto, organized in February under its president, Shigemitsu Mamoru. A second was the maintream Liberal party under Prime Minister Yoshida. A third was the anti-Yoshida group of the Liberals, centering on Hatoyama Ichiro, who had been depurged the year before. Let us examine how the three groups came to be.

In the autumn of 1945, three conservative parties were born in Japan: the Japan Liberal party led by Hatoyama, the Japan Progressive party led by Machida Chuji, and the Japan Cooperative party led by Sengoku Kotaro. Of these, the latter two were the forerunners of Kaishinto. The Progressive party was a carryover of the wartime political party Dai-Nihon Seijikai and as a result included many veteran politicians. Because Hatoyama of former Seiyukai had organized the liberals, the Progressive party was home to former members of Minseito and the Nakajima (anti-Hatoyama) faction of the former Seiyukai.

The Cooperative party, led by Sengoku, a longtime leader of the peasant movement, stood on the platform of cooperative unionism. Later, in 1947, it grew into the National Cooperative party under the secretary generalship of Miki Takeo. By then the platform had shifted from support of the union movement to a more comprehensive concept of cooperation.

Meanwhile, the Progressives enlisted new recruits and became Nihon Minshuto in 1947. Minshuto's party program was more *kakushin* (radical-liberal), calling for eradication of the legacies of Dai-Nihon Seijikai and for "liberation from the old ills of capitalism." The impetus for this transformation came from Shinshinkai, a group of young Dietmen led by Kitamura Tokutaro in the Progressive party. But it was more facelift than transformation as far as most old-timers were concerned; for this reason many bolters from Minshuto sought refuge in Nihon Jiyuto. Ultimately, in 1949, Minshuto would split into two factions, one entering a coalition with Jiyuto and the other remaining in the opposition. This out-of-power faction of Minshuto merged with Kokumin Kyodoto in 1950 to produce Kokumin Minshuto under Chairman Tomabeji Gizo.

Consequently, although Kokumin Minshuto accommodated diverse groups, the goal of cooperation set forth in the party program became increasingly irrelevant. Within Kokumin Minshuto, Miki Takeo led the Kokumin Kyodoto faction, Kitamura Tokutaro represented the Shimpoto-Shinshinkai faction, Ashida Hitoshi—former prime minister in the coalition government with the JSP—stood for the conservatives, and Hayashiya Kamejiro bought up the rear with upper house members.[3] These factional cleavages came to the surface in the course of ratifying the peace and security treaties. Objecting to the party's decision on the two treaties, the Kitamura faction boycotted the ratification session.

Kitamura rested his case for opposition on the following grounds: (1) Okinawa and the Kurile Islands had not been restored to Japan's possession; (2) the two treaties ignored the concerns of Asian nations such as India, which refused to attend the San Francisco conference; and (3) the security treaty did not specify a time limit. In short, he opposed Yoshida's pro-Americanism with his own Nehru-like nationalism and pan-Asianism.[4] It is reported that Kitamura was influenced by the JSP's entreaties.[5] Also critical of the two treaties was Ashida, who nonetheless eventually voted for them. His criticism rested on the thesis that it was a contradiction in terms to declare Japan's willingness to share the defense burden while refusing to rearm. Earlier, in late 1950, he had submitted the Ashida Memorandum to Prime Minister Yoshida stating that Article 9 of the constitution was not incompatible with the possession of a self-defense force. His criticism of the treaties was part of his campaign to rearm Japan, underscoring the wide chasm that separated him from Kitamura within the same party.

As the peace treaty was concluded, former purgees were returning to public life, and thus Kokumin Minshuto was faced with the need to expand. Some of the depurged former Minseito members had organized themselves into the Shinsei Club and planned their own expansion. The two decided to merge, and Kaishinto was founded in February 1952.

Kaishinto's party program called for independence and self-defense for the Japanese nation, the reconstruction of Asia, cooperation, revi-

---

[3]Gikai Seiji Kenkyukai, ed., *Seito nenkan* (Political party yearbook) (Tokyo: Nyususha, 1947, 1948, 1949); Ito Takashi, "Sengo seito no keisei katei" (The origin of postwar parties), in Ito Takashi, ed., *Showaki no seiji* (Politics of the Showa period) (Tokyo: Yamakawa Shuppan, 1983).

[4]Kitamura Tokutaro, *Zuisoshu* (Occasional essays) (Tokyo: Genkyobunkan, 1963), pp. 91–103, 121–34.

[5]Igarashi Takeshi, *Tai-Nichi kowa to reisen: sengo Nichi-Bei kankei no keisei* (Peace with Japan and the cold war: The formation of postwar Japan-U.S. relations) (Tokyo: Tokyo University Press, 1986), pp. 224–28. On the occasion of the party's founding, a dispute developed over whether the word *socialism* should be inserted in the manifesto. Some Kokumin Minshuto Dietmen refused to join Kaishinto.

sionist capitalism, and a role for Kaishinto in the vanguard of progressive national forces. *Independence and self-defense* meant the establishment of democratic self-defense forces. *Revisionist capitalism* was defined more precisely in the manifesto of the founding congress as a willingness to carry out Socialist policies to correct the abuses of capitalism. Among the conservative parties, Kaishinto was the most sympathetic to socialism.[6] Fusing nationalism and egalitarianism is commonplace among revolutionary regimes, but the combination of Asian nationalism and egalitarianism in a Japanese conservative party is rare. Although this brand of *kakushin* can be better appreciated in the context of prewar and wartime *kakushin* ideology, it does reflect the complex factional balance in Kaishinto, comprising the old Minseito (Matsumura Kenzo, Oasa Tadao), Ashida, the Miki-Kitamura group, and the centrist faction under Chiba Saburo.[7]

Nihon Jiyuto was organized around Hatoyama Ichiro, but immediately after its victory in the first postwar election, in the spring of 1946, the leadership was transferred to Yoshida because of Hatoyama's purge. Except for a brief interlude, Yoshida stayed in power longer than anyone else has. Lacking a power base in his party, he vigorously recruited bureaucratic officials into politics and twice succeeded in adding splinter groups from Nihon Minshuto (the successor to Nihon Shimpoto). By 1949, his party boasted 264 members (56.7 percent) in the lower house, a number that assured him the most stable government since the war.

Yoshida held Japan's economic recovery as his primary goal and began trying to whittle down the U.S. demand for Japan's rearmament. But he was disinclined to level with the public about his diplomatic designs, preferring instead to deal behind the scenes. He neglected to restore good relations with the Asian and African nations; his sole concern seemed to be Washington. In economic policy, he followed faithfully the so-called Dodge Line, a policy of retrenchment executed by his loyal lieutenant, Finance Minister Ikeda Hayato.

What was the internal situation in Jiyuto? Although the Yoshida faction controlled the majority in the summer of 1952, a good part of that majority consisted of the followers of Hirokawa Kozen, a profes-

---

[6]On Kaishinto's party program and policies, see Miyamoto Yoshio, *Shin hoshuto shi* (History of the new conservative parties) (Tokyo: Jiji Tsushinsha, 1962).

[7]For Kaishinto's internal situation, whish is still shrouded in mystery, see *Ashida Hitoshi nikki* (The Ashida Hitoshi diary), vols. 1–7 (Tokyo: Iwanami Shoten, 1986); Jiji Press, *Jiji nenkan*, 1949–1953 (Tokyo: Jiji Press, 1949–1953); and Igarashi, *Tai-Nichi Kowa to reisen*.

sional politician. The Masuda faction—under Yoshida, with the help of Sato and Ikeda—vied with Hirokawa, but these bureaucrats were a lesser force. What threatened the Yoshida faction was the Hatoyama faction, which remained in Jiyuto even after Hatoyama had left, held together by Ono Banboku; Miki Bukichi, Ishibashi Tanzan, and others, if and when they were reelected after being depurged, were expected to greatly reinforce the Hatoyama faction.[8]

Thus members of the Hatoyama faction, alive and well in Jiyuto while their namesake was under purge, were expected to support his return to leadership. Moreover, Hatoyama let it be known that he had exchanged a vow with Yoshida that on Hatoyama's return to public life, Yoshida would relinquish power.[9] Hatoyama had no reason to doubt that the promise would be fulfilled.

Hatoyama's basic goals were revealed in a series of moves: He met secretly with John Foster Dulles, newly appointed by President Truman as special assistant in charge of negotiating a peace treaty with Japan, in February 1951. Frustrated by Yoshida's resistance to rearmament, Dulles was trying to find an alternative leader for Japan. Hatoyama fit the bill, as shown in a memorandum in which he proposed rearmament and lifting the purge. On the economic side, his powerful ally Ishibashi went on the offensive in 1951–1952 against Ikeda's disinflation policy at the Finance Ministry and proposed a positive, expanded fiscal policy. In Hatoyama's first speech on returning to public life, he added constitutional revision to his platform to allow rearmament and rapprochement with the Soviet Union. To complete the picture of the Hatoyama faction's policies and ideology, there is Ishibashi's high-priority goal of promoting friendly relations with Asian states.

On all counts, then, Hatoyama was Yoshida's opposite. Hatoyama's foreign policy closely resembled that of Kaishinto, but Hatoyama stood out in his unequivocal demand for a constitutional revision and his more sharply focused economic policies. Internally, his faction—though subdivided under Ono, Miki Bukichi, Kono, Ishibashi, and Hatoyama himself—was cohesive, if only to counter Yoshida.[10] Table 6.1 sum-

[8]Tsutsui Kiyotada, *Ishibashi Tanzan: ichi jiyushugi seijika no kiseki* (Ishibashi Tanzan: A liberal politician's life) (Tokyo: Chuo Koronsha, 1986) should help understand the internal situation in Jiyuto around this time. See also Tomimori Eiji, *Sengo hoshutoshi* (Postwar conservative-party history) (Tokyo: Nihon Hyoronsha, 1977), pp. 46–47.
[9]Hatoyama Ichiro, *Hatoyama Ichiro kaikoroku* (Memoirs of Hatoyama Ichiro) (Tokyo: Bungei Shunjusha, 1957), p. 55.
[10]See Tsutsui, *Ishibashi Tanzan.*

TABLE 6.1.

POLICY OPTIONS OF THE CONSERVATIVES

	Kaishinto	Yoshida	Hatoyama
Constitutional Revision	Handle as a part of occupation system review; not sure whether revision is needed for rearmament	Ignore for the time being	Necessary for rearmament
Defense	Establish democratic self-defense force; no independence without positive rearmament	No formal rearmament but some incremental rearmament	Positive rearmament
Foreign Policy	Autonomous diplomacy; cooperation with Asia; rapprochement with Moscow and Peking	U.S.-Japan cooperation a priority	Autonomous diplomacy; cooperation with Asia; rapprochement with Moscow
Economy	Promote economic planning and cooperative unions; policy poorly defined, unlike Ikeda's or Ishibashi's	Disinflationary balanced budget of Dodge, Ikeda	Ishibashi's positive fiscal policy to stimulate economy

marizes the major programs of Kaishinto, the Yoshida faction of Jiyuto, and the Hatoyama faction of Jiyuto.

How did the three conservative groups act and react with one another until their merger in 1955? We will first follow their respective development in terms of the two most important issues—constitutional revision and rearmament—and then flesh out the skeleton with detailed political history.

Within Kaishinto, the Ashida construction—that because the constitution did not deny the right of self-defense, rearmament was possible without a constitutional revision—was the dominant but not necessarily the unanimous view. Therefore, the party established a subcommittee on defense and constitutional questions with Kiyose Ichiro (former defense counsel at the Tokyo Trials) as the chief investigator. In September 1953, he reported out a conclusion, which became the official view, that upheld the Ashida construction.

Nevertheless, the party's view began to shift. The Sixth Congress in January 1954 resolved to establish a constitutional investigation commission to review the basic law "in view of the circumstances of its origin" but without undermining its "spirit of democracy, peace, progressivism, and international cooperativism." By September, Kiyose, now heading the commission, reported, "It is necessary to entirely revise the Japanese constitution." Among the many points of revision were the right of the cabinet to dissolve the Diet, the nationwide election district system for the upper house, and the plebiscite system to confirm the appointment of Supreme Court justices. On Article 9, the report said that "although Kaishinto construes the existing constitution to mean that the possession of war potential is permitted for the purpose of self-defense, there are contrary opinions. Hence it is necessary to have an authoritative and definitive view." It went on to say that "we renounce wars and the use of arms as a means of solving international disputes, but we must retain the war potential necessary for defending the independence and freedom of the nation." Ultimately Kaishinto took the ambivalent stance that although a revision would be better, self-defense was constitutional even without it.[11]

In the meantime, Prime Minister Yoshida kept telling the Diet that there would be no rearmament even as he upgraded the Police Reserve to the Security Forces. On March 6, 1952, he said, in the upper house's budget committee, "Possession of war potential even for the purpose of self-defense amounts to rearmament, and in this case a constitutional revision is required." But in the face of the Hatoyama faction's intense attack, the cabinet legislative bureau announced the following official

---

[11]See Miyamoto, *Shin hoshuto shi*, chaps. 6 and 7, which summarize the basic information. See also the latest scholarship in Watanabe Osamu, *Nihonkoku kempo kaiseishi* (History of Japan's constitutional revision) (Tokyo: Nihon Hyoronsha, 1987).

position in November: "'War potential' is defined as a force equipped and organized in such a way as to be capable of waging modern warfare," and "it is not unconstitutional to possess a power that falls short of 'war potential' and use it to defend against direct aggression." In this way, the foundation was laid for the latter-day Self-Defense Forces as "armed forces without war potential." This meant that in spite of Yoshida's equivocations, the government was approaching the position originally taken by Ashida: "Self-defense is constitutional."

In 1953 Secretary Dulles took a different tack to push Japan's rearmament: He dangled the offer of military and economic assistance under the Mutual Security Act (MSA) to entice Yoshida's opponents into committing themselves to rearmament. Lest he should be isolated among the conservatives, Yoshida moved closer to Ashida and Kaishinto's position. Thus, in July 1953, Foreign Minister Okazaki Katsuo stated that "in essence the government's policy of incremental expansion of self-defense forces is not at variance with Kaishinto's policy of establishing self-defense forces without a constitutional revision."

Under pressure to conclude the MSA negotiations, Yoshida met Shigemitsu Mamoru, Kaishinto's president, in September and issued a joint communiqué agreeing to "a gradual expansion of self-defense power, establishment of a long-range defense plan, upgrading of the Security Forces to the Self-Defense Forces, and assigning them the mission to cope with direct aggression." This reduced even more the distance between Jiyuto and Kaishinto. In December, Jiyuto, Kaishinto, and Miki Bukichi's Nihon Jiyuto held a conference to work out a joint conservative policy on defense. The result was the twin defense bills—the Defense Agency Establishment Law and the Self-Defense Forces Law—that were submitted to the Diet in March 1954 and passed in June. Although other differences remained among the conservatives, the forging of a common defense policy eliminated one major obstacle to their merger.

Yoshida, in contrast, persisted with his foot-dragging on constitutional revision. After nearly eight years in power, however, he no longer enjoyed a controlling majority in the lower house and was forced to welcome back Hatoyama in November 1953, shortly after Hatoyama's walkout. Yoshida, paralleling his earlier move toward Shigemitsu on defense, had to swallow Hatoyama's condition for return: establishing a constitutional investigation commission in Jiyuto under Kishi Nobusuke, Yoshida's sworn enemy. The commission came into existence in March 1954. In November, Kishi reported the commission's conclusions in the "Outline of the Revision of Japan's Constitution, Draft," which covered a wide range of points. On Article 9, it said that "a minimum of armed forces consistent with national power should be established."[12]

When Hatoyama walked out of Jiyuto to form Nihon Jiyuto in the spring of 1953, Ishibashi, who headed the bolters' policy commmittee, put together a party program calling for the establishment of (1) an investigation commission to amend the constitution and (2) self-defense forces to preserve the spirit of Article 9. A major compromise for Hatoyama, this program reflected the wide currency enjoyed by the Ashida thesis but also represented Ishibashi's long-held belief in a "small Japan." From that time on, Ishibashi interested himself in amending not merely Article 9 but the entire constitution. Hatoyama's position remained unchanged.[13]

In November 1954, Nihon Minshuto came into being. The Jiyuto revisionists, Hatoyama and Kishi, left the party (the second walkout for Hatoyama) and enlisted Kaishinto and Miki Bukichi's Nihon Jiyuto. Nihon Minshuto's party program called for a constitutional investigation commission in the Diet that would become part of the agenda for the Hatoyama government when he assumed power. In the face of intense opposition from the JSP, however, the commission bill did not pass until 1956, well after the LDP merger.[14] In 1957, the commission finally came into being under Dr. Takayanagi Kenzo, a constitutional scholar, and in 1964 delivered its final report to Prime Minister Ikeda, Yoshida's protégé, who ignored it.

Political History (1952–1955)

After his February 1951 meeting with Dulles, Hatoyama began to cast a long shadow on the political scene. But he suffered a stroke and paralysis in June, and during the remainder of the year his followers were forced to wait passively for Yoshida to relinquish power, according to the old agreement.

In July 1952, however, a revolt in Jiyuto touched off a series of anti-Yoshida movements. In Jiyuto, Masuda Kanehichi, secretary general, stood against the four factions under Hirokawa, Ikeda, Sato, and Hori Shigeru. Hirokawa, a party politician, tried to replace Masuda as secretary general with Fukunaga Kenji, a one-term Dietman. But Ishida

---

[12]Miyamoto, *Shin hoshuto shi; Jiji Nenkan* (Tokyo: Jiji Press, 1952).

[13]See Tsutsui, *Ishibashi Tanzan*, pp. 222–26.

[14]See Miyamoto, *Shin hoshuto shi*; Kishi, *Kishi Nobusuke kaiko roku*, pp. 106–7; Kishi Nobusuke et al., *Kishi Nobusuke no kaiso* (Tokyo: Bungei Shunjusha, 1981), pp. 102–3.

Hakuei, another anti-Yoshida man, enlisted Masuda, Ono Banboku, and others and successfully opposed the move. The Hatoyama faction thus came to understand that Yoshida was unlikely to transfer power peacefully to Hatoyama. Simultaneously, Ishibashi, of the Hatoyama faction, was firing broadsides against Ikeda's tight fiscal policy. Not to be outdone, Yoshida resorted to the so-called surprise dissolution of the lower house, catching Hatoyama off guard. During the ensuing campaign, Yoshida expelled Ishibashi and Kono, both confidants of Hatoyama, from Jiyuto and tried to cut off the Hatoyama faction's campaign finances.

The October election was a defeat for Jiyuto. For a while, Hatoyama probed the possibility of a coalition with Kaishinto's Shigemitsu before capitulating to Yoshida's plea to return to Jiyuto's fold. A large number of Hatoyama's followers organized the Jiyuto Democratization League, a party within a party, and, in collaboration with the opposition, succeeded in voting a no-confidence motion against Finance Minister Ikeda. In addition, the league threatened to vote with the opposition in demanding a revision of the supplemental budget. Yoshida thereupon reluctantly agreed to reinstate Ishibashi and Kono and to dismiss his party appointees, the secretary general and the executive committee chairman. Peace was temporarily restored.

During this time, Kaishinto was having its own internal squabbles, as Ashida on the right and the Miki-Kitamura faction on the left struggled to control who would appoint the secretary general and the policy committee chairman. But this was a sideshow whose motive was the Yoshida-Hatoyama fracus in Jiyuto; to outdo the other, both Yoshida and Hatoyama were trying to enlist Kaishinto members. Thus the split in Jiyuto created a parallel fissure in Kaishinto.[15]

In February 1953, Yoshida was overheard to mutter, "damned fool," referring to a Socialist Dietman who was attacking him on the floor. The Democratization League and the opposition jointly voted a motion to censure Yoshida for the insult and followed it up with a vote of no confidence in March. Yoshida responded by dissolving the Diet, whereupon the Hatoyama faction walked out of Jiyuto to form the so-called Hatoyama Jiyuto. Hirokawa, Yoshida's lieutenant until he lost out to Ogata Taketora, joined Hatoyama, who stressed that the split would trigger a reorganization of the conservative regime on the basis of a merger with Kaishinto. Merger among the conservatives became the

---

[15]For all the data and evidence for this section, I have relied on Tsutsui, *Ishibashi Tanzan*. On Kaishinto, see *Ashida*, vol. 4, pp. 244, 245, 249–54.

topic of the day, as the public became concerned over the endless squabbles in the the political establishment.

All the conservative groups—Jiyuto, Hatoyama Jiyuto, and Kaishinto—did poorly in the election, whereas both wings of the JSP advanced. In the voting for prime minister, a move to nominate Shigemitsu was supported by Hatoyama and Sohyo, the General Council of Trade Unions, but the JSP refused to go along; thus the fifth Yoshida cabinet was born. The four opposition parties did manage, however, to vote into the lower house a Kaishinto speaker and a left-wing Socialist vice-speaker. On the following day, Yoshida unexpectedly offered Shigemitsu a cabinet post but was rebuffed.

In July, another attempt to supplant Yoshida took place when left-wing Socialist leader Katsumada Seiichi pushed for a Shigemitsu government by enlisting Hatoyama on the condition that the proposed coalition agree not to submit a strike-curbing bill against the electric and coal unions. But the move was stillborn.[16] In September, the Yoshida-Shigemitsu joint communiqúe on national defense was issued, as noted earlier. But the next day, Kaishinto's Diet members agreed in a plenary session to confine bipartisan cooperation to the defense issue.

Once in opposition, Hatoyama Jiyuto ran into financial trouble, and thus in November, Hatoyama and Ishibashi returned to Yoshida's fold on the condition that he agree to establish a constitutional investigation commission and a foreign affairs commission in Jiyuto. Those followers of Hatoyama who refused to return, the "eight samurai" under Miki Bukichi, organized Nihon Jiyuto. Thus the conservative merger scheme with Hatoyama Jiyuto as the trigger failed.

In February 1954, however, two major corruption scandals involving Hozen Keizaikai and the shipping industry broke out. Public opinion took the view that the conservative establishment was in crisis and that there should be a conservative merger. Behind the scenes there were several moves afoot, including the attempt by Yoshida, Ikeda, and Sato to absorb a breakaway Kaishinto faction and prolong the Yoshida government. Another was the attempt by Miki Bukichi, Kishi, Ishibashi, and Ashida to merge the conservatives and shelve Yoshida, a move favored by Ogata, Yoshida's heir apparent. Ogata, however, wanted to wait for Yoshida's natural death, but Miki and others were ready to slay him politically if necessary.

On March 28, Ogata announced his plan to dissolve Jiyuto and Kaishinto and organize a new party. On April 13, he followed up with a statement saying that "a stable government [based on a merger of

---

[16]*Ashida*, vol. 4, pp. 366–70.

conservatives] is the urgent task of the moment." In the same month, Yoshida's lieutenant, Jiyuto secretary general Sato, was arrested on suspicion of taking bribes. Yoshida's justice minister, on Yoshida's order, nullified the district attorney's arrest warrant. Although the justice minister's action was within the letter of the law, the public exploded. On May 29, the three conservative parties came together in a merger-negotiating forum but failed to agree on a leader. Undaunted, Ishibashi, Kishi, and Ashida called a general meeting of Diet members pledged to forming a new party and began stumping the country in July and August.

On September 19, Hatoyama met with Shigemitsu and agreed to establish a new party based on Yoshida's ouster. In November, Nihon Minshuto came into existence, with Hatoyama as president. In December, the three opposition parties jointly voted no confidence and drove Yoshida to resign. Thereupon, the two wings of the JSP voted with the conservatives to appoint Hatoyama as prime minister.

The end of Yoshida's one-man, eight-year rule was greeted by the euphoria of the Hatoyama boom. In the February 1955 election, Nihon Minshuto won a plurality but fell short of a majority. Now Hatoyama had to pay the price for the JSP's opportunistic collaboration with the opposition conservatives—this time under Yoshida. In the balloting for the lower house speakership, Hatoyama's nominee, Miki Bukichi, lost to Masutani Shuji, the candidate of Jiyuto and the JSP. To consolidate its power in the Diet, Nihon Minshuto's leadership decided on March 27 to pursue a further merger.

There were strong objections to the proposed merger, however, objections rooted in the Yoshida faction of Jiyuto and the former Kaishinto members of Minshuto. Jiyuto was divided into the Yoshida faction, made up of Sato and Ikeda, and the Ogata faction. Naturally, Yoshida, Ikeda, and Sato were wholly opposed to Hatoyama, Miki Bukichi, and Kono and disagreed with Hatoyama's Soviet rapprochement policy.

The former Kaishinto members' objections centered on Miki Takeo and Matsumura Kenzo, who maintained that, in a system made up of two parties (the conservatives and the JSP), a policy failure by the conservatives would mean a transfer of power to the JSP but that the JSP, controlled by its radical left wing, could not be entrusted with such a responsibility. Informally, however, they also feared that Shigemitsu and the former Kaishinto group, already outnumbered inside Minshuto, would further decline in relative power if they were to belong to a single conservative party. Objections from former Kaishinto members in Minshuto were especially strong, and for a brief period Minshuto faced a split. Hatoyama, however, effectively placated the disgruntled conservatives during the summer and early fall. On November 15, 1955, the merger was completed and the Liberal Democratic party was born.

Several theories have been advanced to explain why the conservative merger took place at this point in time. One cites pressure from the business community, which was interested in a stable conservative rule capable of drawing large-scale assistance from the United States via the Mutual Security Act. Another theory holds that the conservatives were shaken by the rapid rise in electoral strength of the radical Socialists and that a unified conservative party was the only answer.[17] A third explanation was that the media played up the desirability of an English-type two-party system but that alternating in power with the Socialist party was premature in 1955; the JSP was committed to domestic class warfare and abolishing the Japan-U.S. security treaty.

It was, however, a more pressing practical concern that drove the two conservative parties toward a merger. In the elections following the San Francisco peace conference, Japan's political scene was split three ways and no conservative party could win a controlling majority. With Yoshida in power, Hatoyama would enlist the JSP's support and make trouble. With Hatoyama in power, Yoshida would retaliate in kind; thus, the executive branch would be unable to manage the Diet. (Hatoyama's failure to appoint Miki Bukichi speaker in March 1954 was the beginning of Yoshida's retaliations.) On April 6 the foreign affairs committee of the lower house passed a motion to censure the Hatoyama government. In May, as a bluff, Jiyuto submitted its own budget to displace the government's. When the budget committee chairman, Makino Ryozo, complained about this move on the house floor, Jiyuto prevailed on the governing party to dismiss him. In late June, Jiyuto threatened to support a motion of censure against Hatoyama's agriculture minister, Kono Ichiro. All the foregoing were manifestations of Yoshida's hatred for Hatoyama;[18] in arguing for a merger, Miki Bukichi was trying to overcome this deep-seated personal enmity in the name of better Diet management.[19]

Conventional wisdom to the contrary, most policy differences among the conservative parties had by this time disappeared. On the constitutional issue, Yoshida agreed to appoint Kishi chairman of Jiyuto's constitutional investigation commission in 1952. (A similar commis-

---

[17]Masumi Junnosuke, *Sengo seiji, 1945–55* (Postwar politics, 1945–55) (Tokyo: Tokyo University Press, 1983), p. 444.

[18]Miyazaki Yoshimasa, *Jitsuroku seihai nijugonen* (Real record of politics for 25 years) (Tokyo: Yomiuri Shimbun, 1970), pp. 162–66.

[19]Mikikai, *Miki Bukichi* (Tokyo: Mikikai, 1958), p. 443.

sion would come into existence in the Diet in 1956.) The conservatives also agreed to enact the twin defense bills, laying the groundwork for the subsequent development of the Self-Defense Forces. On economic policy, Japan's successful recovery strengthened Ishibashi's argument for an expansionary budget. Ikeda would switch to the Ishibashi line through the income-doubling scheme.[20] The only remaining difference—rapprochement with the Soviet Union and China—revived the Hatoyama-Socialist cooperation against Yoshida.

---

[20]See Tsutsui, *Ishibashi Tanzan*, pp. 412–15.

7 | Did *Kokutai* Change? Problems of Legitimacy in Postwar Japan

Nagao Ryuichi

Conflicting Legitimacies[1]

"Something is rotten in the state of Denmark," said Hamlet, doubting the legitimacy of the new regime when the ghost of the legitimate king began haunting the castle of Elsinore. Problems of legitimacy are vitally important to a political regime. The ghost of a legitimate ruler might slay an illegitimate leviathan. When Marx and Engels found the spectre of communism haunting Europe, they believed that the rule of the bourgeoisie was illegitimate. Hitherto, the Communist nations have suppressed any doubts about the revolutionary legitimacy affirmed in Marxism-Leninism, but now the bourgeois-democratic and even dynastic legitimacies are arising from the grave to reassert themselves. The postwar regime of Japan has its own problem of legitimacy, epitomized by the imperial edict that introduced the new constitution:

> I rejoice that the foundation for the construction of a new Japan has been laid according to the will of the Japanese people, and hereby sanction and

[1] I wish to express my gratitude to my colleague, Professor Humphrey D. McQueen, for correcting my English.

promulgate the amendments of the Imperial Japanese Constitution effected following the consultation with the Privy Council and the decision of the Imperial Diet, made in accordance with Article 73 of the said Constitution.

To amend the imperial constitution, five conditions were necessary: (1) submission of the project to the Diet by the imperial order, (2) decision by the House of Peers, (3) decision by the House of Representatives, (4) approval of the Privy Council, and (5) sanction of the emperor. In this procedure, only the House of Representatives reflected the "will of the Japanese people." The semiofficial commentary on the imperial constitution[2] taught that "the right of making amendments to the Constitution must belong to the Emperor Himself, as he is the sole author of it." The de jure author of the new constitution, therefore, must be the emperor. This theory presupposes imperial legitimacy.

The preamble of the new constitution, however, starts with the statement: "We, the Japanese people . . . do proclaim that sovereign power resides with the people and do firmly establish this Constitution." The Japanese people, therefore, are the authors of the constitution. This theory presupposes democratic legitimacy founded on the natural law doctrine of popular sovereignty. There is a blatant contradiction between the edict and the preamble as to who is the author of the constitution.

Because its first draft had been written by Americans who were in the Government Section of the SCAP GHQ, the wording of the preamble follows the U.S. Declaration of Independence. As for the solemn proclamation of the preamble that the sovereign power resided with the people, neither the emperor nor the Japanese people could be sovereign at the time because Japan was not a sovereign state. Both the edict and the preamble were founded on a fiction that concealed the reality of the Allied occupation.

Intellectuals and constitutional scholars dispute the true nature of the constitutional change. This chapter attempts a critical review of the first phase of those disputes: the nature of postwar legitimacy.

At about 11:50 P.M. on August 9, 1945, the members of the Supreme Council in the imperial presence began discussing the war situation in an air raid shelter inside the imperial palace. It was a fateful day for the Japanese Empire: Soviet Russia had declared war on Japan and invaded Manchuria, and the second atomic bomb had been dropped on Nagasaki.

---

[2]Ito Hirobumi, *Commentaries on the Constitution of the Empire of Japan*, translated by Ito Miyoji, 3d ed. (Tokyo: Chuo Daigaku, 1931), p. 141.

The subject under discussion was whether the Japanese government should surrender on the terms of the Potsdam declaration. The minister of war and the chief of the general staff advocated rejecting the declaration because their four conditions for ending the war—(1) maintenance of *kokutai*, (2) disarmament and demobilization on their own initiative, (3) no Allied occupation, and (4) no punishment of war criminals by the Allied powers—had not been fulfilled.

The declaration was pointedly vague on *kokutai* and, perhaps intentionally, avoided referring to the subject of disarmament, though it seemed unlikely that the Allied powers would leave the initiative in Japanese hands. Punishment of war crimes, so forthrightly demanded in the declaration, seemed nonnegotiable.

Foreign Minister Togo Shigenori insisted that, in view of the desperate situation, only the first condition was essential, and the discussion became deadlocked. At 2:00 A.M., August 10, Prime Minister Suzuki Kantaro stepped forward and asked the emperor to decide. The emperor supported the foreign minister, and thus the decision to surrender seemed settled. There remained, however, one condition of surrender that every participant demanded: the maintenance of *kokutai*.

Some took the declaration's vagueness as a rejection of *kokutai*, and so the Supreme Council decided to send a message to the Allied powers stating that "the Japanese government is ready to accept the terms enumerated in the joint declaration . . . with the understanding that the said declaration does not comprise any demand which prejudices the prerogatives of His Majesty as a sovereign ruler." (Here *kokutai* is defined as the "prerogatives of His Majesty as a sovereign ruler.") That message solicited an Allied response.[3]

The U.S. Response

In the United States, specialists in Far Eastern matters had been hotly disputing about how to deal with the imperial institution. The so-called China hands condemned the institution as the ideological and institutional root of Japanese imperialism and espoused its removal. The

---

[3]Herbert Feis, *Japan Subdued: The Atomic Bomb and the War in the Pacific* (Princeton, N.J.: Princeton University Press, 1961), pp. 118–20. One of the best works that followed the process leading up to the promulgation of the new constitution is Kempo Chosakai Jimukyoku, ed., *Kempo seitei keika ni kansuru shoiinkai hokokusho* (Report of the subcommittee concerning the process of constitutional establishment) (Tokyo: Diet, 1961). See also, in English, Theodore H. McNelly, "Induced Revolution," in Robert E. Ward and Sakamoto Yoshikazu, eds., *Democratizing Japan: The Allied Occupation* (Honolulu: University of Hawaii Press, 1987).

Japan hands, however, attributed the rise of militarism to causes other than the imperial system and argued in favor of its preservation as a stabilizing factor.[4]

The first draft of the Potsdam declaration had been written by Eugene Dooman at the request of Joseph C. Grew, the then under secretary of state. These two representative Japan hands were conservative in their political outlook and preferred order to radical reform. They had many friends among the Japanese ruling elite and believed that Hirohito himself was a pro-Anglo-American friend of peace. The twelfth clause of their draft declaration, drafted on May 28, read as follows:

> The occupying forces of the Allied Powers shall be withdrawn from Japan as soon as these objectives have been accomplished and there has been established, in accordance with the freely expressed will of the Japanese people, a peacefully inclined and responsible government. This may include a constitutional monarchy under the present dynasty if it be shown to the complete satisfaction of the world that such a government will never again aspire to aggression.

At that time, Under Secretary of State Grew was in charge of Japanese affairs because Secretary of State Edward R. Stettinius was not interested in Asian matters. The situation changed, however, when James F. Byrnes replaced Stettinius.[5] Possibly under the influence of the opinion of the China hands, Byrnes was suspicious of Grew's conservative approach, and in full control of the final drafting of the declaration at the Potsdam conference, he deleted the last half of the twelfth clause, over the protest of Henry Stimson, secretary of war.

When Byrnes received the August 10 message from the Japanese government, he decided to draft a response without consulting Grew. Grew knocked on Byrnes's closed door twice to offer help; only the second time was he allowed to enter.[6] The answer sent to the Japanese government on August 11 read as follows:

---

[4]Joseph C. Grew, *Turbulent Era: A Diplomatic Record of Forty Years, 1904–1945* (Boston: Houghton Mifflin, 1952); Nagao Ryuichi, "Who Were the Friends and Enemies of the United States in the Far East?: From the Manchurian Incident to McCarthyism," in *Shakai Kagaku Kiyo*, vol. 33, 1983; Nagao Ryuichi, *Amerika chishiki-jin to kyokuto: Owen Rattimoa to sono jidai* (American intellectuals and the Far East: Owen Lattimore and his times) (Tokyo: Tokyo University Press, 1985).

[5]Charles L. Mee, *Meeting at Potsdam* (New York: M. Evans, 1975), pp. 56–61.

[6]Feis, *Japan Subdued*, p. 121; Iokibe Makoto, *Beikoku no Nihon senryo seisaku* (U.S. occupation policy for Japan) (Tokyo: Chuo Koronsha, 1985), vol. 2, pp. 243–44.

From the moment of surrender the authority of the Emperor and the Japanese government to rule the state shall be subject to the Supreme Commander of the Allied Powers who will take such steps as he deems proper to effectuate the surrender terms. The ultimate form of the government of Japan shall, in accordance with the Potsdam Declaration, be established by the freely expressed will of the Japanese people.

This answer contained something new. At Potsdam, the British delegates made several changes to the wording of the final declaration.[7] First, "points in Japanese territory" replaced a blanket phrase, "Japanese territory," as the area to be occupied (Art. 7). This alteration allowed for an interpretation according to which the Allied powers would not be above but alongside Japan, watching the Japanese conduct their affairs. Another change the British introduced was whereas the draft contained no reference to who would remove obstacles to the revival and strengthening of democratic tendencies, the declaration appointed the Japanese government to do so (Art. 10). According to the new formulation, although several "points" would be occupied, the Japanese government would carry out postwar reforms on its own initiative and the Japanese people would freely express their will in establishing a "peacefully inclined and responsible government" (Art. 12). The word *freely* seemed to imply freedom from foreign intervention.

The Allied answer, however, put an end to the possibility of such an interpretation, for it stated that the Japanese government should be "subject to" the Allied powers. For the duration of the occupation, there could be no freedom from foreign intervention because the Supreme Commander Allied Powers (SCAP) would "take such steps as he deems proper" and be the virtual sovereign of the defeated nation. Because the free expression of popular will is incompatible with such a power, that expression would become possible only on the termination of the occupation. The phrase *ultimate form* in the answer presupposed that the Japanese would choose their form of government only when the occupation ended.

The leaders of the Japanese government, after they received the answer, discussed the matter again. The military leaders, Chief of the General Staff Umezu Yoshijiro and Chief of the Naval Staff Toyoda Teijiro, argued against accepting the surrender terms because the emperor's being "subject to" SCAP was incompatible with *kokutai*. Foreign Minister Togo, in contrast, tried to persuade them that the Allied powers did not intend to abolish the imperial institution. At that time,

---

[7]Ibid., pp. 200–201.

he interpreted *kokutai* as the existence of the imperial institution in any form whatever.

The deadlock was again resolved by the emperor's decision on August 14. In the imperial rescript, issued on August 15, there is a passage stating that "we are now successful in preserving *kokutai*."

What Is *Kokutai*?[8]

Literally, *kokutai* means the "body of the state." In ancient Chinese chronicles, the several usages of this word have nothing to do with the Japanese meaning, which originated in the nationalist literature of the Edo period. In Japanese, *kokutai* connotes the greatness of the Japanese nation, the divine authority of the emperor, and the people's unequaled patriotism and allegiance to the emperor. *Kokutai* ideology was emphasized and propagated during the crisis at the end of the Edo period; the Meiji Restoration, which restored the emperor's authority, was regarded as the triumph of the *kokutai* ideology.[9]

Hozumi Yatsuka (1861–1922), the first professor of constitutional law at Tokyo Imperial University, studied in Germany during 1884–1889 under Paul Laband and other scholars and reformulated the word within the framework of the German *Staatslehre*. *Kokutai*, according to him, is the Japanese equivalent of the German *Staatsform*, or the form of the state. In Hozumi's view, forms of the state can be classified with regard to the reigning sovereign. There are fundamentally two kinds of *kokutai*, monarchical and democratic.

Hozumi's other key concept for his theory of the state—*seitai*—corresponds to the German concept *Regierungsform* (form of government). Defining *setai* as the mode of activity of the sovereign, there are, Hozumi taught, two kinds: absolute and constitutional. The distinctive characteristic of a constitutional state is that the powers, especially the legislative and administrative powers, are separate. According to this conceptual framework, an absolute democracy lacks that separation of powers. Hozumi argued that Britain at that time was an absolute democracy because both the legislative and the administrative

---

[8]Nagao Ryuichi, "Ho-shiso ni okeru kokutai-ron" [Discussions on *kokutai* in jurisprudence], in Nagao Ryuichi, ed., *Nihon kokka shishoshi kenkyu* [Historical studies in Japan's state theories] (Tokyo: Sobunsha, 1982), pp. 5–53.

[9]See Richard H. Minear, *Japanese Tradition and Western Law: Emperor, State and Law in the Thought of Hozumi Yatsuka* (Cambridge, Mass.: Harvard University Press, 1970); Nagao Ryuichi's review of Minear in *Law in Japan*, vol. 5, 1972, pp. 209–25.

powers belonged to the majority party in the lower house. The sovereign who reigned but did not rule was for Hozumi only a nominal power. Before the promulgation of the constitution of 1889, Japan had been an absolute monarchy, that is, a combination of monarchical *kokutai* and absolute *seitai;* afterward it became a constitutional monarchy.

So far, there is nothing remarkable in Hozumi's theorizing; however, he went on to a dogmatic thesis stating that although *seitai* might be altered, *kokutai* should not be changed. From these assumptions, Hozumi concluded that parliamentary government was unconstitutional in Japan because it implied an absolute democracy, just as in contemporary Britain. He was regarded, even in his own time, as a reactionary and conceptual jurist who lacked practical sense.

Minobe Tatsukichi (1873–1948), who succeeded to the chair on constitutional law at Tokyo Imperial University, was critical of Hozumi's theory of state and constitution,[10] although he used the German *Staatslehre* as his theoretical frame of reference also. Minobe's mentor was Heidelberg professor Georg Jellinek, who taught that the state was a legal person, represented by natural persons as its organs. Sovereignty therefore lay in the state as a legal person and not in those who served as its organs. One could not thus classify forms of state by who was the sovereign, for even an absolute monarch was not sovereign but an organ of the sovereign state.

According to Minobe, *kokutai* was a cultural concept that meant "unique national character" and had nothing to do with legal or state theory. For Minobe, the only possible criterion in classifying states was how they were organized. If the highest organ of the state was one natural person, it was a monarchy, whereas if the highest organ was composed of the people or their representatives, it was a democracy. Minobe argued that, as both the emperor and the Diet had legislative power, according to the constitution, Japan was a constitutional monarchy with two heads. Careful to avoid unnecessary attacks from emperor worshipers, however, he called the emperor the "highest" organ of the state and the emperor and the Diet (as the legislative powers), "direct" organs.

Besides theoretical constructions about the state and state organs, Minobe made political proposals, which irritated Hozumi and his followers. Minobe argued that the strength of the Japanese emperorship

---

[10]On Minobe, see Frank Miller, *Minobe Tatsukichi: Interpreter of Constitutionalism in Japan* (Berkeley: University of California Press, 1965); Nagao Ryuichi, "The Legal Philosophy of Minobe Tatsukichi," *Law in Japan*, vol. 5, 1972, pp. 165–91.

was its political neutrality, or aloofness and that if an emperor committed himself to a political faction, he would have political enemies within the nation. Emphasizing that emperors from ancient times had carefully and judiciously avoided such commitments, Minobe's interpretation of the constitution tended to nominalize the imperial powers. According to the constitution, the emperor could veto bills the Diet had passed, but Minobe argued that the emperor should not exercise this power and that it would fall into desuetude sooner or later, as did the monarchic power in Britain. In the constitution the emperor was designated as the holder of governmental and administrative power to whom cabinet ministers would give advice. For Minobe, advice was a euphemism; it was the cabinet who should have the full responsibility of government.

Minobe's constitutional theory, generally known as the "emperor-organ theory," had two corollaries. The first one, according to which the state is a legal person, follows from his theory of the state. The second one is a consequence of his assertion that the emperor's powers should be nominalized, and it is this one we want to examine more closely.

The nominalization of the imperial power was a political reality, especially in the Taisho era (1912–1926), when the emperor was weak in body and mind, and thus Minobe's emperor-organ theory became prevalent in the intellectual world. The people at large, however, supposedly believed that all laws and edicts were the will of the divine emperor and that the emperor must be the person who legislated them— "Rationalism for the few, magic for the many" (Jakob Burckhardt). Some called the emperor-organ theory the esoteric doctrine of the Meiji state, and the emperor-divinity creed the exoteric one.[11] Textbooks of elementary education adopted the divine-emperor creed, even in the era of Taisho democracy.

If European fascism was a product of the "revolt of the masses," so was its Japanese counterpart. During the militarist era (1931–1945), the emperor-divinity myth was brought up against the rationalism of the few. In 1935, the emperor-organ theory was stigmatized as sacrilege to the divine emperor and banned as heretical. From that time on, Minobe was regarded as a symbolic martyr of the constitutionalism and rationalist constitutional theory of prewar Japan.[12]

---

[11]Kuno Osamu, *Gendai Nihon no shiso* (Contemporary Japanese thought) (Tokyo: Iwanami Shoten, 1956), p. 132.

[12]For more about the so-called Minobe affair in 1935, see Miyazawa Toshiyoshi, *Tenno kikansetsu jiken* (The emperor-organ theory affair) (Tokyo: Yuhikaku, 1970).

Minobe and the New Constitution

As the war drew to a close, some foreign observers expected that the Japanese people would revolt against the ancien régime and abolish the emperorship. Even Prince Konoye, in his famous memoir to the throne in February 1945, expressed his fear of a Communist revolution. But no such thing occurred; there were no mass uprisings or large-scale antigovernmental movements during the first phase of the occupation. The people were powerless, and their focus was on their daily livelihood. Political power was in the hands of reactionaries and conservatives who, though not militarists, were determined to defend the *kokutai* doctrine. Before the Japan Communist party (JCP) started its anti-imperial campaign, the only threat to the emperor system came from abroad and from SCAP GHQ. At that time there were three problems concerning the emperor system: (1) maintaining the system, (2) whether Emperor Hirohito would be indicted as a war criminal, and (3) whether he would or should abdicate. Those in charge of the government wished to avoid the first two, even at the cost of the third. Thus the problem of *kokutai* remained a hot issue in the immediate aftermath of the war.

The problem of constitutional reform was placed on the political agenda when MacArthur and George Atcheson, director of SCAP's office of political adviser (POLAD) and acting U.S. ambassador, met former Prime Minister Konoye Fumimaro on October 4, 1945. Shidehara Kijuro, who was appointed prime minister a week later, was reluctant to change the constitution under the existing circumstances, maintaining that reforms could be carried out through flexible constitutional interpretation and implementation. This opinion was shared by Matsumoto Joji, a minister without portfolio who was made chairman of the government's committee on constitutional matters.

Minobe Tatsukichi, the onetime champion of liberal constitutional scholarship, accepted the position of adviser to the Matsumoto committee, and many people expected that he would create a new, liberal, democratic constitution. They were wrong. On October 20–22, 1945, in an article in a leading newspaper, *Asahi Shimbun*, Minobe emphasized that the constitution (that is, the Meiji Constitution) embodied democracy, liberalism, and the rule of law; that the practices of the past ten years had been contrary to its tenets; that it was necessary to return to its original meaning; and that the present conditions of social confusion and distress were not favorable for changing the fundamental law of the state.

Minobe was consistent in his contentions because he had espoused a liberal interpretation of the Meiji Constitution in prewar times. After ten years of silence (since 1935, when his theory was banned), however, his attitude seemed to have undergone some changes. In a February 1946 magazine article, he said,

> I am not at all convinced that a revision of the constitution is necessary in order to accomplish democracy in Japan. Appropriate measures can be taken within the framework of the present constitution by way of implementation. There may indeed be room for adjustments in the present instrument, but I don't think we ought to do so at present. It would be better to do it when the people's livelihood is secure and their minds become calmer. But the external situation is such that we are compelled to think about a new constitution.
>
> I strongly believe and assert that the first, third, and fourth articles of the Constitution should not be changed. It is a shallow opinion to believe that democracy and monarchy are incompatible. Democracy in its true meaning is a government which reflects the general will of the people. For thousands of years the general will of the Japanese people has supported the emperor system, and emperors have ruled in accordance with the will of the people. This is the true meaning of *kokutai*. It is merely that, in the militarist era, this idea was abused.[13]

When the new constitution's latest draft (the first draft was written by officials in the government section of the SCAP GHQ and was radically different from the Meiji Constitution) was made public by the Japanese government in March, Minobe criticized it as follows:

> The most important problem of constitutional reform is undoubtedly the problem of the emperor system. The will of the Japanese people supports an emperor system in which the emperor is not merely a symbol but the supreme ruler and the highest source of political authority. Statutes should come into effect only by imperial sanction. High officials of government should obtain their rank and status only through appointment by the emperor. If the draft makes a proposal to give the throne a purely nominal existence, it is attempting a fundamental revision of *kokutai*. It means the destruction of our traditional belief and of the unity of our nation. Our government sent a message to the Allied Powers on August 10, 1945, which stated that it would accept the proposed terms with the understanding that the Potsdam Declaration did not include a demand "which

---

[13]Minobe Tatsukichi, "Minshushugi seiji to Kempo" (Democratic government and the constitution), *Seikatsu Bunka*, February 1946, cited in the Research Division, the House of Peers Secretariat, *Kempo kaisei ni kansuru shoron shuroku* (Collection of opinions on constitutional revision) (Tokyo: House of Peers, 1946).

prejudices the prerogatives of His Majesty as a sovereign ruler." If the new constitution deprives the emperor of all his political power, it clearly violates the understanding stated in the message. I don't believe that the emperor would ever veto a bill the Diet passed. In this sense, the emperor's power is formal. Form is, however, most important in soliciting the obedience of the people. The Japanese people hold statutes and edicts in high esteem because they have been sanctioned by the emperor. Such is the general will of the Japanese people.[14]

As a newly appointed privy councillor, he voted against the new constitution in June 1946.

Miyazawa in the Militarist Era

Miyazawa Toshiyoshi (1899–1976), a disciple of Minobe and successor to his chair as the professor of constitutional law at Tokyo Imperial University, was a man of extraordinarily keen sensibility, penetrating insight, humor—and, possibly, character. A genuine liberal in temperament and an enemy of fanaticism, he was influenced by the Austrian thinker Hans Kelsen, who taught that value judgments were relative and that democracy and liberalism, with their commitment to the idea of tolerance, presupposed the relativism of values. Kelsen was an enemy of philosophical and political absolutism and Karl R. Popper's precursor in criticizing Plato's republic as a totalitarian state.

Miyazawa took over the lecture course of his teacher in the law faculty in 1934, when Minobe retired at the age of sixty. In February 1935, a member of the House of Peers attacked Minobe's emperor-organ theory as a doctrine inimical to *kokutai*. This was also the time of the 5/15 Affair (1932) and the 2/26 Affair (1936), attempted coups d'état spearheaded by young military officers and nationalist fanatics. Irrational activism of the right was on the rise, and liberals and sober intellectuals were forced into silence. In this milieu, the government, which was regarded as relatively liberal among the ruling elite at that time, reluctantly banned Minobe's theory as heresy.

This shocked young Miyazawa, who had just started lecturing from the nation's most authoritative chair. He had to speak before his students, a few of whom were nationalist fanatics monitoring what Minobe's successor would say about the emperor. One story goes that, in Miyazawa's lecture on constitutional law, he skipped over the first four

---

[14]Minobe Tatsukichi, "Kempo kaisei no kihon mondai" (Basic problems of constitutional revision), *Horitsu Shimpo*, April/May 1946, cited in *Kempo kaisei*.

articles of the constitution, which stipulated the sovereign and sacred status of the emperor.

From 1935 to 1945, Miyazawa concentrated on the theoretical analysis and critical reconstruction of traditional dogmas of state and public law, and most of his articles appeared in academic journals. His master in these endeavors, Kelsen, who claimed to be an *Ideologiekritiker*, laid bare the political and authoritarian ideologies inherent in the theoretical dogmas of the traditional German *Staatslehre*. In their writings, both Kelsen and Miyazawa seemed resigned to the fact that law and the theory of law were impotent in times of turmoil.[15]

Kelsen had emigrated from Germany when Hitler seized power. As a citizen of an insular nation, Miyazawa found emigration impossible and so had to lecture, year after year, on that most dangerous subject, the emperor, before the vigilant ears of fanatical students. Understandably then, he sacrificed some of his intellectual integrity. Some of his writings, however, give the impression that he came to believe what he was compelled to write.

Miyazawa's textbook on constitutional law, dry and careful in tone, refrained from expressing opinions on controversial issues. On *kokutai* he wrote as follows:

> It is necessary for a state to have its own basic principle. The principle must be unchangeable. If it is altered, the state loses its identity. The basic principle of our nation is expressed in the first article of the Constitution, which stipulates that the Empire of Japan shall be ruled over by emperors of the dynasty that have reigned in an unbroken line of descent for ages past. This principle has its origin in the divine mandate written in the ancient chronicles. Emperors are scions of the Sun Goddess, by whose mandate they have ruled and will rule our nation forever. This principle is called the *kokutai* of Japan.[16]

---

[15]"Das Ideal einer objektiven Wissenschaft von Recht und Staat hat nur in einer Periode sozialen Cleichgewichts Aussicht auf allgemeine Anerkennung," in Hans Kelsen, *Reine Rechtslehre* (Berlin: Franz Deuticke, 1934), p. viii. Friedrich von Gerber, the father of the "juristic method" in constitutional theory, once said, "An age when one principle of organization takes the place of another, when all the political relations are in ceaseless unrest, and when the status quo is threatened by revolutions, is not favorable for jurisprudence. It is an age of politics, not of law." It seems that contemporary Germany is in not a legal but in a political age. Miyazawa Toshiyoshi, "Kohogaku ni okeru seiji" (Politics in public law jurisprudence), *Hogaku Kyokai Zasshi*, vol. L, Bk. 7, 1932; also found in *Koho no genri* (Principles of public law) (Tokyo: Yuhikaku, 1967), p. 69.

[16]Miyazawa Toshiyoshi, *Kempo Ryakusetsu* (Fundamentals of constitutional law) (Tokyo: Iwanami Shoten, 1942), pp. 72–73.

One might argue that these passages are *mots d'esclave*. In any case, Miyazawa was too able to limit himself entirely to academic activities. He sometimes commented on contemporary matters in journals for generalist intellectuals, including several he might later have regretted. Soon after Pearl Harbor, he contributed an article to the journal *Kaizo* entitled "Twilight over the Anglo-Saxon Nations" in which he said:

> December the eighth! It was on that day that all the Japanese people were strained, excited, and overjoyed. As soon as I finished my lecture, I hurried to the refectory in order to listen to the radio. There I saw many colleagues standing at attention and listening to the imperial proclamation of war. "Now we have no alternatives. Our empire can and shall break through all the obstacles for the sake of our existence and self-defense," the announcer read. Prime minister Tojo made a vigorous speech. "We did it at last," we uttered with a sincere, bright smile. The feeling that we were now facing the inevitable made our mind clear. This was the moment at which all the Japanese people wholeheartedly felt their Japanese blood circulating in their veins. . . .
>
> The true root of the present war is the hegemony Britain and the United States have claimed in Asia. They have asserted that maintenance of the status quo in this area is international justice. What appalling self-righteousness. They came to Asia from distant quarters of the earth in order to usurp the spoils. Their justice is nothing but keeping these spoils for themselves. We shall now make them realize their fundamental errors. We must expel the Union Jacks and the Stars and Stripes from Asian seaports and liberate Asia from their influence. The sun is setting for the Anglo-Saxon nations. The sun is rising for Asian nations. Let the Greater East Asia War be the first page of an Asian renaissance!

Three and a half years later Japan was defeated. When Miyazawa learned of the surrender, he murmured, "Now I can sleep without fear. Maybe I will be able to get a decent cup of coffee."[17] In Japanese, such bathos is called a dragon's head with a snake's tail.

The August Revolution

On October 19, 1945, Miyazawa contributed an article to the newspaper *Mainichi Shimbun*. The points he made closely paralleled Minobe's:

> We must emphasize that our constitution is quite compatible with democratic tendencies. Its principle is constitutionalism. Everyone knows that constitutionalism consists in a guarantee of people's freedom and

---

[17]Hidaka Rokuro, "Senso taiken to sengo taiken" (The experiences of the war and the postwar), *Sekai*, August 1956, p. 51.

people's participation in government. Liberalism and democracy are the two principles of constitutionalism. During the militarist era, constitutionalism was rejected. What is necessary today is the full recovery of true constitutionalism, which is inherent in the Constitution. Another important point is the flexibility of our Constitution. We can do many things without rewriting its articles. We can reject the political influence of the military, democratize the upper house and change many things within the framework of the present Constitution.

Miyazawa played an important part in writing the draft constitution of the government's Matsumoto committee. That conservative draft maintained the basic structure of the imperial constitution, but in February 1946, SCAP rejected it. On February 3, MacArthur ordered the Government Section of GHQ to write a new draft, which the Shidehara cabinet accepted with great reluctance. On March 6, the government issued as its own the draft constitution that had been written by the Americans and somewhat revised during discussions with several Japanese government representatives.

Even when faced with this latest reality, Minobe did not bend, but Miyazawa converted to a new theoretical assumption, the so-called August Revolution theory. According to this theory, monarchical sovereignty was abolished and popular sovereignty established when the Japanese government accepted the Potsdam declaration and the Allied answer of August 11, which stated that the ultimate form of government should be established by the "freely expressed will of the Japanese people." Such a transfer of sovereignty was, Miyazawa said, a legal revolution, even though not accompanied by street fighting and bloodshed. He first espoused this theory in a magazine article in March 1946,[18] wherein, as a newly appointed member of the upper house, he criticized the government for dishonestly failing to acknowledge the change in *kokutai*.

His new theory invited criticism. Sasaki Soichi,[19] former professor of the Kyoto Imperial University and the most authoritative constitutional theorist in prewar times besides Minobe, argued that the word

---

[18]Miyazawa Toshiyoshi, "Hachigatsu kakumei to kokumin shuken-shugi" (The August revolution and popular sovereignty), *Sekai Bunka*, May 1946; also in Miyazawa, *Kempo no genri* (Principles of constitutional law) (Tokyo: Iwanami Shoten, 1967), pp. 375–99.

[19]Sasaki Soichi, *Tenno no kokka-teki shocho-sei* (Emperor's character as the state's symbol) (Tokyo: Kobunsha, 1949), pp. 51–52; Soichi Sasaki, *Nihon koku kempo-ron* (Discourse on Japan's constitution) (Tokyo: Yuhikaku, 1949), p. 90ff.

people in the Potsdam declaration and its answer meant the Japanese people as a nation, not the people in contrast to the emperor, and that the freedom of the people to express their will meant freedom from foreign intervention. He concluded that the declaration and its answer guaranteed that the Allies would not intervene in determining the forms of the state, that the Japanese would choose according to their own constitutional procedures.

Others argued that the Japanese government in August 1945 had promised to democratize Japan only gradually[20] and that Japan had not changed from a monarchy to a democracy in an instant, as Miyazawa taught. At some future time, Japan might change its political structure in fulfillment of its promise, but for the time being *kokutai* remained as it had been. These arguments held that Japan had promised only *evolution* in August 1945, that the act of acceptance did not imply a sudden *revolution*.

During the occupation, prewar Japan was depicted as in the Dark Ages, thus a radical departure from the past was demanded not only by the SCAP bureaucracies but by left-wing intellectuals and the younger generation, who knew only the worst aspects of the prewar regime. Miyazawa's August Revolution theory appealed to this group and became prevalent among postwar intellectuals.

More recently, however, the August Revolution theory has begun to seem artificial and legalistic. The objective of the Allied powers in 1945 was to induce the Japanese government to surrender; the democratization of Japan was for them at best a secondary consideration. Opinions among Japanese specialists differed as to how far postwar Japan should be democratized. Grew and Dooman, the writers of the draft of the Potsdam declaration, had lukewarm opinions. To infer a democratic revolution from the documents they created justifies ex post facto the unexpectedly radical reforms carried out by MacArthur and his staff.[21]

---

[20]Kanamori Tokujiro, minister without portfolio and in charge of constitutional matters in the first Yoshida cabinet (May 1946–May 1947), emphasized this view in the Diet.

[21]See Nagao Ryuichi, "Kokumin shuken to tenno-sei" (Popular sovereignty and the emperor system), and "Futatsu no kempo to Miyazawa kempo-gaku" (The two constitutions and Miyazawa's constitutional theory), in Nagao Ryuichi, *Nihon hoshiso-shi kenkyu* (Tokyo: Sobunsha, 1981), pp. 304–20; Nagao Ryuichi, "Kempo ronso no makugire" (The end of the constitutional debate), and "Hachigatsu kakumei-setsu noto" (A note on the August revolution thesis), in Nagao Ryuichi, *Nihon kokka shiso-shi kenkyu* (Tokyo: Sobunsha, 1982), pp. 129–47.

The Legitimacy of the Postwar Regime

Political regimes need to legitimize themselves. Japan's postwar regime had a peculiar need of self-legitimation because its existence was dictated by its former enemies. Philosophers have put forward differing principles of legitimacy: John Locke and his followers proposed a democratic legitimacy wherein the popular will becomes the ultimate basis of all government. According to this theory, governments that are established by way of coups d'état or revolutions acquire legitimacy if they are supported by the popular vote. Jeremy Bentham espoused a utilitarian legitimacy: Any government that brings about the greatest happiness of the greatest number is the best government.

Max Weber distinguished three types of legitimacy: charismatic, traditional, and legal. Charisma played an important role at the beginning of the postwar regime, first the emperor's and then MacArthur's.[22] MacArthur's charisma faded when he advocated dropping atomic bombs on China and was dismissed; the emperor's charisma appealed primarily to the older generations. Moreover, emperor worship and postwar democracy are so different that the former can hardly be the basis of legitimacy for the latter.

Kokutai would seem to be the principle of traditionalist legitimacy; in reality, however, it is the principle of legitimacy during a specific historical period, that is, from the Meiji Restoration to the end of World War II. Historians point out that, in the long history of Japan, emperors have almost always been outside the political arena as either moral authorities or bearers of cultural tradition.[23] The Meiji Constitution, which ascribed supreme power to the emperor, was an exception to and an aberration of that tradition. Ishii Ryosuke, a legal historian, contends that the new constitution resumed the age-old national tradition.[24]

Miyazawa's August Revolution theory is a legalist construction and legitimation of the postwar reform by SCAP, whereas Minobe doubted the legitimacy of the new constitution from a standpoint of traditionalist legitimacy. Miyazawa's theory replaced the traditionalist concept of legitimacy with a legalistic one. (MacArthur's concept of legitimacy

---

[22]Nagao Ryuichi, "MacArthur and the Postwar Democracy in Japan," *Japan Echo* 1, no. 2 (February 1974):69–78.

[23]Watsuji Tetsuro, *Kokumin togo no shocho* (The symbol of national integration) (Tokyo: Keiso Shobo, 1948).

[24]*Tenno* (The emperor) (Tokyo: Kobundo, 1950).

at that time may have been a Lockean natural law doctrine of freedom and democracy.)

Confucius said that "the orientation of men of high aspiration is justice, whereas the orientation of common people is utility." Ideologues have disputed whether tradition or democracy is the basis of legitimacy for Japan's postwar regime. The common people, however, have accepted the regime because it brought them peace, freedom, and prosperity. Most people who vote for the LDP belong to this category. The JSP and the JCP have been kept from power because these people preferred utility to justice.

After the occupation ended, the ghost of nationalist legitimacy revived and started to campaign against the "imposed constitution." Assessment of the success of that campaign is difficult for several reasons.

First, although there were varieties of opinions concerning postwar reforms among conservatives who advocated revising the constitution, few rejected all the postwar values. Some constitutional scholars declared the new constitution was null and void because it was dictated by foreign powers and violated the principle of *kokutai*. Most conservatives who claim to be liberals or democrats, however, called for only partial revision of the new constitution and by so doing implicitly accepted postwar legitimacy.

Second, leftists and liberals supported the new constitution and its democratic legitimacy. Miyazawa's August Revolution theory, though too artificial for the general public, was welcomed by leftists and liberals because it rejected legitimizing the new regime through *kokutai* doctrine. Although some radicals rejected the postwar democracy as capitalistic or bourgeois, their influence was negligible.

The *kokutai* defenders and democracy champions are still hotly debating. Emperor Showa's death provided an occasion to review the problem. The Communist party, consistent with its program to abrogate the emperor system, did not issue a mourning statement, instead restating its harsh opposition to any effort by the government or the conservatives to enhance the "imperial myth." Other radical leftists demonstrated their opposition to the emperor system by holding a rock concert on the funeral day and vandalizing *hinomaru* (the rising sun emblem). The government and the media in their attention to rites behaved as if they were loyal subjects of the traditional emperor but otherwise avoided any commitment to *kokutai* ideology.

Up to now, I have avoided defining *legitimacy*, the key concept of this discussion, which political philosophers present as the ultimate justification of regimes, whereas sociologists see it as why the governed accept those regimes. Imperial or democratic legitimacy belongs with the philosophers. If the majority of Japanese accept any political theory, it must be some utilitarian notion according to which any political regime that brings them prosperity and happiness is legitimate. The LDP has governed Japan for more than a generation, claiming by its name to be liberal and democratic. Espousing sometimes nationalist and sometimes internationalist causes, it has behaved sometimes like a traditionalist and sometimes like an innovator but has always promoted economic prosperity. Thus the LDP is the symbol of the political philosophy of the majority.

8 | The 1955 System: The Origin of Japan's Postwar Politics

Kataoka Tetsuya

By a commonly accepted definition, the 1955 System refers to the system of party politics established in the fall of that year when the parties in (the conservatives) and out (the Socialists) of power confronted each other. The conservatives in the Liberal Democratic party (LDP) have been in power ever since. For reasons explained in the introductory chapter, I maintain that the 1955 System is still in existence today and that it will remain in existence so long as U.S.-Japanese security relations remain what they are, with the United States playing the dominant, protective role. The 1955 System has defined the characteristics of Japan's postwar politics. In this chapter, I survey the history of the system between 1945 and 1960.

As is true of many things Japanese in the postwar era, the 1955 System carried a deep U.S. imprint because changing Japan's political system was the highest desideratum of the United States during the occupation. But the system as it emerged was not the one intended by occupation policies. The Americans defined the parameter and provided materials without which the system could not have been born, but the Japanese exercised their discretion to fashion a system that ensured a degree of insulation from the United States. What is fascinating about the system is that it was not an accident but followed the conscious design of one intelligence, that of Prime Minister Yoshida Shigeru.

The story begins with Japan's 1945 diplomatic exchanges with the United States for terms of surrender. The Potsdam declaration was drafted and pushed by Henry Stimson, army secretary; Joseph C. Grew, former ambassador to Tokyo and then acting secretary of state; and the Joint Chiefs of Staff, who felt that unless the United States scaled down its demands for unconditional surrender and destruction of the Japanese monarchy, Japan might fight on to the bitter end or capitulate to the Soviet Union. The declaration, then, set forth specific terms of surrender; addressed itself to the Japanese government rather than to the Japanese people; demanded "unconditional surrender" of the Japanese armed forces, not of the government; and stipulated a "peacefully inclined" government based on the "freely expressed will of the Japanese people." Stimson said that "the monarchy is a small problem compared with victory."[1]

In July and August, following the issuance of the declaration, however, there were major reshuffles and attendant policy changes within the Truman administration, as documented by Theodore Cohen, a direct witness.[2] Secretary of State Stettinius was replaced by James Byrnes, who in turn replaced Grew as under secretary with Dean Acheson. Stimson also resigned from the army in September. The State Department spearheaded the drive to liquidate the monarchy, colliding with the Joint Chiefs of Staff (JCS), who wanted to use the emperor to accomplish peaceful disarmament and occupation. Leon V. Sigal posits that conflict between the State Department and the JCS as the major cause of U.S. ambiguity on the disposition of the emperor and the emperor system.[3]

The Japanese government split on the declaration, with the peace faction and the Foreign Ministry insisting that the declaration guaranteed the safety of the throne and the army mistrusting that interpretation. With the destruction of Hiroshima and Nagasaki on August 6 and

---

[1]Iokibe Makoto, *Beikoku no Nihon senryo seisaku* (The U.S. occupation policy for Japan) (Tokyo: Chuo Koronsha, 1985), II, 243.

[2]Theodore Cohen, *Remaking Japan: The Occupation of Japan as New Deal* (New York: Free Press, 1987).

[3]Leon V. Sigal, *Fighting to a Finish: The Politics of War Termination in the United States and Japan, 1945* (Ithaca, N.Y.: Cornell University Press, 1988), p. 154.

9 and the Soviet declaration of war on August 9, however, on August 10 Japan indicated its willingness to accept the declaration provided that the "prerogatives of His Majesty as a sovereign ruler" not be altered. In their reply of August 11, the Allies neither affirmed nor denied the Japanese condition but stated that from the moment of surrender the authority of the emperor and the Japanese government to rule would be "subject to" the authority of the Supreme Commander Allied Powers (SCAP). The Japanese government understood that the United States was keeping open the possibility of liquidating the monarchy; nonetheless it surrendered with a unilateral declaration stating that *kokutai* (the emperor system) was saved because without it the military would not lay down arms.

In early September Washington made public its major policy directive, SWNCC 150/4, the Initial Postsurrender Policy toward Japan, which indicated that eliminating the emperor system was indeed one policy alternative for the occupation commander. In addition, SWNCC 150/4 set forth sweeping political and economic programs to make Japan into something radically different through a combination of constitutional revision, political and economic purges, liquidation of *zaibatsu* combines, and so on. Another directive stated that Japan's surrender was unconditional and that the United States was not bound by any contractual obligations to Japan.[4]

Thus the fate of the emperor and the monarchy was to be determined through the process of constitutional revision. The Japanese government of Prime Minister Shidehara, duty-bound to safeguard the integrity of the throne, fell back on its interpretation of the Potsdam declaration. Two of Shidehara's cabinet ministers in particular, Yoshida Shigeru and Matsumoto Joji, strongly objected to any concession on the Meiji Constitution as a direct threat to the throne. In an "extraordinarily dangerous and inherently inflammable situation,"[5] MacArthur, trying to emulate his father's benevolent treatment of the Filippino rebel leader Emilio Aguinaldo, struck a bargain with Shidehara to save the emperor in exchange for Japan's accepting popular sovereignty and the

---

[4]For SWNCC 150/4, see John M. Maki, *Conflict and Tension in the Far East: Key Documents, 1854–1960* (Seattle: University of Washington Press, 1961), pp. 121–23. SWNCC 181/2 can be found in *Foreign Relations of the United States* (hereinafter *FRUS*), 1945, VI, 712.

[5]D. Clayton James, *The Years of MacArthur* (Boston: Houghton Mifflin, 1985), III, 22.

war-renoucing article in the new constitution. The emperor, then, was held hostage to Japan's good conduct during the most critical phase of the reforms, thus ensuring their success.[6]

Having written the constitution to save the emperor, MacArthur wanted to perpetuate it for all time as the monument to his rule, which he saw as comparable to Caesar's occupation of England and France. From this point on, until his dismissal in April 1951, MacArthur's entire career was devoted to this task; not even the outbreak of the Korean War would force him to deviate from this end.

The constitution was not the only legacy of the occupation; other items included the decimation of the old ruling elite, the rise of the Socialist party, and the preservation of Japan's central-ministry bureaucracies. All these were accomplished by the purge that was ostensibly directed at ultranationalists. According to E. H. Norman's Marxist theory justifying the purge, the civilian bureaucracies, the military, and the *zaibatsu* financiers constituted the triumvirate of Japanese militarism, and thus there was no reason to spare the bureaucracies from the ravages of the purge.

Hans H. Baerwald, the administrator of the program in Tokyo, tells a somewhat different story. The Ministry of the Interior was abolished, the Justice Ministry was reorganized, and the Imperial Household Ministry, reduced in size; the bureaucracies, however, remained intact (see table 8.1). Eighty percent of the military and 17 percent of the political elites, including nearly all the conservatives at the national level, were purged, but only 1 percent of the bureaucrats. *Shinninkan*, the administrative vice-minister class, lost only 48 percent. The political elites were professional politicians and thus resented the fact that the SCAP enlisted the bureaucracies to administer the purge. This unevenness, the result of "indirect government" in the occupation, tallies with the fact that MacArthur could not rule without the administrative expertise of the Japanese bureaucracies, although the Japanese had no autonomy under the unconditional surrender.

The Socialists also gained by the purge, not as an indirect consequence of the purge of the conservative politicians but by the occupation's purpose of establishing what MacArthur called a "moderate force" in Japanese politics. The purge was the instrument, and the Socialists

---

[6]*FRUS*, 1949, VII, 747. Handing over the SCAP draft of the constitution to Yoshida and other ministers, General Courney Whitney remarked that they could remain in power only if they made a "sharp swing to the left." Takayanagi Kenzo, et al., *Nikonkoku kenpo seitei no katei* [The process of drafting Japan's constitution] (Tokyo: Yuhikaku, 1972), I, 322–28.

TABLE 8.1

	Purges by Elite Categories[a]	
	Number	Percent
Military	167,035	79.6
Political	34,892	16.5
Ultranationalist	3,438	1.6
Business	1,898	0.9
Bureaucratic	1,809	0.9
Information media	1,216	0.5
	Purges of Bureaucratic Elite	
	Number	Percent
Total number screened	42,251	100.0
Total number purged	830	1.9
Shinninkan[b] screened	87	100.9
Shinninkan purged	42	48.3
Chokuninkan[c] screened	1,974	100.0
Chokuninkan purged	164	8.3
Soninkan screened	40,190	100.0
Soninkan purged	624	1.55

[a]These statistics include only those screened, not those who retired or resigned and subsequently were provisionally designated.
[b]Ministers and privy councilors by imperial appointment.
[c]Vice-ministers and senior civil servants by imperial appointment.
From Hans H. Baerwald, *The Purge of Japanese Leaders under the Occupation* (Berkeley: University of California Press, 1959), pp. 80, 82.

were the beneficiary.[7] MacArthur also used the purge as the primary means of defending his constitution, favoring the Socialists because they favored the constitution. The purge, then, is the second instance

[7]See the article by Courtney Whitney, in Government Section, Supreme Commander for the Allied Powers, *Political Reorientation of Japan, September 1945 to September 1948* (Washington, D.C.: GPO, 1949).

of MacArthur's intervention in Japan's constitutional affairs. In addition, he called two elections in close succession, in 1946 and 1947, to see that the JSP would emerge triumphant and force the reluctant Socialists to form a coalition government with the Ashida-led former Minseito. MacArthur spared Ashida from the purge and gave him the mandate to enter the coalition.

The purge program resulted from a peculiar marriage of the theories of unconditional surrender and New Deal socialism. Unconditional surrender was based on the theory that regarded wars as crimes to be punished in a court of law. New Deal socialism as applied to Japan was embodied in the works of E. H. Norman, a Canadian Communist, who, in his straightforward Marxist analysis that he learned from the *kozaha* school of Japanese Socialists, attributed the will to war or peace to the social structure. According to this view, a certain class was warlike and others were peacefully inclined. In the case of Japan, the culprit was the "arrested" or incomplete state of bourgeois-democratic revolution as represented by the Meiji Restoration. The feudal remnants in Japan had to make way for a peace-loving society, for it was the semifeudal ruling class that had committed the crime against peace.

The two theories combined to form a purge without trial, appeal, or due process, with the objective of removing a class of people, a number too large for judicial treatment. The purge was therefore handled administratively; one and a half million Japanese had their personal histories investigated, 900,000 were reviewed, and 210,000 were purged.[8] A SCAP directive said that "individual guilt . . . is irrelevant" but that it had "no objection to the establishment of a Commission of Inquiry, . . . providing that the individual is first removed from public office."[9] The purgees were driven from office and, in the case of *zaibatsu* officials, deprived of "the means of production" (i.e., private property).

Although individual guilt was supposed to be irrelevant, the purgees were nonetheless branded ultranationalists because that label justified such a punishment. The Americans who knew what was going on seemed to have pangs of conscience, but the deed was done. Although there were undoubtedly some unrepentant, dyed-in-the-wool militarists, the SCAP created 210,000 "militarists" and "ultranationalists" who, they knew, had a reason to resent the occupation. Furthermore,

---

[8]Baerwald, p. 45. Kusayanagi Taizo, *Nihon kaitai* [Japan dissolved] (Tokyo: Gyosei, 1985), p. 351.

[9]Government Section, Supreme Commander for the Allied Powers, *Political Reorientation of Japan, September 1945 to September 1948* (Washington, D.C.: GPO, 1949), p. 18.

the purge fell most severely on the professional politicians.

MacArthur, obsessed with preserving the constitution, identified the purged politicians as the threat to it, and thus they became constitutional revisionists. The bogey of Japanese militarists did not stop there, however, but became the controlling factor in America's subsequent foreign policy toward Japan. The Eisenhower administration and its secretary of state, John Foster Dulles, dearly wished to find allies in Japan who would take the cold war alliance seriously, but their only friends were Yoshida and the Socialists; the revisionists would not come on board without a constitutional revision, which Americans were taught to fear by MacArthur and Reischauer.

In 1948, Washington's cold war–induced reversal reached Japan in the form of NSC 13/2, authored by George F. Kennan. Japan then became, not a former enemy to be punished, but a precious asset to be denied the Soviet Union, husbanded as a U.S. garrison, and enlisted as a possible ally. The State Department, the earlier champion of punitive peace, had leapfrogged MacArthur and begun pushing for "rehabilitation" and policy reversal. MacArthur had earlier frozen State out of the occupation administration because it threatened the emperor. Now State was trying to curtail MacArthur's influence by demanding a major policy reversal. Later the conflict would evolve into one between State and the Joint Chiefs of Staff (JCS) over the terms of peace with Japan.

MacArthur's natural inclination was to dig in his heels and reject outside interference in his domain. Thus, the MacArthur who advocated magnanimity for Japan became the MacArthur who refused to undo the "new deal" because he thought he would lose Japanese confidence if he were to scuttle the constitution. Because of MacArthur's stonewalling, Washington dispatched Joseph Dodge, a Detroit banker, to Tokyo to take over Japan's economic rehabilitation. But political rehabilitation, such as lifting the purge and constitutional revision, had to be postponed until MacArthur was dismissed. That postponement would have a major impact on subsequent developments in Japan.

America's turnaround in 1948 shocked the *kakushin* forces as much as it pleased the conservatives. Both the JCP and the JSP chose to believe that they had been betrayed by the Americans, although the JSP—the ruling party at the moment—let the Communists do all the protesting. The left began to distance itself from the United States and to move toward Moscow, whereas the conservatives began to see Washington as a potential friend. The center—the Socialist right wing and former Minseito —was falling out, and a major political realignment was under way. In the general election of 1949, the Socialist center was reduced from 143 seats to 48; former Seiyukai won a whopping 266 in the 466-seat chamber, up from 131; and the Communists, who were already waging open guerrilla warfare, shot up from 4 to 35. The Socialists, after prolonged soul-searching, concluded that their future lay in opposing the United States under the left-wing leadership. The "domestic 38th parallel" was emerging.

The 1949 election sowed the seeds of the 1955 System in other ways as well. In 1946, Hatoyama Ichiro, who founded the successor to Seiyukai and who was about to head the government after the election of that year, was purged. Yoshida became the leader of former Seiyukai and prime minister, a highly unwelcome development at the Government Section (GS) of SCAP GHQ because of Yoshida's resistance to the new constitution. The GS, by appointing a Socialist prime minister, ensured that Yoshida would be kept out of power after the 1947 election. When Yoshida threatened the Ashida-Socialist coalition again in 1948, the GS intervened in former Seiyukai's internal affairs to eliminate him. Many of the party professional politicians, who resented their discriminated status in the purge, vented their resentment at Yoshida, the quintessential bureaucrat, by siding with SCAP's nominee. Although the GS intervention was in the end aborted by MacArthur, Yoshida had discovered his vulnerability and thus decided to surround himself with faithful followers recruited from the ranks of bureaucratic officials, who were successfully returned in the election of 1949. This was the beginning of the so-called Yoshida School of bureaucrats-turned-politician, who would go on to array themselves against Hatoyama and his cohorts of professional party politicians.[10]

The election was a triple victory for Yoshida. He now had his own loyal faction; his party had won an impressive majority in the election that was regarded as a riposte to SCAP's ideologically motivated meddling; and the conservative victory coincided with the rightward shift in Washington's policy, with which MacArthur complied, by establishing rapport with Yoshida. Now he was the cold war ally of the United States.

Beginning in 1946 several schemes for peace treaties had been debated in Washington. Early U.S. plans were so punitive that they had to be abandoned. In the end the peace plan for Japan was determined by three powers: the Japanese government supported by Douglas MacArthur, the State Department, and the JCS and the Pentagon. Amaz-

---

[10]Masumi Junnosuke is the best source for these fracases. See *Sengo seiji, 1945–1955* (Tokyo: Tokyo University Press, 1983), I, chap. 2, sec. 3.

ingly, it was the Japanese government's plan, authored by Yoshida during his first prime ministership in 1947, that dominated U.S.-Japan
relations for nearly forty years.

Yoshida envisioned a Japan nursing its wounds for a few decades
under U.S. protection but without injuring its amour propre, which
meant he was willing to countenance a small constabulary force for
domestic peacekeeping but ruled out any overseas military role. To
secure U.S. military protection, Yoshida was willing to lease bases to
the U.S. armed forces in Okinawa in peacetime and in Japan proper in
an emergency; he insisted, however, that this exchange—military bases
for protection—was fair and that it entitled Japan to an equal status.
Until 1948, moreover, his ideas enjoyed the support of the conservatives
and the JSP.[11]

The JCS's position was straightforward and brutal: It did not want
to relinquish the privileges of the occupation army for the foreseeable
future; that is, it did not want a peace treaty at all. Its proposed status-
of-forces agreement, for instance, would be based on the U.S.-Philippine
agreement rather than on the NATO agreement. At the same time, the
JCS wanted to rearm Japan with conventional capabilities and, after
the outbreak of the war in Korea, began entertaining thoughts of using
Japanese troops there. In contrast, the State Department, represented
by John Foster Dulles, argued eloquently for a nonpunitive and generous
peace according formal equality to Japan. Having dropped its objections
to Japan's rearmament in 1950, the State Department became as insis-
tent as the Pentagon on rearmament. Dulles in particular felt that
military self-help and a regional collective security role were the sine
qua non of independence and equality.

However, the bureaucratic interests of the State Department and the
Pentagon were involved in their respective positions. The military stood
to lose control of Japan to the State Department with the conclusion
of a peace treaty; in Tokyo, SCAP would give way to a U.S. ambassador.
In its efforts to beat the Pentagon, was the State Department only paying
lip service to Japan's equality and independence?

Being an old hand at government bureaucracies, MacArthur seems
to have understood the State Department–Pentagon conflict and sought

---

[11]Martin E. Weinstein misunderstands the role of domestic politics in Japan's
foreign policy, but his description of the germination and continuity of the
national security policy is good; see his *Japan's Postwar Defense Policy, 1947–
1968* (New York: Columbia University Press, 1971) and Michael Yoshitsu, *Japan
and the San Francisco Peace Settlement* (New York: Columbia University
Press, 1983).

to steer a midcourse. Although he repeatedly assailed the JCS and the Pentagon as being "imperialistic,"[12] he also sought to restrain Dulles's demand for rearmament because it would jeopardize his constitution. The bottom line of the U.S. demand was bases, not rearmament. So MacArthur's compromise split the difference: The State Department got the peace treaty and an independent Japan would volunteer to enter into a base-leasing accord. MacArthur justified his alternative with the constitution and Dulles had to accept it for the time being.

The Truman administration was under fire from the Republicans in the Senate who were up in arms over the "loss of China" and frustrated by their prolonged minority status. In fact the appointment of Dulles, a Republican, as chief negotiator was intended as a move toward bipartisan foreign policy. In this context, MacArthur, the darling of the Republicans and their potential presidential candidate, held the key to Dulles's managing the two treaties through the Senate ratification process. If MacArthur criticized the treaties, Dulles was doomed. Hence the two entered into a bargain: In exchange for MacArthur's endorsement of the treaties, Dulles agreed to Yoshida's token rearmament thus keeping the constitution intact.[13] This decision superimposed the no-war constitution on its antithesis—the anti-Communist military alliance—in the security treaty.

Yoshida's amour propre, however, was not satisfied, and his continuing resistance to rearmament caused Dulles to penalize him by de facto continuing the occupation. For instance, the United States could wage war against the Soviet Union or China from the Japanese bases without consulting the Japanese government; the U.S. forces were authorized to put down domestic disorder in Japan and were immune from trial in Japanese courts for common crimes. Yoshida's domestic foes now openly criticized him. The revisionists maintained that Yoshida's refusal to do away with the constitution and to rearm was responsible for Japan's unequal status and united with the JSP to put treaty revision on the agenda of postoccupation politics. The JSP split over the ratification of the treaties: The right wing reluctantly swallowed the peace with the United States but rejected the security treaty; the left wing rejected both.

Thus the peace and security treaties split Japan three ways and created an unstable system. Yoshida and his followers stood in the middle, siding with the revisionists to maintain the security system

---

[12]*FRUS*, 1950, VI, 1134–35; ibid., 1951, VI, pt. 1, 1286.
[13]*FRUS*, 1951, VI, 822–23.

but siding with the Socialists to limit Japan's military burden. Yoshida explained his stance as follows:

> We can never pull off the so-called rearmament for the time being, nor is there any interest in it among the people. On the other hand it is not something that justifies the government's initiative to impose on them. The day [we rearm] will come naturally if the livelihood recovers. It may sound selfish, but let the Americans handle [our security] until then. It is indeed our god-given luck that the Constitution bans arms. If the Americans complain, the Constitution gives us an adequate cover. The politicians who want to amend it are oafs.[14]

For Yoshida's purposes, then, the right-wing Socialists, such as Nishio Suehiro, who were interested in rearmament or bipartisan foreign policy were useless. He needed allies who were unequivocally committed to constitutional defense and disarmament, and only the left-wing JSP fit the bill. Thus in 1951 Yoshida sent an emissary to Suzuki Mosaburo and Katsumada Seiichi, both of the left-wing JSP, to ask for their assistance in mounting an antirearmament campaign.[15] The Socialists, who had just been cripplingly defeated in the 1949 election, found a new nationalist cause: serving Japan's interest in standing up to the American colossus.

The United States resumed pressuring Japan to rearm, with Yoshida if possible and with Hatoyama if necessary, and to revise its constitution after San Francisco. Vice-President Richard Nixon was dispatched to Tokyo in 1954 to own up to America's "mistake" in writing the constitution of 1947.[16] Thus Yoshida's late 1954 isolation and resignation, which he fought with the help of the JSP, may be attributed in part to Washington's pressure. This U.S.-Japan tension and the JSP's role in it explain the party's resurgence at the polls in the first half of the 1950s.

The Socialists' power in the lower house of the Diet grew between the first postwar general election and that of 1958 (see table 8.2). The JSP started out with ninety-four seats in the first election, 1946, which was held after the first round of purges removed the competition, and went on to capture a plurality in 1947. With SCAP's blessing, the JSP

---

[14]Miyazawa Kiichi, *Tokyo-Washinton no mitsudan* [Secret talks between Tokyo and Washington] (Tokyo: Jitsugyo no Nihonsha, 1956), p. 160.

[15]Igarashi, "Peace Making and Party Politics: The Formation of the Domestic Foreign-Policy System in Postwar Japan," *Journal of Japanese Studies*, Summer 1985, p. 350.

[16]*The Memoirs of Richard Nixon* (New York: Grosset and Dunlap, 1978), pp. 129–30.

TABLE 8.2

ELECTION RESULTS IN THE LOWER HOUSE
(by number of seats)

Year	Conservative Parties	Japan Socialist Party			Japan Communist Party	Others
		Left	Center	Right		
1946	272		94		5	129
1947	291		143		4	34
1949	333		48		35	50
1952	325	54		57	0	30
1953	310	72		66	1	17
1955	297	89		67	2	12
1958	287		166		1	13

formed two coalition governments with a conservative party in the next two years. Still dominated by the right wing at this stage, it had the potential to grow into a loyal opposition through merging with a wing of the conservatives. In 1948, however, the coalition government fell victim to political corruption, which coincided with the rightward shift of SCAP and its abandonment of the Socialists. In the 1949 election, the bottom fell out of the Socialist center, and both Yoshida and the Communists made stunning gains.

In 1951, in the midst of the Korean War, the peace and security treaties were signed. The JSP split over the issue; the left wing of the JSP was discovering the appeal of anti-American neutralism and nationalism, which helped it overtake the right wing at the polls. At the same time the Communists, overplaying their hand in a violent putsch, lost all thirty-five seats in 1952. A sizable number of voters were also shifting loyalties between the JCP and the JSP, which caused much anxiety among Japan's conservative leaders. The expanding JSP captured one-third of the Diet seats in the 1953 election, enough to block constitutional amendments, and began to entertain hopes of winning the government in two or three more elections.

During 1952–1953 the increasingly powerful Socialists began to intervene boldly in conservative politics. Yoshida's power was dwindling in the last years of his rule, and the Socialists frequently voted with Hatoyama to embarrass the government. Because no one of the three groups had the commanding majority, irresponsible and opportunistic combinations carried the day and further eroded the prewar party alignments. The fast-growing JSP was becoming an arbiter between the warring conservative groups, further enhancing its stature.

At last, in the fall of 1954, Socialist support made it possible for Hatoyama to overthrow Yoshida, and the proximity to power induced the two wings of the JSP to merge in October 1955. The fear of the unified Socialists in turn induced the conservatives to carry out a merger of their own one month later, creating the Liberal Democratic party. The two mergers were touted in the media as the return of a two-party system, but the conservative power brokers who engineered the merger were pursuing five distinct goals.

First, they wanted a stable conservative government capable of receiving major assistance in the form of Mutual Security Act (MSA) grants from the United States. Both the revisionists and the Keidanren leaders assumed that Japan would enlist in the anti-Communist alliance and become an arsenal of the free world, in stark contrast to what Japan has since become. Constitutional revision and rearmament were thought of as natural preconditions for integrating Japan militarily and economically with the United States. Second, to eliminate the conflict between Hatoyama and Yoshida, they were prepared to isolate and oust Yoshida, if necessary. Third, both political and business leaders, agitated by the sudden expansion of the radical JSP, were determined to keep power out of its hands.

Fourth, most of the anti-Yoshida leaders were professional politicians who saw an alternating two-party system as a natural benchmark of democracy and were fully prepared to return to the conditions that prevailed in 1947–1948, when the Socialist-conservative coalition faced former Seiyukai in the Diet. Fifth and finally, the merger was to herald the return of professional politicians to power. A great deal was at stake in the merger of the conservatives who dreamt of a very different Japan in concept, makeup, and policy.

Unfortunately for the revisionists, however, they were soon embroiled in a series of foreign policy encounters with Washington that undermined their goals. Just before the LDP's 1955 merger, the Republican administration of President Dwight Eisenhower began trying to discredit the Yalta agreement's concession of the Kurile Islands to the Soviet Union. The point at issue was whether the islands of Habomai, Shikotan, Kunashiri, and Etorofu, lying immediately to the north of Hokkaido, were part of the Kuriles Japan had abandoned in San Francisco. There is not enough space to go into the full dispute here, but suddenly Washington was interested in supporting the maximum claims of Japan in contrast to the minimalist attitude taken by Dulles in 1951. Moreover, to "help" Japan make the maximum claims against Moscow, Washington began provoking armed collision over the disputed territories by conducting armed reconnaissance.[17] The rising U.S.-Soviet tension proceeded alongside Nikita Khrushchev's thaw toward Japan, posing sensitive problems for Hatoyama, Yoshida, and the Socialists.

I believe that Secretary of State Dulles wished to see Japan move in tandem with the Federal Republic of Germany on rapprochement with Moscow. Being a divided government, the West German government could hope for nothing more than an exchange of ambassadors, repatriation of prisoners of war, but no peace treaty. But the Hatoyama government wanted a full peace treaty, and Moscow sought to encourage him with an offer to return two of the four islands as a territorial settlement. Inadvertently, Hatoyama walked into the cockpit of the East-West struggle. Yoshida saw in the rift between Dulles and Hatoyama a chance to enhance his standing by opposing Hatoyama. The LDP merger, which was to culminate in the containment of Yoshida, turned out to be a draw instead, as the Hatoyama group's draft party program stalled on the issue of a foreign policy plank.[18]

The end of the treaty dispute came in August 1956 when Dulles issued a demarche that supported Yoshida's position. The United States, Dulles said, would take away Okinawa and the Bonin Islands, still under U.S. occupation, for itself if Japan were to accept only two islands in the Northern Territories and cede the other two to the Soviet Union.[19] This effectively ended any hopes for the peace treaty, and Hatoyama was forced to scale down his rapprochement to the German formula. The setback eclipsed Hatoyama's star, but in a last gamble in the fall, he submitted a small-election-district bill to displace the multi-member, single, nontransferable ballot system with the single-member, winner-take-all system.

Although the single-member district was designed to restore the

---

[17]In October 1952 and November 1954. See Wada Haruki, "Sanfuranshisuko kowa to chishima retto" [The San Francisco peace conference and the Kurile Islands], *Sekai* November 1980, pp. 233–49; Wada Haruki, "Chishima retto no han'i ni tsuite [On the boundary of the Kurile Islands], *Sekai*, May 1987, pp. 147–61; Wada Haruki, "'Hoppo ryodo mondai' no hassei" [The origin of the 'northern territories issue'], I, *Sekai*, April 1989, pp. 153–69; Wada Haruki, ibid., II, May 1989, pp. 205–23. See also Kubota Masaaki, *Kuremurin eno shisetsu* [The emissary to the Kremlin] (Tokyo: Bungei Shunjusha, 1983).

[18]See my comments and footnote on Tsutsui's chapter, in the introduction.

[19]See *New York Times*, August 28, 1956, p. 1; *Asahi Shimbun*, August 29, 1956, p. 1.

prewar alternating two-party system, Miki Bukichi, who masterminded the scheme, did not see the JSP as the loyal opposition. The small-district bill therefore was accompanied by wholesale gerrymandering to eliminate the bulk of Socialist seats. I believe that Miki intended thereby to reduce the Socialists to impotence and drive the remnants into coalition with one of the conservative parties, as happened during the occupation. Because that would also make constitutional revision possible, the JSP went into a do-or-die campaign against what it called the "Hatomander" scheme. The JSP was probably aware that the professional politicians regarded it, the beneficiary of the purge, as an American stooge.

Although the Socialists resorted to all sorts of parliamentary tactics to filibuster the bill, their numbers were too few. The beleaguered Socialists' rescue materialized in an unexpected quarter, however, when Masutani Shuji, speaker of the lower house and a Yoshida protégé who had been spending his declining years in honorary sinecure, suddenly became a crusader for "parliamentary democracy." Thanks to his collusion with the Socialists, the bill died in the upper house.

Hatoyama himself called the vote "the biggest loss of the Hatoyama government," but it was more than that: The cause of the revisionists suffered irretrievably. Although Kishi Nobusuke replaced Hatoyama and resumed the fight, his chances of reversing the tide were bleak after the events of the summer of 1956.

I posit that the LDP's politicians saw in the events of that summer the hopelessness of improving Japan's status: The road to equality through equal burden-sharing was closed; the constitution and rearmament were impossible. On top of that Dulles denied Japan's diplomatic autonomy by closing the door on Moscow. Japan was now effectively reduced to client status, with the United States in charge of its security and diplomacy.

This also meant, however, that Japan no longer faced any external threat and that the LDP could afford internal squabbles. Thus in December 1956, when Ishibashi Tanzan was elected as the LDP leader to succeed Hatoyama, the LDP's factions made their formal debut, thereby institutionalizing the alignments that had emerged when the Yoshida-Hatoyama cleavage crosscut the Seiyukai-Minseito division.

Factions—each with its own head office, staff, campaign organization, sources of funds, and a sort of "shadow cabinet" for government and party posts—form around powerful politicians who have ambitions to be prime minister. Most factions thus resemble a party. The LDP, which is made up of factions, therefore lacks cohesion and is unable to articulate a long-range program as political parties are supposed to do, according to an authoritative study by Watanabe Tsuneo.[20] But Watanabe misses the LDP factions' most vital trait: They never displace the party. Factions remain factions because the party serves a distinct purpose that no faction can serve. The LDP exists to maintain the U.S.-Japan security tie by containing the JSP. On this issue, all the factions always come together.

Ishibashi Tansan, who in early 1957 fell ill, was succeeded by Kishi Nobusuke, who had ambitions of revising the security treaty and, on the strength of that successful revision, of revising the constitution. With the JSP's endorsement, Kishi launched himself on revising the security treaty. However, although bipartisan activism on foreign policy continued, after the Soviet launching of Sputnik and China's "Great Leap Forward," both in 1957, the Japanese Socialists seemed persuaded of Mao Tse-tung's observation that "the East wind prevails over the West wind." During the Quemoy crisis in the Taiwan Strait in 1958, then, the Socialists did a volte-face. The revised treaty, they now insisted, would involve Japan in wars provoked by America's "brinkmanship." Therefore the Socialists covertly preferred the existing security treaty to a revised and more equal one, though they kept up their adamantly anti-American rhetoric: "American imperialism," said JSP chairman Asanuma, "is the common enemy of the Japanese and Chinese peoples."[21]

Secretary Dulles's decision—in the midst of treaty revision—to involve Japan in a national security crisis was a fatal tactical mistake. Kishi had launched Japan on the treaty revision primarily to improve Japan's status vis-à-vis the United States. Although the revisionists were receptive to Dulles's plea for Japan's self-reliance on conventional defense, defending Quemoy, Chiang Kai-shek's honor, and Washington's "brinkmanship" was an extreme test of Japan's loyalty, and none of America's allies would have passed it. Dulles effectively switched the issue from status to security, and not even the revisionists would pick Dulles's chestnuts out of the fire of Quemoy. Ironically, Dulles proved Yoshida's selfishness to be correct.

In the political fallout of the Quemoy crisis, Kishi was deserted by both the JSP and his revisionist friends just as the treaty revision reached its final phase. Eisenhower and Dulles, Kishi's only friends, were now

---

[20]*Habatsu* [Factions] (Tokyo: Kobundo, 1964), chapter 1.

[21]The JSP's reversal in the summer of 1958 is one of the best-kept secrets in the party's history, and I cannot document the internal debate. From this point on the JSP followed the policy of denouncing the treaty but of relying on it de facto.

fully committed to supporting him against the Communists, domestic and foreign. Others would offer help but only in exchange for favors. One stunning development during the Quemoy crisis was that Yoshida, who watched Kishi get mired in troubles partly of Yoshida's making, offered to help. Now that the treaty itself and the American connection were in jeopardy, Yoshida decided to switch sides.

But his help had a price tag. Yoshida demanded that Kishi name Ikeda Hayato, Yoshida's protégé, as his successor and that the treaty be revised in accordance with his wishes. (In 1951 Yoshida had asked for a fully equal treaty in exchange for leasing military bases, but he was penalized by Dulles for refusing to rearm.) This time Yoshida was in a position to dictate to Dulles, and, in the 1960 treaty,[22] he got what he wanted.

The issue that caused the rioting and turmoil was not the substance of the treaty but Kishi's alleged dictatorship. The media and the Socialists demanded unanimity (read *consensus*) in the ratification vote and assailed the "majority rule" as "violence of number." Kishi was branded a dictator for having forced a majority vote. At a critical moment, then, the issue was switched from the security treaty to "democracy"; thus the mob violence in the final days of ratification was not anti-American but anti-Kishi, and his retirement saved the day for the security treaty. The issue-switching enabled Japan to make a subtle statement to Washington; by sacrificing Kishi, the "lackey of American imperialism," but not the security treaty, Japan retained the military protection but kept the United States at arm's length.[23]

In 1955, five years before the crisis, when Hatoyama was prime minister, the economic miracle had begun. The engine of Japan's wartorn economy sputtered, shuddered, and began to hum. Because no one at the time understood what was happening, no one took credit for it. Most people felt that economic growth of more than 10 percent in real terms per year was unsustainable. Prime Minister Ikeda Hayato, Yoshida's protégé who displaced Kishi, seized on the "high-speed growth" and hammered out a campaign platform for the election of 1960 that elevated the policy of growthmanship to the first principle of Japan's conservative rule: the income-doubling plan. At that same time, he saw to it that Kishi did not get credit for the successful treaty revision. Instead Ikeda talked of "patience and tolerance" toward the JSP, which, combined with high-speed growth, was the origin of the appeasement policy that Kent Calder calls "crisis and compensation."

---

[22]Weinstein is correct in seeing Yoshida's design in the 1960 treaty, but he is mistaken in ignoring the vital role played by Kishi in getting that result.

[23]See this interpretation fully developed in Kataoka, *The Price of a Constitution*, chapter 8.

When Yoshida's policy was established as orthodoxy, subtle but distinct traits came to mark the body politic. The conservative establishment became semipacifist and anemic toward defense, thus placing Japan on the outer fringe of the Western alliance system. The LDP shelved constitutional revision, and the JSP accepted the security treaty de facto. The Japanese began to speak earnestly of the distinction between *tatemae* (facade) and *honne* (reality)—between the constitution and the security treaty. From 1960 on the LDP began blanketing Japan with self-abnegating injunctions including the three principles of nuclear disarmament (whereby Japan pledged not to possess, manufacture, or introduce nuclear weapons), two bans on export of weapons and arms, the decision not to spend more than 1 percent of gross national product on defense, and the like. But the security ties with the United States remained in place.

After the 1960 upheaval, the politics of Japan settled down to tranquility on the basis of collusion cum tension between the government and the opposition. Critical votes raising systemic questions were seldom taken because a "consensus"—an acquiescence in the impossibility of breaking the Yoshida-JSP cooperation—had developed. This, then, was the origin of the vaunted "consensus" decision making of Japan. Consensus decisions thus originated in Japan's postwar politics, not culture; if anything, culture was shaped by politics.[24]

As Yoshida's friends would later say, Japan became a new Venice, no longer concerned with the status question and devoting itself to economic development. Karel van Wolferen would find the new Venice and its seemingly stateless condition enigmatic.[25] As I have shown, the primary reason for this condition lies in the constitution written by MacArthur and accepted by Prime Minister Yoshida and the Socialists. As the gulf war has demonstrated, the new Venice is deficient, and a movement looking toward constitutional revision and political realignment may soon be on the way. Japan's "statelessness" was after all a mirage maintained by the cold war.

---

[24]See Sato Seizaburo, et al., *Bunmei toshiteno ie-shakai* [The ie-society as a civilization] (Tokyo: Chuo Koronsha, 1979), for a contrary thesis.

[25]*The Enigma of Japanese Power: People and Politics in a Stateless Nation* (New York: Knopf, 1989).

Index

Agricultural Cooperation Act, 93
Agricultural cooperatives, 94, 97
Akiyama Konosuke, 106
American revisionism, 32. *See also* Revisionism
Anpo utility thesis, 25
Arita Hachiro, 101
Asanume Inejiro, 67–68, 75
Ashida Hitoshi, 11, 56–64 passim, 105, 120; Ashida Construction, 125; Ashida Memorandum, 58–59, 121; elitism of, 58; nationalism of, 63; on rearmament, 59–61; on tradition, 64
Atcheson, George, 141
August revolution theory, 146
Ayabe Kentaro, 106

Bad Godesberg, 30
Baerwald, Hans H., 3
Boss-type leadership, 66
Byrnes, James F., 136

Calder, Kent E., 24, 168
Chiba Saburo, 122
Cohen, Theodore, 17, 152
Collective security, 13
Consensus, 24, 167

Conservatives: as kakushin, 122; merger of, 109, 110, 112, 115, 129
Cooperative party, 120

Defense bills, 126
Democratic forces, 8
Democratization League, 128
Dodge, Joseph, 157
Dodge Line, 122
Domei, 35
Domestic 38th parallel, 10
Dooman, Eugene, 136
Dower, John W., 8
Dulles, John Foster, 22, 27, 56, 123, 126; accepts the constitution, 10; reneges on the security treaty, 10

Emperor fascism, 67
Emperor-organ theory, 140

Factionalism, 13; debut of, 165. *See also* Watanabe
Fallows, James, 2
Flanagan, Scott C., 95
Four Principles of Peace, 21, 87
Fukunaga Kenji, 127
Fukuzawa Masao, 91–92

Greater East Asia Conference, 101
Grew, Joseph C., 136

Hakone conferences, 23
Haragei, 66
Hatoyama Ichiro, 11, 56, 105, 107, 110; cabinet of, 114; collides with Dulles, 12; elected PM, 130; in Hatoyama Jiyuto, 128; platform of, 123; rapprochement to Moscow, 115–16; Hatomander scheme, 165
Hayashi Chikio, 96
Hayashi Kentaro, 19
Hayashi Kisaburo, 106, 109
Hayashiya Kamejiro, 121
Hellmann, Donald, 27
Hirano Rikizo, 71, 81, 83
Hirokawa Kozen, 122, 127, 128
Horiuchi Kensuke, 101
Hozen Keizaikai, 129
Hrebner, Ronald J., 96

Ikeda Hayato, 13, 108, 128
Imperial legitimacy, 134
Income-doubling plan, 25, 167
Indirect rule, 4
Inoki Masamichi, 18
Inukai Ken, 112
Ishibashi Masatsugu, 85
Ishibashi Tanzan, 14, 56, 123, 127
Ishida Hakuei, 127–28
Ishihara Shintaro, 32
Ishimoda Shou, 18
Item Y Purge, 29
Ito Takashi, 29
Iwanami, 19

Japan Communist party, 86
Japan Farmers' Union, 93

Japan Socialist party (JSP): as centrist force, 80; as Yoshida's ally, 161; neglected farmers, 93; New Manifesto of, 65; merger of, 86, 163; Nichirokei of, 71, 72–73, 74, 75–76; organizational transformation of, 89–90; political culture of, 67; purge of, 85; Realists of, 65, 69; Seventh Congress, 70, 85; Shaminkei of, 65, 69, 71, 74, 76; split of, 71, 162; structural reform, 42; third coalition, 84; volte face on treaty revision, 166
Japan Socialist party left wing, 68
Japan Socialist party right wing, 73–75 passim; decline of, 84
Jiban, 28, 39, 97
Jiyuto, 122. See also conservatives
Johnson, Chalmers A., 10, 16, 47
Joint Chiefs of Staff, 159

Kaishinto, 120; founded, 121; left wing of, 108; on constitution, 125; platform of, 112
Kakushin, 4, 8, 46
Kakushin Doshikai, 101
Kankoro, 88
Kase Toshikazu, 103
Kataoka Tetsuya, 87
Katayama Tetsu, 76, 83
Kato Takao, 106
Katsumada Seiichi, 21, 129
Kawakami Jotaro, 35, 71, 75
Kawakami Shuji, 61
Keenan, Joseph, 102
Kennan, George F., 4–5, 35, 82, 143, 157
Kido Koichi, 102
Kindai Bunka, 18

Kishi Nubusuke, 13, 27, 103, 106, 109, 116, 126
Kitamura Tokutaro, 61, 120
Kiyose Ichiro, 125
Koenkai, 28, 40, 98
Kokumin Minshuto, 120
Kokutai, 135, 138
Kono Ichiro, 11, 116
Kono Mitsu, 75
Konoye Fumimaro, 141
Kosaka Masataka, 25
Kozaha, 86

Land Improvement Act, 93
Liberal Democratic party: founding of, 12, 29, 131, 163; factions, 48; mainstream, 49; in one-party dominance, 14
Liberal party, 120. *See also* Jiyuto

MacArthur, Douglas, 3–4, 5, 160; sabotages reverse course, 157
Machida Chuji, 120
Maruyama Masao, 20
Marxism, 16–22 passim
Masuda Kanehichi, 123, 127
Masumi Junnosuke, 30
Masutani Shuji, 13, 165
Matsumoto Joji, 141, 153
Matsumoto Shun'ichi, 115
Matsumura Kenzo, 104, 106, 130
Matsuzaki Tetsuya, 95
Media, 53
Miike Coal Mine, 44
Miki Bukichi, 35, 123, 165
Miki Takeo, 41, 105, 120, 130
Mikuriya Takashi, 101
Militarism, 23
Ministry of International Trade and Industry (MITI), 47
Minka, 18

Minobe Tatsukichi, 139–43 passim
Minshuto, 61–62. *See also* Minseito
Miwa Juso, 75
Miyake Shoichi, 94
Miyazawa Kiichi, 25
Miyazawa Toshiyoshi, 143–47
Miyoshi Hideyuki, 107, 110
Modernization, 15, 23
Money politics, 15
Mutual Security Act, 74, 126

1955 System: 1, 3, 13; paradigm of, 5–6; maturation of, 36
Nagai Yonosuke, 26
Nagao Ryuichi, 32
Nakano Yoshio, 21
Nakasone Yasuhiro, 15, 53
New middle mass, 25
Nihon Jiyuto, 129
Nihon Minshuto, 105, 120, 130
Nihon Saiken Renmei, 103
Ninagawa Torazo, 91
Nishimura Eiichi, 69, 72
Nishio Suehiro, 35, 66–68, 71–77
Nixon, Richard M., 161
Nomura Kichisaburo, 56
Norman, E. H., 17, 154, 156
Northern Territory, 163
NSC 13/2, 82, 157

Oasa Tadao, 104, 106
Ogata Taketora, 35, 108
Ogura Hirokatsu, 18
Okazaki Katsuo, 108, 126
One-third barrier, 89, 95
Ono Banboku, 35, 123
Ota Saburo, 103
Otake Hideo, 21, 30

Packard, George, 27

Peace Problem Symposium, 20, 70
Political Affairs Research Committee (PARC), 50
Political culture, 95–96
Political realignment, 157
Politician-bureaucrat rivalry, 11–12, 50
Pollution, 45
Potsdam declaration, 32, 136–37, 152
Prestowitz, Clyde, 2
Purge, 3–4, 154

Quemoy crisis, 13, 166

Realists, 1, 25. *See also* Japan Socialist party
Rearmament, 73–77 passim, 109
Regional development, 43
Reischauer, Edwin O., 1, 22
Reverse course, 4–5, 82. *See also* NSC 13/2; Revisionism
Revisionism, 4, 6, 149; in America, 32
Revisionist capitalism, 122
Richardson, Bradley M., 95
Ronoha, 17, 86

Saito Hiroshi, 101
Saito Takao, 76
Sanbetsu, 31, 85
Sasaki Soichi, 146
Sato Eisaku, 110
Sato Seizaburo, 95
Sawada Renzo, 109
SCAP. *See* Supreme Commander for the Allied Powers
SCAPINs (SCAP Instructions), 11
Seamen's Union, 75
Security treaty, 160
Seitai, 138

Sekai, 19
Sengoku Kotaro, 120
Shidehara Kijuro, 11, 141
Shigemitsu Mamoru, 29, 84, 102, 105, 107, 108, 113, 114, 115, 116, 129
Shindo Eiichi, 57
Shinsei Club, 121
Shinshinkai, 120
Shiratori Toshio, 101
Showa Denko, 81
Shutaisei, 84
Sigal, Leon V., 152
Small-district bill, 12, 164
Social change, 38–39, 51–52
Social Progressive party, 81
Sohyo, 15, 31, 84, 88–90
Soka Gakkai, 95
Sone Eki, 69, 72, 74
Soviet peace talk, 163
Standard history, 7–8
State-War-Navy Coordinating Committee (SWNCC) 150/4, 4, 10
Stimson, Henry, 136
Suekawa Hiroshi, 18
Suma Yakichiro, 106
Supreme Commander for the Allied Powers (SCAP), 80–81, 85, 86, 92, 141, 146, 158
Supreme Council, 134
Surrender terms, 135. *See also* Potsdam declaration
Suzuki Mosaburo, 21, 35, 70, 83, 87
SWNCC 150/4, 4, 10

Takano Minoru, 84. *See also* Sohyo
Takayanagi Kenzo, 127
Tanaka Kakuei, 15, 41, 50–51, 94
Tani Masayuki, 103, 109

Tani Satomi, 30
Tatemae/honne, 168
Three principles of nuclear disar-
    mament, 24, 31, 168
Three Principles of Peace, 70, 72.
    See also Four Principles of
    Peace
Three-way division of politics, 3–
    4, 6–7, 77, 107, 131, 160
Togo Shigenori, 135
Tomabeji Gizo, 120
Tsutsui Kiyotada, 28
Two-party thesis, 107, 117, 130

Uchida Kenzo, 3

Van Wolferen, Karel, 2
Violence of number, 167

Wada Hroo, 68–71
War potential, 126
Ward, Robert E., 97–98

Watanabe Tsuneo, 14, 100, 165.
    See also Two-party thesis
Willoughby, Charles A., 81–82

Yokota Kisaburo, 18
Yoshida School, 158
Yoshida Shigeru, 6, 8, 11, 18, 107,
    129; basic line of, 88; fifth cab-
    inet, 129; final victory of, 167;
    no-confidence against, 128; on
    the constitution, 126, 153; on
    rearmament, 109, 125, 126,
    161; ouster of, 164; peace
    terms of, 159; rescues Kishi,
    167; surprise dissolution of,
    cabinet of, 128
Yoshino Genzaburo, 19
Yo-yato hakuchu (government-
    opposition equilibrium), 37

Zaikai, 47
Zoku, 50

About the Editor

KATAOKA TETSUYA is senior research fellow at the Hoover Institution. A graduate of Waseda University, he received his doctorate in political science from the University of Chicago and has taught at Vassar College, the State University of New York at Buffalo, and Tsukuba University. He is the author of *Resistance and Revolution in China: The Communists and the Second United Front.*